DURING the epic defense of Bataan, José Calugas, mess sergeant of Battery A, Philippine Scouts, saw a gun of a battery not his own put out of action by casualties among the crew. He was a mess sergeant, and it was not his battery. To save and then to help man the gun was a job that lay wholly outside the scope of his duties. But he ran to the endangered battery across one thousand yards of bursting shells and bombs—under conditions where to have moved five or ten yards in the open would have been hazardous in the extreme. He was given the Congressional Medal of Honor, highest military award in the gift of the American people.

Out of a thousand heroic deeds by the 75,000 Filipino soldiers who fought in Bataan—21,000 of whom lie in nameless graves—the award to Sergeant Calugas stands both as fact and as symbol. As fact it stands single and isolated—one man's dazzling exploit rising above myriad lesser ones. But it also stands for something greater than itself; it stands for the courage of a whole people—a courage that has passed the gruelling test of fire.

My people are now wrapped in silence, a nation of prisoners. Calugas and the other Filipino and American soldiers who fought for America in the Philippines are today behind the barbed wire of Japanese concentration camps. Your War Bond will help hasten their deliverance. Don't let them down!

CARLOS P. ROMULO

# MOTHER AMERICA

BOOKS BY CARLOS P. ROMULO: MOTHER AMERICA
I SAW THE FALL OF THE PHILIPPINES

# MOTHER AMERICA

## A Living Story of Democracy

BY CARLOS P. ena ROMULO

DOUBLEDAY, DORAN & COMPANY, INC.
GARDEN CITY, NEW YORK 1943

PRINTED AT THE *Country Life Press*, GARDEN CITY, N. Y., U. S. A.

*Dedicated*
*To the Filipino soldiers who fought and died*
*beside Americans on Bataan and Corregidor*
*in defense of the Philippines,*
*and to their brothers in the Far East—*
*the one billion inarticulate Orientals who are daring*
*to lift their eyes toward the dazzling hope*
*of freedom.*

## AUTHOR'S NOTE

THE FIRST FOUR DOCUMENTS included in the Appendix are the Magna Charta of the Philippines. They show the important steps in the evolution of the Filipino people to self-government. That the Filipinos believed in democracy and thought along republican lines even before the advent of American rule in the Philippines is shown by I—The Constitution approved by the Philippine Republic in 1899.

# PREFATORY NOTE

THIS is a living story of democracy. It is political science personalized. America's work in the Philippines is a masterpiece in human relationship because it is *human*.

I write it as a Filipino who is one of the beneficiaries of Philippine-American collaboration. I write it so that America may know what she achieved in the Philippines. I write it also for the world—that subject races may be informed of how the Filipino people increasingly fought for their freedom, and that sovereign nations may profit by the example of America. For America was the only sovereign nation in the Far East that in its hour of danger was able to count on the loyalty of its subject people.

I write as a private citizen of the Philippines. The views expressed in this book are mine and are not official. I presume to speak for no government. But I am convinced I bespeak the sentiments of all my Filipino comrades-in-arms who fought in Bataan and Corregidor. We know why and what we fought for there.

My acknowledgment goes to President Manuel L. Quezon, who granted me leave of absence without pay from the Philippine Army and later placed me on inactive military status; to General Douglas MacArthur, for having sent me to America from Australia on special detail; to Harold Matson, for valuable advice and help; to Evelyn Wells, my loyal friend, for research and co-operation; and to Solomon Arnaldo of the office of the Commonwealth of the Philippines, for the appendices.

I must not forget to dedicate a few words of appreciation to the memory of the late Very Reverend Father James M. Drought, Vicar General of the Maryknoll Mission, with whom, before his untimely death, I discussed various portions of this book.

CARLOS P. ROMULO

# CONTENTS

# INTRODUCTION. WHY AMERICA?

THAT was a dramatic meeting in mid-ocean that marked the signing of the Atlantic Charter!

Startling as light to a blacked-out world was the news of the secret meeting between Roosevelt and Churchill, August 10, 1941, off the coast of Newfoundland, and the creation of the Charter with its voicing of the Four Freedoms:

". . . to see established a peace which will afford to all nations the means of dwelling in safety within their own boundaries, and which will afford assurance that all the men in all the lands may live out their lives in freedom from fear and want. . . ."

Men in all the lands!

To millions all over the earth, of all colors and creeds, this democratic premise of the Atlantic Charter was the beginning of a dream, a hope, and a prayer. But to Franklin Delano Roosevelt the Charter was an actuality. He knew it could be accomplished on world-wide scale. He had seen it work in the Philippines.

When, back in 1934, he approved the Tydings-McDuffie Independence Act promising independence to the Philippines on a definite date, July 4, 1946, he was virtually putting into effect the Atlantic Charter.

One year after the signing of this epochal bill I found myself seated next to the President of the United States on a platform at the University of Notre Dame. This leading American Catholic university was awarding its degree of Doctor of Laws to the President and to me, a Filipino editor from the Philippines.

Sitting on that platform by the President, receiving, with him, the highest honor conferable by a great university, and seeing around us the leaders of America's governmental hierarchy, I felt proud, as any man would be. President Roosevelt represented the world's greatest nation; in a humbler way I represented the Philippines. Above our heads hung the American and Filipino flags. After the hoods were laid over our shoulders and our citations read, the Notre Dame choir sang the national anthem of the Philippines, followed by "The Star-Spangled Banner."

I joined in the singing of both songs with equal emotional fervor. They were equally mine. And I was thinking: "Where else in the world, in the entire history of the world, could this scene be duplicated—a representative of a subject race sharing the same platform with the head of a conquering country and being awarded the same honor? Where else could this happen, save in America?"

It seemed to me that what was happening was symbolic of the joint efforts of two nations and of all that had been accomplished in the Philippines by America. This honor paid me by Notre Dame was less a personal award than it was a tribute to the protective guidance of America over our group of islands on the opposite side of the world.

I could remember a small boy who wore no shoes, who lived in the provincial town of Camiling, a town of nipa shacks and tin-roofed houses under which the pigs and goats lived. There was little sanitation, few roads, no telephones nor public libraries in Camiling. That boy beside the Camiling River—where the herb doctors brought the older boys for the primitive rites of circumcision—I was that boy.

That I had come the long way from Camiling to Notre Dame was due to the public-school system in the Philippines as introduced by America. It was part of the economic, intellectual, and spiritual progress developed in a foreign country by America.

Within forty-two years, the span of my lifetime, the Philippines have changed destinies. My country achieved the short cut to democracy under the kindly guidance of Mother America.

Shortly before the turn of the century we revolted against Spanish rule in the Philippines. Ours was a struggle against poverty, exploitation, and greed that accompanied the corrupt rule under Spanish kings. America interrupted our fight for freedom on the eve of victory—took us over.

In the beginning we resented America as violently as we had resented Spain. There was much adjusting to be done by both Filipinos and Americans before peace finally came to the Philippines. It was not an easily attained peace. There were many accusations and misunderstandings.

In the beginning America groped in the Philippines, but throughout the stumbling and groping she never failed to consider that paramount element—the dignity of the human soul. We were regarded by the Americans as fellow humans. In other parts of the Far East, we knew, men were treated like cattle by their conquerors.

Slowly our suspicions and resentments were overcome. Slowly, under the most remarkable colonial guidance in history, an Oriental nation was converted to faith in democracy.

President Roosevelt, in his speech that day at Notre Dame, defined Philippine independence. It was virtually an outline of what would later be known as the Atlantic Charter.

When it came my turn to speak I prophesied the sacrifice of Bataan. I said:

"If war comes, or fresh conquests from whatever source, we shall oppose it to the death. To the Philippines the United States has been a generous benefactor, a loyal and true friend, and, if we can honor that debt in no other way, we can pay with our lives."[1]

This was December 9, 1935.

Exactly six years later to the day we began the payment of our debt to America with our lives, when the first Japanese planes swept over Manila! Then, for the first time in history, men of a subject race lined up to die beside their former conquerors.

Our loyalty to American principles was sealed in Filipino blood on Luzon, Bataan, and Corregidor.

The week before Japan attacked the United States I attended in Java a secret conference of native leaders, representing seventy-five million Indonesians. We spoke of the war all knew was bound to break at any moment.

"Our only salvation, here in the Far East," one of the leaders said, "is for all of us to unite—Chinese, Hindus, Burmans, Malays,

[1]See Appendix.

Filipinos, Indonesians—and form the Pan-Malayan Union, under the protecting influence of America."

I asked:

"Why America?"

All the leaders were ready with the answer.

"In view of America's record in the Philippines, she is the only nation we can believe in and trust."

This is Asia's response to America's sole experiment in colonization. The democratic treatment in the Philippines has achieved a miracle in trust and hope, not only among the Filipinos, but among all the peoples of the Far East. This miracle was accomplished within this century. Within the span of forty-two years, in my country, East and West have settled the differences of color and points of view.

Through the Philippines, doorway between the hemispheres, the Orient has looked to America and caught its first glimpse of freedom.

# MOTHER AMERICA

# 1. WHAT IMPERIALISM MEANS TO THE FAR EAST

---

THE WORD "IMPERIALISM" means little to the average American. It brings to his mind, if anything, certain ready-made phrases of Kipling: "Little brown brother," "The white man's burden," "Hewers of wood and carriers of water." The singing voice of the British Crown did much to popularize the theory of the superiority of white skin over brown, and that East was East and West was West.

During the battle of the Philippines I sometimes remembered Rudyard Kipling. How I wished he had been with us on Bataan! I should have liked showing him miles of fox holes piled with American and Filipino bodies and asked him to repeat over that mingled flesh "never the twain shall meet."

Nevertheless, Kipling's poems have come to express to the Occidental mind the manifestation of imperialism. The American, with his characteristic willingness to give the other fellow the benefit of the doubt, frequently has been led to believe that imperialism was fashioned out of some critical national need, as a means of helping the less privileged. If he is the traveling type of American and visited the Far East before this war began, he has seen the works of the colonial policies laid over the gilt and grime of antiquity. He has been shown magnificent public buildings, civic improvements, beautiful residential districts set amid squalor, good roads, peace and order—the outer manifestations of colonization.

More than likely he was impressed. Having for himself no autocratic desires or ambitions, the American was apt to come to the conclusion that the native was being benefited by all these. He perhaps reported to his fellow Americans that the British and

Dutch were fine colonizers, that backward countries certainly took a change for the better under their guidance, and that the native subjects seemed better off under imperialism than if under their own rule.

To the average American, the word imperialism has carried no odious implication since 1776. He may even regard it as conveying some sort of blessing to those whose destinies come under the glittering authority of a crown.

As an American he has forgotten his far-off resentment of crowns, and the fact that, two hundred years ago, he knew no peace until he had thrust off the galling yoke of imperialism. He can have no possible concept of the meaning of that word—imperialism—to the Oriental. Because, in America, he can tell off any other American in any matter pertaining to public welfare, and at the top of his lungs!

A whisper of complaint in the Far East can be regarded as high treason. And yet, before war started, there were many such whisperings in the Far East. As a Filipino and a fellow Oriental I heard them up to the very hour before the attack on Pearl Harbor. But the fact is important that I was allowed to hear them, not as the trusted fellow Oriental, but because, to the nationalists of Malay and French Indo-China and India, I represented America.

I was the Filipino, the Americanized, Westernized Oriental, who had been given every privilege of democracy under the American flag, and of whom these men of the subject Orient said wistfully:

"How lucky you are!"

Even that was said in whispers. Because in the Far East the government represents the Crown, and any criticism of the Crown is treasonable. Representatives of sovereignty, wishing to impress the natives with the infallibility of government which is the Crown, set themselves up in Asiatic countries in the full trappings of power. The Governor General appears before the dazzled populace in splendid uniform and wearing all his decorations. He is surrounded by strong forces, changes of guard, colorful ceremonials, presentations, and pageantry.

Dramatic and costly ceremonials are held in the palaces of the Far Eastern governors. These are staged to strike awe in the native and impress his simple mind with the life-and-death authority of the

Crown. The native sees and is awed, and behind the façade of glitter he is aware of naked bayonets and knows they are waiting for him if he does not conform to every order of this foreign authority, and over his awe terror forms. He knows if he edges too close to the impressive scene he will be hit over the head or bayoneted by a member of that watchful guard—a man perhaps of his own race. He may even be shot.

I have watched the faces of natives before such spectacles, seen them cringe under the blows of native police as they edged too near, and understood their sullen, watchful silence.

The native remains silent, for even if he dared criticize the injustices that invariably breed under the shadow of power he has no way of making his protests heard. He has no voice and no representation under kings. Sometimes, in Far Eastern countries, one or two natives would be pointed out as holding relatively important places of power. "See!" I was told, "the goodness of the Crown! These natives are holding positions of rank, just like white men."

But such men are quite aware that they are set in places of seeming authority for the sake of appearances. Ostensibly they are there to represent their people; in reality they are there to uphold imperialism. Represent it they must, if they wish to hold their positions, and it invariably happens that these men draw back from their own people into the imperialistic point of view where they are comfortable and well provided for.

Insignificant minority as such men are, they know their jobs will vanish if they dare move against the dominant current of power. Often, in time, they come to look arrogantly upon their fellow natives.

Since this type of puppet official does not represent the native, the native dares not go to him with his problems. To the native such false representation is injustice. To him, injustice and imperialism are one. Speak to him, this voiceless, helpless Oriental, the word imperialism, and if he trusts you, you will see his hatred!

Let me, being both of the Occident and the Orient, explain the inner source of this hatred for the benefit of those I consider my fellow Americans. For until Joe Doe of Brooklyn understands the human longings and problems of John Chang of Canton or Batavia there can be no true understanding between East and West. And until that mental chasm is bridged a permanent, intelligent peace cannot be developed and maintained between the West and the Far East.

To the Oriental the word imperialism has come to represent the presence in his country of white men in spotless clothing, who sip gin slings all day with their pampered women, in places the native is forbidden to enter. Apparently they never work, and pay no taxes, while the Oriental's miserable bowl of rice is nearly taxed out of existence. Yet the foreigners continue, in some mysterious fashion, to grow richer and richer. Incredible are the fortunes taken out of the Far East by white men! To the Oriental such fortunes are beyond his comprehension, but he is capable of asking how the foreigners are able to grow rich in his country, while he himself must pull a rickshaw all day and every day, in searing sun or pouring rain, to earn two dollars in a seven-day week.

On this sum he and his family must live, cooking, eating, sleeping, breeding, dying—often of starvation—in the streets, his children disfigured with the skin diseases that come of hunger and filth, his wife giving birth to those children on the sidewalk, on a filthy mat, like an animal whelping. He sees the twisted bodies of men like himself waiting disposal in the street, dead of hunger—a sight familiar to everyone who has visited the Orient. He is slow in movement, and a well-planted kick from a white foot restores him to activity—this I have seen as has every traveler in China, Hong Kong, India, French Indo-China, Burma, Java, Singapore.

He drags his rickshaw or burdened cart past magnificent residences, and realizes that such palaces are built by men who do not work, who spend much time carousing, which, he knows, has been made possible by the Crown. So he comes to hate imperialism. Hating imperialism, he hates the white race.

John Chang, average man of the Orient, was not often able to express this hatred. For one thing, he was, as a rule, too ignorant. In certain countries under imperialism the ratio of education is as low as 5 per cent. Also, he was afraid. But the moment came when he was able to protest his long years of humiliation and resentment with action, or, rather, with lack of action. Imperialism tottered in the Orient, and he did not step forward to hold it in place. The white man lost face in the Far East and John Chang had no pity.

The Oriental's hatred and fear of imperialism spoke at last in Burma, French Indo-China, Thailand, Singapore, Hong Kong, and Java, when he did not protest, but accepted, Japan!

Only the Filipino did not gloat over the fall of the white man. Only in the Philippines did the Oriental Filipino fight invasion by the side of his white brother.

In the Orient, long before war started, I watched imperialism die. There is no death without cause. Imperialism perishes only when it deserves to die. Kings do not always perish on guillotines. That is only the final step toward dissolution. They die first in little ways and little places—when their subjects scramble for food in gutters running with typhoid, when a starving native crawls meekly to a sidewalk's edge to die of hunger, when a well-shod shoe is planted on a scrawny buttock, and a baby's heavy head falls back from a starved breast empty of milk. Unpleasant and unrecorded are the little stories leading to the death of kings.

The Filipino fought with the white man's America because he believed in that America. He was not alone in that trust. It is universally shared by his fellow Orientals. All over the Far East, wherever I traveled before the outbreak of war, I heard this expressed in many tongues. The Oriental's suspicion toward the white race does not include America. He has seen in the Philippines the American principle of fair play expressed for the first time in the Oriental.

Everywhere else in the Far East he became familiar with exploitation and pillage, the bleeding of his country's riches, and the reduction of his living condition to an animal status by white men operating under a protective imperialism.

How differently America proceeded in the Philippines!

And the Oriental, as I know him, realizes this and has a pathetic desire to set his case before America.

Only America can re-establish contact between the white and

colored races in the Far East. Only America can rebuild a trust broken under centuries of imperialism.

America can do this. She is the only white man's country that can.

She did it before, in the Philippines.

## II. THE ORIENTAL LOOKS TO DEMOCRACY

DEMOCRACY, like imperialism, is a word taken for granted by the average American. It has been part of his national blood stream since 1776. It is as much a part of his daily living as his newspaper, so why get excited about it? That he is free and equal to any man he takes for granted. If he must fight to uphold that theory, he does so, as willingly as he would uphold his flag.

But the word "democracy" has a far different meaning to the Oriental mind. I wish every American could know how wishful a portent that word holds for John Chang—common man of the Orient!

From my point of vantage in the Philippines, facing both East and West, and being myself both of the Occident and of the Orient, I have watched the crosscurrents of ideology. I made a point of discussing democracy with the people of Far Eastern countries I have visited, and with their leaders in the nationalistic movements that so often, by motivating the downfall of imperialistic rule, become preludes to democracy.

In every Asiatic country I heard the same words, as if the same man were speaking. The same complaints were voiced, and the same pathetically eager questions asked of our life under American guidance in the Philippines.

The Oriental asks about democracy—and what does he mean by democracy? And what has it meant to men like himself under a white government?

These are his questions:

"Is it true that you, fellow Orientals like ourselves, have the right to govern yourselves under a white government? Is it true that you have the right to vote in the Philippines? Has it actually happened that in your country white men have been punished, some even by death, for crimes against natives?

"Is it true that you are paid fair wages, like white men, and own the produce raised on your own land, and send your children to public schools and even colleges built by Americans?

"And do you attend the club functions and social affairs given by the American, and does he visit in your home and you in his, and do you look upon him as a friend?

"Is it true that if you do not like some point in the American law that you can send an objection as far as America, and it will be listened to with respect?"

He asks such things for corroboration only, knowing they are true. And he invariably adds, wistfully and with envy:

"How wonderful! If only we could do the same."

For that is the dream of all men, to be equal and free. Even the goose-stepping Teuton carries that dream—to him his aim of being set above all the earth is his concept of being free. He is willing to submit to any regimentation in order to attain the superiority which to him is freedom.

The Oriental of the Far East dares to dream of freedom because he has seen it in action—he knows of the democratic example set by America in the Philippines.

Mind you, he has not read of these things! He cannot read—this average Oriental. He has perhaps never heard a radio nor seen a newsreel. And he dares not talk, unless he is brave enough to join the steadily growing secret movements of nationalism. But he has ears. He can listen. No matter how hard his life may be, no matter how remote his Asiatic village, he knows that in a country not far from his own men of his own color were likewise conquered by white men and still permitted to retain their self-respect. His fellow Orientals, the Filipinos, were permitted to exercise self-government under the American flag.

And he wonders, this outcast in his own country, this lingerer beside doorways he may not enter! In the Philippines, he knows, there is no doorway forbidden the Filipino. And this, he thinks enviously, is democracy. He thinks such thoughts and tells you about them, if he trusts you.

"If we could rule ourselves—how wonderful! That is being free. That is the thing you call democracy. But this imperialism we have is death, and no change could be the worse for us."

I heard this argument all over the Far East before Japan invaded. I answered it the best I could.

"Japan would be worse. Japan would be imperialism of the rankest order."

But they shook their heads in denial—these men who were subject to foreign crowns.

"No change could be worse for us."

I told them in the words of the speech made that day at Notre Dame in the presence of the President of the United States:

"If war comes, the Philippines will fight with America."

The leaders of the brown-skinned people would answer me reasonably, "We would hold with that point of view, if we were under a government such as you have in the Philippines. We would be willing to fight for a country like America."

That is Asia's answer to imperialism, its response to the democratic principle of the American fair deal.

I have no desire to denounce the policies of certain imperialistic countries which have paid heavily for their sins of omission or commission, nor their representatives in the Far East. Nor do I wish to hold to the premise that America's colonizing experiment in the Philippines was a matter of unstained, glowing altruism. America, the youngest, most impulsive, most human of the world's nations, is no angel. She has made her mistakes. But, as a country, she has ever been willing to admit and underwrite her errors.

I am not going to pretend there have been no cases of American exploitation in the Far East. There were a few Americans in Manila as greedy as the worst. But—and this is the subtle difference—such men were not permitted to represent America, and America as a government did not uphold their position, as imperialistic countries too often have upheld their exploiting representatives in the Far East.

The Oriental has been made aware of this difference. Imperialism upholds exploitation—democracy at its weakest merely condones it. An important difference to the native caught under the wheel! The distinction, in his mind, between imperialism and democracy.

The most benighted native knows the difference between fair and unfair treatment. No matter how difficult his life may originally have been, he knows it is made worse for him by imperialism. As his own master he might starve, but he would not be beaten while asking for a handful of rice.

Most important of all to his proud if downtrodden soul is the fact that from the very start of American occupation in the Philippines his fellow Oriental was met, not so much on the basis of equality, as on that of one human to another.

In all his dealings with the Filipino the American never failed to recognize what the imperialist overlooked in dealing with other races—the dignity of the human soul. I cannot overstress the importance of this fact. There may be several explanations for this attitude. It may be due in part to the American mind, which carries with it, even in transplantation, his inherent belief as voiced in the Declaration of Independence, that all men are created equal. Or it may be due to the fiercely independent quality of the Filipino nature and the fight he put up to maintain his dignity and impress the American with his passion for independence. The Indonesians protested the rule of the Dutch, the Hindus fought the English, only sporadically; but we carried on the fight against American occupation for three years and after that waged vigorously the political contest for independence.

This adventure in altruism, as it has turned out to be, has not failed to pay rich dividends. Economically, the Philippines paid. Spiritually and physically they paid, in America's worst hour. But America's reward extends beyond the Philippines. It is in the trust of millions of anxious brown faces, turned over the horrors of contest away from all other white peoples toward her, Mother America. America's is the reward of the proselyte—she who has never attempted to force upon other countries her concept of democracy.

In this lies America's reward and America's power. The Far East is in upheaval, but over it lies the glow of American victory.

It is to America that the Oriental turns at this time with a prayer for understanding. I heard that cry all over the Far East. Wherever I traveled native newspaper editors and correspondents told me hopelessly:

"If only we could tell our side to America! But the imperialistic press never gives us a chance. We can't get any news through to America."

Native nationalist leaders were as bitter.

"We will open our hearts to you as a fellow Oriental," they told me, "and tell you how we think and what we believe should be done. But what good will it do? What we tell you will never be printed in America."

They were wrong. I wrote their side of the Asiatic problem and America did print it; it was published in more than a hundred newspapers in North and South America, and that these articles won their Filipino author America's Pulitzer prize is another example of American fairness.

That is America—always willing to look at the other fellow's side, hear his story, give him credit on equal terms. And that, to the Oriental, is democracy. He likes—he trusts—that word democracy. Trusts it, because he knows it held unfailingly to its every premise for forty-two years in the Philippines.

In other countries in the Far East natives were reduced to the level of animals, but in the Philippines, from the very beginning, the Americans regarded us as men.

Final proof of the efficacy of this treatment came in 1941 when, for the first time, Orientals turned against Orientals to fight beside white men—to uphold democracy.

Why this Philippine defense of our white conquerors?

Why did the Filipinos, almost to a man, feel so strongly bound to America?

To understand this fully we must go back, and not so very far back, to within my own lifetime, when the Philippines were still under the Spanish Crown.

# III. THE PHILIPPINES UNDER IMPERIALISM

SHORTLY before the turn of the century, when I was born, imperialism presented a haggard face in the Philippines. Poverty, injustice, and exploitation had lasted too long under the Spanish kings.

The tao, or common man, was helpless under the exploitations and cruelties of the hated Guardia Civil—representative in the Philippines of the Spanish Crown.

Juan de la Cruz as we call him—the Juan Tao or John Doe of the Philippines—was a virtual serf under the land-renting or Kasama system.

Kasama is a Tagalog word meaning partnership. But the partnership under Spain was that between master and slave. The system held the Filipino population in bondage to Spain.

Living was cheap in the Philippines. The rivers and seas were teeming with fish; fruits and coconuts grew everywhere. But the country has never been self-sufficient. Food remained, and still remains, a problem. Rice, milk, canned goods of every kind, were imported.

The fact that the Philippines is an agricultural country and its people pastoral gave birth to many wrongs. Rich Spanish landowners held the land. They rented small portions to the Filipino in need of a farm. The poor tao, owning nothing but his carabao or water buffalo, was "employed" to work the land. A sum of money was advanced toward his hire, and out of this he must build his hut and purchase seed and farming tools. He was to live on the land and repay this primary loan out of the rice he was able to produce.

As a rule, due to the uncertainty of crops, he found the loan impossible to repay. The debt increased year after year and was handed down through one generation after another. Children many times removed from the original borrower toiled in the rice fields to pay a debt that never could be paid, that had swollen in size for perhaps a hundred years.

Ignorant, in debt, and at the mercy of the unscrupulous, the tao had no means of protesting the power of the rich landowners. He was a serf. He had no voice in his own government under the Guardia Civil. He had no government.

Harassed, tyrannized, and persecuted, Juan Tao was at the mercy of a too-remote rule. Luzon was half the world away from the courts of Spain. Had it been nearer, the story would have been different. The Philippine Colonial Governor General was advised by the Viceroy of Acapulco, Mexico, which was the terminus of the Spanish Government.

Spain itself was torn in the throes of change and dissolution. The Philippines were far-off tatters of its former glory. It was ruled by despotic Spanish officials who fattened on graft. Even the progressive change of street lighting in Manila from coconut oil to kerosene was accomplished by scandalous graft charges.

Law was in the hands of the feared and hated Guardia Civil. "They are worse than the bandits!" people said helplessly of them. And bandits were everywhere.

But no Filipino dared protest anything done by the men who worked under the Captain General. Evil stories were told. Men were arrested—no one knew why. They were tried behind locked doors. They vanished—no one knew where.

No one dared question the actions of the dread Guardia Civil.

To own his own plot of land, to earn a decent living, to educate his children, were not for the Filipino tao under Spanish rule. Education was in the hands of friars, some of them unscrupulous, who collaborated with the landowners in holding the Filipinos in slavery. The imperialists did not think it wise to expose the subject tao to the dangers of learning—a theory shared by all autocratic powers. And rightly. Education has ever contributed to the downfall of kings.

The average Filipino child was taught at home by mother and grandmother, then attended a school conducted by the village priest. At best he could look forward to learning the alphabet and his prayers. The Filipino who did succeed in attaining priesthood was considered unfit to have in his care the keeping of souls. Education and ambition were detriments to a poor man's son.

Our greatest patriot, Rizal, tells of a Filipino schoolmaster who had purchased maps and pictures from his meager salary and petitioned the Spanish authorities for a roof for his schoolhouse—an abandoned warehouse—to shield these treasures from the torrential rains. He was logically adjudged an agitator and suspended from teaching.

As the last century drew near its close resentment deepened among the Filipinos. Every debacle in the shaky politics of Spain had its resultant flurry of misery for the Philippines.

The Filipinos are peace-loving, fun-loving, pastoral, quickly moved to love or resentment. For three hundred years we had resented Spain. By this time Spanish blood was in ours. There was much intermarriage. Spanish colonists were numbered among our relatives and friends. We still resented Spanish rule.

It was not Spain we hated, but its corrupt representatives. It was not the Church we protested, but those friars who had yielded to greed in dealing with the helpless Filipinos. And in this situation it is interesting to note a characteristic of the Filipino: that he could remain loyal to the Church while turning against some of its unworthier representatives.

In this he was Oriental—he could forget the substance and remember the shadow. The same attitude controlled his actions later in dealing with America. He saw in his faith a sound and sane principle; he remained faithful to it. By the same precept he would later defend democracy, having found it sound and sane and to his liking.

We were well aware how much we owed to Spain in the Philippines. But from the very beginning we had protested the presence in our country of a foreign power. We showed our resentment to the first European to touch our shores. Ferdinand Magellan, sailing under the Spanish flag, discovered the Philippines in 1521 in the first circumnavigation of the world, and claimed and named them in honor of a Spanish king. He was killed in open combat by a native Filipino—first protestant of imperialism in the Philippines.

The missionaries accomplished where the conquistadores failed. Half a century later the Spanish friars came with the first colonists to the Islands. The good fathers went in small groups or even alone into the forests, to live with the natives and attempt bringing them to a Christian faith.

The native Filipinos, of Malayan stock and speaking many dialects, were simple and responsive. They capitulated wholeheartedly to the white missionaries. They turned to the white man's God. Never again would they be true Orientals.

Spanish authority followed in the wake of the children of God, and while we learned quickly to distrust that authority, our allegiance to the Catholic Church never faltered. Certain friars came in time to be hated; these we would fight, as we fought all exponents of imperialism. Such men represented, not the Cross, but the Crown.

Spain brought us closer to Europe. The sixteenth century found us occupying an important position on the charts of commerce. Ours was the most easterly tip of the Spanish Main!

The fabulous galleons came regularly to our shores, returning to Spain across the Pacific, along the coasts of California, Mexico, and South America. Among other treasures they carried back shawls of great beauty embroidered by Filipinos, to be known henceforth as Spanish shawls. And for two years we were British!

In 1762 Spain warred against England, and thirteen British ships appeared in Manila Bay. The British tars bombarded the Walled City and captured Manila.

Two years later the war ended and the Philippines were given back to Spain.

Despite the vices and injustices of imperialism we benefited greatly and learned much from Spain. The good priests taught us our prayers and tillage of the land. Spiritual, social, and agricultural advances were made under the guidance of the Church. It established the University of Santo Tomás—the oldest university under the American flag—older than Harvard.

The good Spanish families set us examples of culture and social living. Many of our leading families in the Philippines are Spanish. The Spanish are part of us, our traditions, our blood, and our very lives.

That we are more of Occident than Orient the Filipinos owe to Spain.

The Spanish taught us to sing in European fashion. Oriental music has no chromatic scale and its songs are strange to Occidental ears. They became equally strange to the Filipino, for we came to love the sentimental love songs and laments of Cadiz and Castille. We learned to play guitars under barred windows, to watch hopefully in the wake of watchful duennas for a smile's flash under a veil. We even learned to kiss as Europeans do. The Malayan kiss is primitive—the mouth placed close and a swift intake of breath, as babies kiss while learning.

Our concept of morality and marriage became Occidental. Our attitude toward women is that of the West, not the East. We regard women with an exaggerated and sentimental respect, as most Europeans do, not like the Oriental, who accepts them as beasts of burden or things of pleasure.

So upon our basic Oriental structure was superimposed Spanish culture and belief in the Christian God during a process that lasted three hundred years.

Spiritually, economically, and intellectually, we were of the Occident. The Occident also gave us that most dangerous of weapons, the printing press. During the last half of the last century presses were brought to the Philippines from Spain. Limited at first to religious publications, they gradually widened their scope until between 1840 and 1872 fifty newspapers were founded in the Islands.

Men who learn to read learn to question. The Filipino is inherently a freedom-loving individual, and he had not ceased to chafe against foreign rule since the arrival of Magellan. Out of the hearts of the common people came a Tagalog myth that persisted through the centuries.

This hopeful legend, similar to one that exists in many forms among oppressed peoples, dealt with a King Bernardo who had been held prisoner in a cave in the Luzon hills for hundreds of years. The legend prophesied that someday the king would burst his shackles and stretch his giant frame, and stride over the Philippines, stamping to death all the hated members of the Guardia Civil.

The voice of the legendary Bernardo was heard before the century ended.

As always with restless people, protest began among those who had been given means with which to think. The rebellion against

Spain was started by young men who had tasted the freedom of education. Some had studied in the Spanish university in Manila and others had gone abroad to study in France, Germany, or Spain. These returned with a new and indignant awareness of the way men lived in other lands.

They told of progress made in other countries; they listed the wrongs and injustices of their own. Why, they demanded, were the Philippines not permitted to advance? Why was the Kasama system of hire permitted to hold the Filipinos as peons of the land? Why was the land in the hands of the few?

And why, they wanted to know, should not the Philippines have roads and railways and commercial enterprises, like other countries?

The young men told stories of outrages—graft, violence, rape, murder—perpetrated under the guise of Spanish authority. They cited the tragedy of Kalamba, which is the Lidice of the Philippines. Humble men in the village of Kalamba had dared protest claims to their land, and were driven out before Spanish guns. The body of one was actually dragged from its grave and tossed to the village dogs by way of showing contempt for a Filipino who had dared ask for justice!

These rebellious young thinkers began addressing those they trusted as "Citizens of the Philippines!" in the same fierce way men had voiced in France the first defiant words of the "Marseillaise." Such words were spoken by the discontented, in locked rooms or behind the covers of books.

Among their voices was that of our nation's greatest hero, José Rizal.

What Harriet Beecher Stowe had been to the American Civil War, José Rizal was to our revolution against Spain.

He was of pure Malayan blood. He studied at the University of Santo Tomás and in Germany and Spain. He returned to the Philippines fired with indignation against a system that held his countrymen to the level of serfs. He became a member of the Young Filipino party, a liberal group struggling to attain justice. He wrote— his books were like flames. His greatest book, *The Reign of Greed*, bared the vicious system of imperialism and its resultant injustices.

It became the *Uncle Tom's Cabin* of the Philippines. It gave impetus to the revolution; it brought death to Rizal.

This book was dedicated to three Filipino priests who were the first martyrs of the rebellion. In 1872 the rapidly growing liberal party had incited the native garrison in the Cavite arsenal to mutiny against their Spanish officers. The three priests were garroted in reprisal.

Rizal was hounded by the Spanish authorities. He set out for Europe, by permission of the authorities, having enlisted in the medical corps of the Spanish Army that was going to Cuba. He was arrested in Singapore and returned to Manila, where he was charged with treason and exiled to Mindanao. Evidence that helped convict Rizal was his moving dedication of *The Reign of Greed* to the three martyred priests of Cavite.

Nevertheless, he came back to his beloved Manila. He was not an agitator. He was not a believer in violence. He was a patriot who loved his country—who returned home.

The Spanish authorities were afraid of the influence of Rizal. They committed the last of the fatal errors that would cost Spain the Philippines.

Rizal was publicly executed by a firing squad in Manila, in December 1896.

Rebellion flared up with his death. A young Filipino leader, a laborer, Andres Bonifacio, summoned his waiting forces and marched against imperialism.

At Balintawak, a village outside Manila, there is the statue of a Filipino holding aloft a bolo and the flag of the revolution. It is called the "First Cry of Liberty."

On this spot shortly after the death of Rizal, Andres Bonifacio and his band of Filipino patriots struck the first Philippine blow against Spain.

## IV. REVOLUTION AGAINST SPAIN

EMILIO AGUINALDO was only twenty-seven years old when Andres Bonifacio led the uprising against Spain.

He had been born in a barrio in Cavite. Education served to make the young man resentful of the lot of his fellow Filipinos. He joined Andres Bonifacio's Katipunan, which was the Filipino challenge to imperialism.

This organization had been primarily made up of the liberal nationalists, who asked for fair treatment from the Spanish rulers. It was not unlike the groups of nationalists that developed before this present war in Indonesia and India and other Oriental countries under imperialism.

The requests for equality made by this early group had been denied. By 1896 it was no longer liberal or pacific. Its members were avowedly for rebellion. They prepared, bought guns and ammunition, trained in secret. "Reform by violence" was the new motto with which they launched their attack on Spanish rule, first under Bonifacio, then under the command of Aguinaldo.

It was a time ripe for rebellion. Spain had weakened as a world power. The Spanish Crown was being supported with increasing shakiness in the Philippines. Spain had never maintained a competent standing army in the Philippines to uphold Spanish authority. There were only a few hundred Spanish soldiers in the Islands. The majority of troops were Filipinos, serving under Spanish officers.

And now Spain, tottering on the last legs of her greatness, had need of her soldiers elsewhere. She was hurrying her best troops out of the Philippines, to Cuba.

There were rumors heard in the Philippines of growing difficulties between Spain and the United States. Spain had been growling in the direction of America and America was beginning to show her teeth in answer.

The Filipinos watched this situation hopefully. We had long admired Yankee ingenuity and America's fight for freedom against the English Crown. The rebellion of 1776 was cited as a source of inspiration by such leaders as Aguinaldo. In a way America had become our ideal among nations. She was the symbolism of our own unrest.

Our revolution against Spanish rule began with a concerted attack on the Guardia Civil. The Spanish authorities tried to suppress the revolt with superior weapons and trained forces. But they were fighting true revolution, which is a spiritual force and comes from the very soul of a people.

Three hundred Filipino leaders were flung into the Spanish prisons. Those convicted of being rebel leaders were executed. Manila and five other provinces were declared in a state of siege.

Prison and death could not stop the revolution. The Spanish authorities had tried the argument of death before. They had martyred Rizal, but his soul, like John Brown's, continued its heroic march toward freedom.

Aguinaldo's forces swept over one Spanish stronghold after another, until the last Spanish representative begged for mercy.

On December 12, 1897, Aguinaldo signed the pact of Biak-na-Bató—one of the most important documents in Philippine history.

This treaty promised, among other things, the Filipino equal representation with the Spaniard. The Filipinos believed it ended a struggle for equality that had lasted three hundred years.

Aguinaldo retired to Hong Kong with indemnity and thirty-five members of his staff. There he learned that the promises made by the representatives of Spain were not being upheld by the Spanish Crown. Madrid was not living up to the promise of Biak-na-Bató.

Members of the Katipunan were persecuted. Men who had taken part in the revolution were hunted down and jailed. A resurgence of terrorism swept Manila. Aguinaldo's work had not been finished—the Philippines were not entirely free.

This was the state of affairs when an incident in Cuba, on February 15, 1898, rushed our destiny to a strange conclusion.

News traveled slowly then, and my father, learning from Spanish friends that on this date the U.S.S. *Maine* had been blown up in Havana Harbor, little dreamed the explosion would rock the farthest provinces of the Philippines. He, with others who had taken part in Aguinaldo's revolution, received the news with personal interest.

Cuba was only eighty miles off the American coast. Surely the planting of a mine there could not affect the Philippines. Let the Americans and Spanish fight, for virtually this made the Americanos allies with the Filipinos! So the Filipinos decided, following the delayed reports from the other side of the world. They were delighted when President McKinley took a firm attitude toward Spain. They rejoiced when America went to war with Spain in the wake of a cry:

"Remember the *Maine!*"

Aguinaldo hurried back to Manila. He returned, with his fellow revolutionary leaders, in an American transport, provided by the American Commodore George Dewey, who chanced to be stationed with his Asiatic fleet at Hong Kong. Dewey approved Aguinaldo's return and allowed him to be supplied with arms.

Waves of revolutionists swept before Aguinaldo, reopened the rebellion with new fervor, and declared the Philippines forever independent of Spain. They fought as only patriots can fight, wiping out Spanish fortresses the length and breadth of Luzon. They declared the Philippines an independent republic and Aguinaldo its President.

At last only Manila remained in the hands of the Spanish. Within its ancient walls were trapped the last of the Guardia Civil and the remnant forces of the Spanish artillery. Aguinaldo and his army surrounded the city.

Spanish ships anchored in Manila Bay held back Aguinaldo's taking of the capital. But he knew Manila must fall—it was only a matter of days. There was neither water nor food in the city, and famine and disease worked in behalf of the besiegers. The water supply had been cut off. Terrible rumors came over the old walls. Every animal in the city was eaten, down to the house cats.

The revolutionists could afford to wait.

The rebellion would end with the fall of Manila, and after three hundred years the Filipinos would be free.

Then a strange thing happened.

The American Dewey and his ships appeared in Manila Bay. It was said later in the Philippines that Aguinaldo was beside Dewey that day on his flagship. From the shore Aguinaldo's victorious army watched the battle of Manila Bay and the destruction of the Spanish ships by Commodore Dewey's Asiatic fleet. This was May 1, 1898.

Aguinaldo and his forces were delighted with this unsolicited American aid in their war against the Spanish forces. They had no way of knowing that Dewey and his ships were in Manila Bay in reprisal for the Spanish mine planted under the *Maine*.

Dewey had been ordered to destroy the Spanish squadron and capture the Philippines—Spain's stronghold in the Far East. He had issued soothing propaganda: "We are not here to fight you, but to protect you."

Protection was the last thing the Filipinos wanted. They were cocksure of victory.

Aguinaldo requested a conference with Dewey. He had but one question:

"Will the United States recognize my government?"

We of the Philippines, and certainly Aguinaldo, have always believed Dewey assured the Filipino commander that the United States had no intention of colonizing the Philippines. Aguinaldo claimed that Dewey promised him America would give complete independence to the Philippines. This Dewey would deny. Aguinaldo bolstered this belief from his knowledge of American democratic ideals.

"I have studied attentively the Constitution of the United States," Aguinaldo decided, "and in it I find no authority for colonies, and I have no fear."

Touching words, in view of what was to follow!

In the wake of Dewey's bluejackets men in khaki came pouring into the Philippines—the first American soldiers ever to leave American soil.

Among their military leaders was a Major General Arthur Mac-

Arthur, who, and his son after him, were to have much to do with shaping subsequent history in the Philippines.

The concerted attack on Manila began with the arrival of Mac-Arthur's brigade. The American forces ignored Aguinaldo's siege and began bombarding the city from both harbor and shore.

Without water or supplies, ridden with malaria and typhoid, fired on by both American and Filipino guns, Manila fell.

The white flag lifted over the old wall and American forces marched into the historic capital: MacArthur's men. Dewey's men. Greene's men. Merritt's men. But not Aguinaldo's men!

They were stopped at the gates of Manila. They were forbidden to enter the city. It was this—the capital—Aguinaldo wanted! He was forced to retire with his troops to a suburb in the outer city.

This was the beginning of Filipino indignation against the American forces. Aguinaldo was no longer grateful to the foreigners who had helped write the last chapter of Filipino protest against Spain.

Then the Filipinos learned that the war between America and Spain was over and that the Philippines, overnight, had been made part of America.

We, half a world away from Havana Harbor, who had known little of the troubles in Cuba, were losers in the contest between the United States and Spain. The battle of Manila need never have been fought. The rich but tattered royal prize that was the Philippines was the spoil of victory.

The Philippines, with more than seven thousand islands and ten million brown-skinned inhabitants, had been ceded to the United States by Spain for twenty million dollars.

I was an infant when this happened, but I was to be nourished to manhood on the indignation and despair of my elders who had fought in the revolution against Spain and known the sweetness of victory—only to find that victory tossed aside as a sop to appeasement.

This was the way the Filipinos felt when their country was taken over by America. We would suffer from this resentment many years.

To be frank, the Philippines were acquired by America in her only outburst of imperialism. The outburst did not come from a desire for power. It was salve applied to the wounded pride of a great country. It was a response to a slogan: "Remember the *Maine!*"

The American military authorities explained why they were in our country. "To develop the country. To open up the Philippines to commerce."

Such phrases were fine-sounding, like Dewey's statement that he came to protect the Philippines. The usually good-natured, easygoing Filipino had discovered much in his brief war against Spanish tyranny. He had learned he was a fighter. He had won his revolt against Spain. Had he turned against one foreign rule only to submit to another? No matter how beneficent that rule might be, in the minds of men who had fought for independence it was still tyranny.

The insurgents rallied in swelling forces around Aguinaldo. On February 4, 1899, hostilities broke out in a Manila suburb between American and Filipino forces.

Our revolution against America—which the Americans would term insurrection—began.

# V. REVOLUTION AGAINST AMERICA

As a NATION we were thoroughly aroused by 1899.

"The Filipinos are not a warlike people," General Arthur Mac-
Arthur said of us at this time. But we had waged and won our revolution against Spain and had no intention of submitting to America's
claims on our country. The Americans were in the Philippines
without our consent.

It was the determination of every Filipino man, woman, and child
to drive them out.

We fought American occupation for three years. From the beginning it was a hopeless contest. The United States was rich in
resources and man power; it could pour whole armies of soldiers,
well trained and well equipped, into our country. Within four years
American transports had landed 125,000 khaki-clad Yankees on
Luzon.

Without proper training or organization, with primitive weapons
and ancient guns, the Filipinos fought to hold the Philippines.
Tribes from remote provinces swung bolos beside their college-
educated countrymen. Natives of types we of the cities had never
seen came down from the hills to fight with bows and arrows. Even
the children formed brigades and threw rocks at the American soldiers, who stood helpless before such ludicrous but telling on-
slaught.

Both armies fought mud, pestilence, and the dangers of the jungle.
Aguinaldo's men had the additional handicaps of lack of food,
equipment, and transportation. It was the same sort of hopeless war
that would be waged forty-two years later on Bataan, when Filipinos and Americans yielded to the superior forces of the Japanese.

Major General Henry W. Lawton of the American forces said of the Filipinos during this time:

"Taking into account the disadvantages they have had to fight against . . . they are the bravest men I have ever seen." American occupation was achieved by 1900.

After hundreds of small battles the revolution ended from the American point of view when Aguinaldo went into retreat in the mountains and organized warfare stopped. But the Filipinos did not know they were beaten. Aguinaldo was still their King Bernardo, held captive in the mountains and waiting his chance to free the Philippines. The Filipinos went on fighting as guerrilleros.

Guerrilla warfare began in 1900 with the new century. This mode of fighting, as old as war itself, is particularly adaptable to the Philippine terrain. There are forests in Luzon so impenetrable that they are capable of sheltering entire armies. Thick foliage forms a waterproof roof against the torrential rains. There are trees with hollow trunks that can provide shelter for half-a-dozen men, and caves behind shores and rivers impossible for any but a native to locate. In such places the scattered forces of Aguinaldo went into hiding, to sally out in surprise raids that harried and baffled the American forces. They were aided and abetted by the townspeople. Again, it was everybody's war—everybody was in the fight.

There was no "walkie-talkie" then, no telephone to carry communication between the secret lines. Orders in code were drummed through the forests on bamboo. This was the bamboo telegraph that would sound again in the Philippines when the Japanese invaded. Guerrilla warfare was revived after the Philippines fell to the Japanese. Modern devices aid its efficiency, but as a mode of fighting it remains savage and elemental.

Guerrilla warfare comes from the inside of a people—it is waged, encouraged, and aided by the people. It cannot exist without the loyalty of the general population. The guerrilla army must be fed, armed, sheltered, protected, and kept informed by the civilians.

As the son of a guerrillero father I learned much of the methods of these fighters.

Townsmen, countrymen, or guerrilla at large worked under the very noses of the occupying forces. The most peaceful citizen by day might be a prowling tiger by night. Your next-door neighbor, a man of sedentary occupation and mild manners, might be the leader of a guerrilla band. Such men were inured to dangerous living and hardship. The guerrilla fighter trained by night. He became a master marksman who used his gun only when necessary, not only to save ammunition but to keep from exposing himself to the enemy. He carried food on his person and went hungry, to accustom himself to semi-starvation. He learned to suffer pain without whimpering, because a sound might betray him to the enemy. He learned to endure rain and heat and jungle discomfort and knew which herbs of the forest were useful in warding off jungle diseases. Wounded, he nursed his wounds in silence until he could reach a physician that could be trusted. Captured, he died without speaking.

The guerrillero of the town was in constant touch with the guerrillero in the hills. He sent messages of advice or warning to those in hiding by the bamboo telegraph, church bells, or messenger. Arms, ammunition, and provisions were received and dispatched in strange ways, under mounds of dried cogon grass or in carts heaped with buffalo dung.

Women played an active part in the campaign. They maintained much of the communication between the guerrilla forces. Housewives haggling with vendors in the market place might be discussing in code the movement and troop numbers of the Americans. Mango and guava prices they argued were translatable into terms of arms and men to the farmer-vendor, who served as courier to the forces hiding in the surrounding hills. At nightfall, driving his empty cart homeward, he would pause to relay his information to other couriers waiting along the roads.

Women patched the clothing of the fighters, prepared bandages, medical kits, and food, and left these on kitchen tables in the evening. In the morning all would be gone.

The youngest child knew he must observe much and tell nothing. He might be playing ball outside his home when an American sentry appeared at the corner. The ball would fly in an open window—the guerrillero father within would be warned in time.

War such as this is impossible to stamp out. The Americans realized it would continue indefinitely in the Philippines unless some means could be found to convince the Filipinos that American intentions were friendly.

Certain officers decided upon more violent steps to quell what the Americans called the "insurrection," but which we of the Philippines termed our second revolution. The American forces continued to spread through the occupied towns and fought back as best they could the surprise sallies of the Filipinos. But to bring the guerrilla forces to terms they would have to learn two things: where were the guerrilla leaders hiding, and where were the ammunition and guns hidden?

American soldiers asked these questions of captive Filipinos.

The ugly chapter began.

Filipinos were encouraged to talk by means of the rope and water cures. The rope method was a slow strangling and a painful release to life. This was repeated.

The water cure was revived from the Inquisition. A man's stomach was pumped full of water and then jumped upon until it emptied. This was repeated until the victim was unconscious. Then he was revived, and the process repeated.

But the tortured Filipinos did not talk. The hidden guerrilla army remained hidden. Even Filipinos who by this time had become sympathetic to the Americans and were willing to accept the occupation refused to talk under torture.

All through the year 1900 the guerrilla fighting continued. By this time a great deal about the Filipinos and the Philippines was finding its way into the American newspapers. Americans talked of Luzon, Zamboanga, Iloilo—strange names for American-held places.

There was much sympathy for the Filipinos in the United States. A definite wave of "anti-imperialism" swept the country. Added indignation followed reports of the "cures." Aguinaldo of the Philippines became surrounded by a symbolic aura, not only to his own people, but to many sympathizers in the United States.

No less an authority than Washington investigated the reports of the rope and water cures. Officers who had been in charge of such cases were found guilty, reprimanded, fined, and dismissed from the Army. Several received prison terms.

Impossible to translate the effect of such reprisal on the military mind! Consider, then, its effect on the simpler reasoning of the Filipino. He was impressed and awed that the United States he had been fighting as a tyrant should take such pains to uncover and punish tyranny.

It was our first experience with American justice. Its effect was recognizable. As American officers were punished, more and more Filipinos brought in their guns and ammunition and yielded to the American military heads. Among these one of the most respected by the Filipinos was the father of Douglas MacArthur. General Arthur MacArthur was one of the first of the Americans to win our wholehearted trust.

As Military Governor he held the Philippines under martial law, policed the country, imprisoned and tried captured insurgents, and deported those found guilty. He was stern, courteous, and fair. He issued the proclamation of amnesty that promised a reward and no punishment to anyone turning over a rifle to the American authorities.

Thousands of Filipinos took advantage of the amnesty by turning in their arms and taking the oath of allegiance to the United States.

General MacArthur established in the Philippines the writ of habeas corpus which is the foundation stone of the American Bill of Rights. This was a daring act in a country still at war. And in this turbulent year 1900 he organized the Filipino Scouts, the military organization composed of Filipino soldiers under American officers which later became the nucleus of the American armed forces in the Philippines.

Many of these were Filipinos who had fought in the revolution against Spain and the revolution against America. Proud of their new organization and their new uniforms, they told their friends: "This General MacArthur is a great man!"

Stories spread of this American leader. His friendly, democratic attitude toward the Filipino soldiers was often cited. He was one with his men, they said. He was also a hero—he had been awarded the Congressional Medal of Honor for valor in the Civil War. His son would wear that medal later in recognition of Bataan and Corregidor.

Officers like General MacArthur helped quell the revolution by the weight of their personal integrity. But the guerrilla fighting continued. Without sufficient arms, food, medicines, or hope the guer-rilleros carried on the three-year-old fight against America.

It was General MacArthur who reasoned that the resistance would never end while Aguinaldo remained free. The Philippine leader, who was encamped in the mountains with his movements handicapped by the sick wife who had to be transported by litter, had become a legend and the symbol of freedom to his people.

"Capture Aguinaldo," MacArthur ordered finally, "but capture him alive."

In March 1901 Aguinaldo was taken prisoner by General Fred-erick Funston, by a ruse. Pro-American Filipinos went to the lead-er's camp pretending to be Aguinaldo sympathizers. With them were American officers disguised as prisoners. General MacArthur received the captive Aguinaldo with the respect one military leader tenders another. The result of their meeting was agreement and complete understanding, and out of that understanding came the full capitulation of Emilio Aguinaldo with his historic proclamation that brought peace to the Philippines:

"The country has declared unmistakably for peace. . . . By ack-nowledging and accepting the sovereignty of the United States throughout the entire Archipelago, as I do now without any reser-vations whatsoever, I believe that I am serving thee, my beloved country."

The words ended protest against America.

Following Aguinaldo, leader after leader, fighter after fighter, made his way into Manila and took the pledge of allegiance to the United States of America.

Aguinaldo retired under pension to serve as head of the Philip-pine Veterans' Association.

So the last of the fighters for freedom laid down his arms.

But the people—that was a different matter. Juan Tao had fought and sacrificed too long and too bitterly to capitulate in spirit to American rule. The common Filipino who had struggled to hold his country was still to be convinced of the friendly intentions of America. In his own fashion he continued his fight for freedom.

# VI. AMERICA IN THE PHILIPPINES

THE FILIPINO at the beginning of this century had reason to distrust the American.

The record set by the white man in the Orient was not calculated to inspire trust in Oriental minds. Invariably his presence in a Far Eastern country brought grief and degradation to the natives. The entire history of the Orient was a gigantic object lesson teaching us to suspect and fear all peoples with white skin.

The Americans had taken the Philippines by ruse and violence and we were not going to make their occupancy any easier for them. So we prepared ourselves for sullen and secret opposition—the Oriental's age-long defense against the more powerful Occidental.

From the beginning there were difficulties in our way. In the first place, we were no longer true Orientals. In speech and manner and way of living we were like our first white conquerors, the Spanish. The first Americans to meet the Filipinos on other than fighting terms were surprised to find how many characteristics we shared with them.

We had far more in common with the Americans than with our neighbors and close relations in near-by Asia.

This mutual discovery came about after General MacArthur had restored peace and order to Luzon and authority moved from military to civil government. On July 4, 1901—American Independence Day and our first under the Stars and Stripes—military law was abolished and American government was established in the Philippines. William Howard Taft became the first Civil Governor.

The year previous he had formed the Philippine Commission,

assuring for the Philippines legislative authority for the passing of revenue-raising laws, the establishment of an American educational system and civil courts, and promising, most important to our minds:

"The Philippines for the Filipinos."

We could not place faith in that pledge. We had suffered too long and too deeply—as all the Orient had suffered—under the rule of white men. We took it for granted that while improvements might be awarded the Philippines under the new American rule, they would be for the benefit of the Americans and not for us. We reasoned that the Americans were there to take advantage of us. That had been the immemorial procedure of white men in the Orient.

The coming of peace sent the majority of the American soldiers back to the United States. Others remained in the Philippines to enter business or trade, and of these not a few made fortunes. They were joined by a migration of Americans from the States, come, we had no doubt, to prey upon us, the defeated.

These, the first non-military Americans in the Philippines, arrived with preconceived notions of our country and of us. Much had been printed about the Philippines in American newspapers during the war with Spain and our own revolt against American occupation. Also, many American soldiers, returning home from the first American war sally off home soil, spread lurid and gory tales of the Philippines.

The American civilian arrived with the expectation of facing life in an uncivilized, almost savage country, inhabited by people who wore G strings and lived in trees. He was surprised to find a country that, while not as advanced as his own, was certainly not primitive. While education was not as yet a free and public institution, still the seeds of it were everywhere. Set among the nipa shacks were handsome Spanish *casas*, balconied and patioed, of the type of architecture that would later make Hollywood delightful as a residential city. In such a house in Camiling, wherein I was born, was antique furniture brought centuries before by galleon from Spain.

These homes of the well-to-do Filipinos and Spanish held many of the refinements the American associated with the better homes of his own country. Culture was European, instigated by the early

Spanish and developed by Filipinos who had traveled or studied in Europe. Social living was regarded as one of the fine arts, and the hospitality of the Filipinos was lavish and warmhearted, like that of Spanish hidalgos.

The American was astonished to find a definitely established school of Filipino literature. There were many excellent Filipino artists, schooled in the finest traditions of the Old World.

He found the Filipino's songs, his manner of dancing in couples, his attitude toward women, sentiment and morality, and his political ideology were far closer to the American than the Oriental.

Unlike other Orientals, we Filipinos do not speak of "face," but rather of honor or dignity, and we term it *amor proprio*, as a sophisticated American may speak of his *amour-propre*. Unlike most Orientals, we have a deep love for life and a reluctance and respect for death.

Like the Americans, we love a jest, even to the point of practical joking. We have an overwhelming desire to be thought well of and liked. We are friendly and smile easily. From the beginning it was difficult for us not to smile at the white invaders. And, most important of all, we were fellow Christians. Filipinos and Americans worshiped the same God.

Yes, it was difficult for us to dislike the Americans. Nevertheless, it was our determination, as the century and American rule began, to stand firm and not yield an inch to the usurpers.

The Americans found the Filipinos united against them solidly. As a people we were determined neither to give nor to accept anything from them. The very babies shared this determination. I remember how I glowered from a distance at the American soldiers bivouacked in Camiling and made up my mind nothing should make me speak nor smile at the "foreign devils."

The Filipino's passion for freedom and democracy was as strong as the American's. Before the Americans came we had set up our own Philippine republic based upon democratic precepts. We distrusted the professions of a democracy that had set another aside to substitute its own.

The American did not fail to consider our point of view. Like the Filipino, he is both friendly and a fighter. Also, he is curious and has an honest interest in other people. But he is neither so friendly nor curious as he is fair and open-minded. He has his prejudices but is always willing to hear what the other fellow has to say. We learned this very soon about the American. And we had a great deal to say. We were not a submissive people. Our language was richly descriptive—we were able to make our objections and intentions known.

Our intentions were for the maintenance of self-respect. We were speaking to men qualified by heritage to understand. The American, being an American, knows that only self-respect can command respect. People who voluntarily stretch their necks under yokes are treated with contempt. This is the human law.

We had battled America three years for our self-respect. The American had fought for his in 1776. It is to the credit of us both that we met in the Philippines, in 1901, on equal terms.

There were, as I have said, ugly cases of cruelty and injustice in the beginning. But these things did not go unpunished under American law. Any Filipino with a story to tell was listened to with respect. Every complaint was investigated.

It took us some time to reach the astonishing conclusion that white blood did not outweigh colored under the blind goddess set up in the new American courts. Slowly we realized that white men were invariably punished by their fellow white men for crimes against Filipinos.

The Filipinos learned that if Americans cheated or abused them they could go to the American officials and obtain redress. There was to be no American exploitation in the Philippines. Individual cases of greed there would be, human nature being what it is, but exploitation was never permitted by American law. The law books of the Philippines are filled with testimony to this effect.

In one case an American usurer who was fleecing his clients was arrested by Filipino police, tried by a Filipino judge, prosecuted by a Filipino fiscal, and imprisoned in a jail under a Filipino warden and Filipino guards. All this, under American law, under the American flag. Never would justice have taken such a turn in a country colonized under imperialism.

In several cases American attorneys who took advantage of the ignorance of Filipino clients were disbarred for malpractice, as they would be in the United States.

Beyond legal justice in the Philippines, we learned, justice in a more powerful form awaited us, in a place called Washington, D.C. To this, the very source of American democracy, we could send our Filipino spokesmen to speak of matters important to the Philippines, and these men would be treated with respect and their words weighed by the most highly placed men in America.

Even the great American hero General MacArthur appeared before the Senate Committee there and testified to the treatment of Filipinos by American soldiers. Such consideration of subject peoples had never been shown before in the entire history of colonization.

Let us be realistic in analyzing American policy in the Philippines.

Although on the whole it was benevolent and libertarian, it was not entirely altruistic. It was based both upon good business and good will.

America had never before had the experience of having conquered another nation. It had none of the arrogance of the seasoned colonizer. From the beginning the American made friends with the Filipinos, and every change made in the Philippines was to Filipino advantage. The changes were swiftly made and decisive.

Following the advent of civil government American money became legal tender, based upon gold instead of silver.

The civilian police were organized and Filipinos and Americans alike were protected by a native constabulary officered by Americans. These instigated a system of law and order unknown under the Guardia Civil. Banditry was driven back into the mountains and vanished. Graft was no longer the principal source of an official income. Educated Filipinos were admitted to the Civil Service.

One of the first acts of the Philippine Commission was the extension to the Philippines of the benefits of Civil Service "based on merit."

Important words, these "based on merit." They are keystones in the building of democracy.

Other American improvements were the appropriation of $1,-000,000 for the building of roads, $3,000,000 to improve Manila Harbor, and the establishment of the judiciary, supreme court, a bureau of forestry, health department, and agricultural bureau, and provision for the scientific mapping of the Philippine Islands.

President Theodore Roosevelt, signing the act that established civil government in the Philippines, also provided for the purchase of tremendous areas of land held by the great Spanish landowners who had fled to Spain before the fury of our revolution against Spanish rule.

The passing of the landowners brought about the decay of the unjust aspects of the Kasama system that had so long kept the Filipino peasant enslaved to the land.

# VII. MATERIAL ADVANTAGES

Not only the rich Spanish, but the wealthy Filipinos as well, had taken advantage of the pernicious Kasama system of hire. All took advantage of the low Filipino labor scale.

In the Philippines, as in other countries, it was an accepted precept that the poor should remain poor. This was changed by the first Americans to take up residence in the Philippines.

Juan Tao—the common man who saw this century begin in the Philippines—lived with his family in a single-room thatched hut under which the livestock found shelter. They were exposed to pestilence and the elements and perpetual hunger. If he farmed, his small profits were often poured into the bottomless pit of the family debt. As a laborer or servant he might earn as much as ten dollars a month. His wife might earn ten or even twenty-five cents a day weaving hats or grass cloth on a native loom, or she embroidered for a pitiful wage. Their children were born without medical attendance. Nearly all children were malnourished and uneducated. They might become servants in more fortunate families for their board and clothing and two and a half dollars a month. Usually this money was paid to the servant's parents. The father "borrowed" a sum, perhaps fifty dollars, from the employer in return for the hire of his daughter or son. Month after month the two-and-a-half-dollar "wage" was deducted from the debt. In other words, the servant worked for nothing.

It was part of the Kasama system of hire that held the serf to the land.

The Americans put an end to this idyllic if unfair system. They did not take advantage of Filipino poverty and the cheapness of labor. They did not take advantage of the fact that Filipino money was half the value of their own. They paid what was in their eyes full value—which was twice that of the values we had set.

Many of those first Americans, not wishing to be bothered with the details of housekeeping in a strange country, boarded in Filipino homes. This made for a closer relationship between us.

Those who set up housekeeping taught us equality. They refused to use the Kasama system of hire. They hired house people at ten dollars a month, with food and clothing, because they did not think it fair to pay less. Also, where our servants had lived day and night in the house and were subject to duty at all hours, the Americans gave their servants time off to themselves, and let them live, if they liked, in their own homes.

This opened the eyes of our servant class. Servants in the Filipino families began demanding the same wages.

The vendors who brought their products in from the country had their vision scaled to larger profits. If a chicken cost fifty centavos, which is twenty-five cents in American money, the Americans paid in pesos, which made a chicken worth fifty cents, or double in value. And the American paid without haggling. Such lavish buying also doubled the price of eggs.

To the American this doubled price was reasonable; to the poor vendor it was manna.

The carpenter who asked fifty centavos for his work was paid fifty cents, which was a whole peso, or double his usual pay.

The American, by appraising values according to his own standard, which was twice that of ours, raised the standard of living for the Filipino.

There were other practical advantages developed in the Philippines.

The Americans introduced sanitation.

There was no sewerage system before the Americans came. Even in Manila filth ran in open drains through the streets. Epidemics wiped out thousands yearly in the city. When I was a child nearly every Filipino was pock-marked. Now such marks of disease are seldom seen.

Heavy rains were prayed for, to wash filth from the streets and bring about cessations in the recurrent epidemics of smallpox, malaria, and bubonic plague. Mosquitoes bred in the swamps and rats scuttled underfoot in the towns. Cures were left to the discretion of the herb doctor, who was helpless before the annual reapings of pestilence and plague.

Shortly after the American occupation the usual epidemic of smallpox and bubonic plague swept Manila. The Americans promptly stamped out both. They distributed rat poison and killed off the plague-carrying rats. A vaccine farm was established; eighty thousand Filipinos submitted to vaccination. The first underground sewerage was laid.

Disease vanished in proportion.

Up to this time the only public hospital in Manila was maintained solely for the care of lepers. Thirty thousand Filipinos had died of this horrible disease that had been introduced into the Philippines from Japan. Members of the American Medical Corps rounded up the lepers that were roaming the streets. The city was ransacked for those who went into hiding. The segregation of the lepers checked leprosy. Hospitals were built and medical care was no longer a luxury possible only to the rich.

Schools opened, and education also was no longer the privilege of the rich man's child. The son of the poorest tao could take advantage of opportunities once given only to the sons of the don. He could attend Philippine public schools, high schools, universities, and all without cost and in his own country.

As the years passed the new generation of Filipino youth developed not only intellectually but in actual physical stature. Filipino youth grew taller and stronger as improved health conditions, physical-training methods introduced by the new school system, and the rise in wages developed the standards of living. Where once it was unusual to see six-foot Filipinos they now became common.

The Americans built roads that opened up the interior, developed transportation and the spread of commerce and civilizing influences. The trip from my home town Camiling is now a matter of several hours from Manila by car; but when I was a child I watched my father set out on that journey with the sense of watching the start of adventure. My father traveled first by water in a banca, or river boat, then in a cart drawn by a carabao, then in a pony cart, and a hilly stretch was made in a hammock carried by men. The final lap was by steam train. In all, the trip required two weeks of arduous travel!

This trip from Camiling to Manila is typical of the advances made by the Philippines under American rule.

America had taken the Philippines, but it was giving in return the best it had to offer in democratic advantages and civilized methods. The benevolent policy of America toward the Philippines was like none other in history. Certainly it was different from any white authority we had known in Asia.

Only by reviewing the attitude of other countries toward their conquered can you evaluate the work of America in the Philippines. We were not exploited. We were not despised. We were not made to feel ourselves members of an inferior race. We were looked upon from the beginning as underprivileged but acceptable partners, to be developed and encouraged until we had proved our worth.

Gradually, as the years passed, more and more political advantages were placed in Filipino hands. Filipinos were trained and appointed to government posts.

In 1907 elections were held for the first Philippine Assembly. The first Philippine Legislature under America met. One hundred thousand votes were cast by Filipinos.

In the face of such treatment it was impossible to maintain our resentment of America. Gradually our suspicions were overcome.

The increase in wages, the development of our country, the spread of the American school system, and above all the sense of fair play and good will, helped bring about our conversion to American democracy.

But there were other factors, which, to the seemingly inscrutable Oriental mind, weigh more than rice, which is the Eastern equivalent for gold.

# VIII. OF HIGHER VALUES

OF MORE VALUE than rice, to my people, was the Americans ordering by legislative enactment a national holiday set aside to honor our Filipino hero Rizal.

Rizal the native, the rebel, had died for his defiance of white authority on the Luneta in Manila. His Spanish executioners had him stand with his back to the firing squad that he might be shot from the rear as a traitor, but at the last minute he whirled to face the blast of gunfire. Rizal made a victory out of the shameful death decreed by the authorities. Now a statue rose to his memory on the Luneta, on the spot where he had fallen, and under American law December 30 became Rizal Day, our Filipino Independence Day, honoring the day of his death.

Other gestures, seemingly unimportant and of little practical value, were not overlooked by us. They were gratefully accepted along with the more tangible benefits brought to us by America.

These are the imponderables that weigh so much more than material things in the Oriental scales.

How deeply valued were certain acts of courtesy offered by the American Governor General, Henry L. Stimson, upon his arrival in Manila! He ordered that for all parties given at Malacañan Palace (the equivalent of the White House) the invitations should be equally divided between Americans and Filipinos. Less apparent, but no less appreciated as a gesture of respect, was his order that all the official balls at Malacañan should open with the Philippine ceremonial dance, *rigodón de honor*. Governor and Mrs. Stimson themselves learned the dance that they might take part. This dance was among our most beloved traditions. There were wet eyes among my people the first night the *rigodón de honor* was danced under American rule at Malacañan!

Seemingly small, such gestures, but they proved to us the sincerity of the American avowals of democracy. And these gestures were proffered by the highest in authority—by such men as the Governor General and by leaders in Washington.

In other sections of the Orient I have seen spiritual hurts offered the native, imperceptible to white vision, but blows to the pride of the sensitive and easily hurt Oriental. The Filipino is Oriental in his pride. Only to him it is not "face" but the personal dignity of the individual.

Of more lasting importance to us than any material advantage was the fact that the Americans seemed to like us and enjoyed living among us. This was first made apparent by the schoolteachers.

The significant year 1901 that brought America to the Philippines also brought, under proviso by the Philippine Commission, one thousand American schoolteachers. They scattered through five hundred towns to teach several thousand Filipino teachers English and improved methods of American education. These women and men were the real missionaries of democracy. Many lived with us in our homes. They seemed actively interested in us. They shared our meals, social activities, and habits of living.

The schoolteacher never took advantage of his superior position in the community. He might live with the upper stratum of the town, but he was always willing to listen to the troubles of the underprivileged. He became known for his sympathy for the underdog.

Simple people distrust authority. Many a poor Filipino who got into trouble and feared the police went to "teacher" with his story. The schoolteacher persuaded the native to go to the native police, and went along with him to headquarters. So it was the poor tao who first concluded that the American was a person to be trusted.

The Americans practiced infiltration in the Philippines, but it was a campaign based upon equality and good will. What came about eventually I can only describe in the simple phrase—we had fun together.

Manila, with Americans and Filipinos living together in perfect understanding, became the gayest city in the world. It was host to two hemispheres—the most cosmopolitan city in the Orient. And it was the only city in the Orient, as the Philippines was the only country in the Orient, where every native was smiling and friendly.

Travel through British Malaya, India, Java, Burma, Indonesia—you do not see open, friendly faces! Never have I seen more sullen and suspicious looks than those on Javanese faces before the outbreak of war. Resentful of tyranny, contempt, oppression—these people were frank in their hatred of white authority when the chance came.

But everyone who has visited the Philippines will remember us as a smiling race. We did not lose our ability to smile under American rule.

Nearly all Orientals smile readily, with the single exception of that lone wolf, the Japanese. It is only when the Oriental has reason for suspicion that he becomes sullen and unfriendly. Our suspicions were laid by the strongest evidence of friendliness, therefore we smiled. We formed friendships with the Americans that were personal and lasting. The Americans liked giving parties in their homes and in hotels. So did the Filipinos. There were always Filipino guests at the American affairs. And no Filipino thought of giving a party without inviting some of his American friends. This was not compulsory. It was not playing politics nor the social game. It was Manila! It was part of its life and gaiety and unforgettable charm. Our parties were incomplete without the presence of the Americans; they, in turn, seemed to enjoy our companionship. Our native costumes added greatly to the picturesque charms of social life in Manila.

We continued to wear with pride the embroidered costumes of our native country. Even our wealthy Filipinas—women who went by Clipper every year to buy clothes in New York and Paris—wore the bright *camisas* of our native land.

There was a constant exchange of courtesies between races. The Philippine Columbian Association, composed of Filipino graduates of American universities, gave parties every year honoring in turn the Chinese, the Spanish, the Japanese, and the Americans as represented by the Rotary Club. Each group in turn responded with a Filipino party in our honor.

The membership of the Rotary Club was two thirds American,

yet the second year I was a member I, the youngest member and a Filipino, was elected president.

There were no closed doors to the native in the Philippines.

The Army and Navy Club forbade Filipino membership and yet, long before the war, the Gridiron Club, composed of Americans and Filipinos, held parties in the club.

For one American who might behave unpleasantly toward a native in the Philippines there would be ten to outweigh him in friendliness. Take so irrelevant a matter as the contest of the Polo Club.

The first polo club in Manila was built by the Americans in the days when the Filipinos were still nursing their bitterness. It was limited to American membership. The Filipinos did not mind; they did not play polo anyway. But as the years passed they took an interest in the game, bought ponies, and learned to play. The crisis came when one of the most popular Filipinos in Manila applied for membership and was blackballed.

Among the more indignant members of the club were the Elizalde brothers, wealthy industrialists and exporters who stem from one of the oldest and most highly respected Spanish families in the Philippines, and who later, because of their love for the Philippines, became Filipino citizens. They withdrew from the club and with their friends organized another composed of both Filipinos and Americans. This, the Los Tamaraos Polo Club, became the leading polo club.

Through our American friends we formed friendships with people in the United States. When the more fortunate of us visited America we did not feel alien. We felt at home. American schooling, motion pictures, popular songs, magazines, newspapers, had made us familiars of the United States.

I have visited other white countries and left them infuriated and with a sense of having been debased. On a recent lecture tour through the United States I visited two hundred and fifty American cities and did not experience one unpleasant incident.

These—the immeasurable gifts of equality and good will that are America—were beyond price to us, the Westernized Orientals.

Of greatest importance to us was the confidence the Americans placed in the Filipinos. The placing of legislative power in Filipino hands was valued, not so much for the exercise of that power, as for the fact that it displayed growing confidence in our ability.

Slowly, through the years, the last of our suspicions and resentments were overcome.

Slowly there was completed our long but thorough conversion to democracy. It was complete in 1941—in time for Bataan!

To understand the inner mechanisms of this victory one must first understand the workings of the Oriental mind.

# IX. HIS WAYS ARE PECULIAR

THE MISUNDERSTANDING between East and West is largely due to the Occidental's failure to understand and respect the Oriental point of view and the Oriental's failure to understand and trust the Occidental.

A significant advance of the present war is the distribution among our armed forces of pamphlets calculated to make the United States soldier understand and respect the people he will meet in other lands. This is a typically American gesture. Mother America expects her wandering doughboys to make a good impression in foreign countries.

An equally sincere effort on the part of other white men in the Far East would have done much toward preventing the present crisis between East and West.

The Oriental mind has ever been an insoluble mystery to the white man. In turn the white man's ways are equally perplexing to the Oriental. This mutual mystery must be solved if understanding is to be brought about between East and West.

I know that many a white man is prone to blanket the Oriental under the damning conclusion: "He is a liar. You can't trust him. He is slippery."

That white man might be astonished to learn that the Oriental condemns him in almost the same words. The white man should modify his criticism. Instead of saying the Oriental does not tell the truth, he should say, "If he does not tell the truth to me, it is because he suspects me." For nearly all Orientals are suspicious, and with reason, of all white men. A dog, a child, a man cringes when afraid. The dog shows his teeth if he dares. The child and the man will lie in self-defense.

The Oriental regards the white man as a slippery character who will get the better of him in the end, because this has always been the rule in the Orient. The white man, according to the Oriental, comes to him in the guise of being a civilizing influence, and proceeds to grab everything in sight.

This pale foreigner, the Oriental suspects, is in his country for the purpose of robbing him of all he may possess. He believes that should he trust the white man, the white man will inevitably betray that trust to his own advantage. Has he not seen this happen again and again? Therefore, why be frank and open?

Truth is an important thing, to be given only the trustworthy. The sad truth remains that the Oriental does not think the white man can be trusted.

The sadder truth is that his theory has been too often upheld by unscrupulous white men in the Orient. It has seldom profited the native of the Far East to take a white man into his confidence.

The Oriental is not evasive and given to subterfuge with his fellow Orientals. He has no reason to mistrust his own people. But the Oriental is not untruthful, unless he is taking direct refuge from fear.

Truth is relative, and to understand the Oriental veracity you must understand his ways of speech and thought which are difficult indeed for the white man to interpret.

There are not only shadings in speech and idiom but nuances in Oriental courtesy as well that make the Oriental out a liar to the Occidental. In turn, the failure of the white man to recognize these shadings makes him appear boorish and overbearing to the pained Oriental.

While the people of the Orient differ according to race and geographical location, they share certain common characteristics that are essentially Oriental.

Let me, being neither of the Occident nor the Orient, but a Westernized Filipino who shares the viewpoints and problems of both hemispheres, translate for the benefit of the Occident the "inscrutable" Oriental mind.

The Oriental is not mysterious. He operates on age-old simple patterns and believes in simple precepts of behavior centuries old. Chinese, Hindoo, Indonesian, and Japanese hold to the basic Oriental thought pattern with minor differences. In the Japanese these differences have become intensified with tragic results.

Even the Westernized Filipino retains certain characteristics that are basically Oriental.

In the Philippines we have a Tagalog saying handed down from our Malayan ancestors:

"Life is short, and well I know it is only a minute long. Therefore, I want this minute to stay with me as long as it can, for who knows what may happen to me tomorrow?"

This sums up the universal Oriental objection to haste.

There is a cant expression among white men that "you cannot hustle the East." This fact is extremely annoying to white men. But the Oriental has a cosmic outlook upon eternity. He is an introvert. His wish is to live quietly, inwardly, as much as possible alone with his thoughts. When his work is done, as it will be in good time, he wishes to return to his thoughts.

Haste is an indignity. The Oriental is not racing against time, for why should he? Time, he knows, is infinite; it will beat him in the end.

The white man wonders at the serene and unlined faces of elderly Orientals. Their look is serene because, no matter how hard their outward life has been, inwardly they are at peace.

The white man's incessant "chop-chop!" or demand for hurry, is a constant affront to the dignity of the Oriental soul.

Happiness, if you examine the fundamentals of his belief, is a reflection of the soul. No matter what bodily discomforts are his, if the soul is at peace, the Oriental is content.

No wonder the Occidental finds this difficult to understand! He must have conveniences and even luxuries to be content. The average white man plans his life around a Ford, a home, a radio, an electric refrigerator, two movies a week, and "a chicken in every pot."

John Chang, his Oriental prototype, does not know of these things. He is happy without material comforts, money, or progress in the Occidental sense, because to him happiness is not measured in terms of comfort but in the inward satisfaction which is his aim in existence. He can be happy if he has a bamboo bed to sleep upon, a dish of rice and vegetables to share with his family. His family is his universe, and his happiness depends upon its unity. He reaches the apex of his day seated with his household around the common bowl of rice. In this patriarchal state he is the supreme ruler, the sire, the head of his wretched but beloved dynasty. This is carried to an unpleasant extreme by the Japanese in the Shinto, where the entire nation is one family and the Emperor is supreme father of all.

Give this John Chang of China, Burma, Java, or India one hundred dollars, and it would not make him happy at all. Such riches would be meaningless to him. But give him a five-cent piece and he is overjoyed. He can see in concrete terms the supplying of his simple wants. He can buy a great bowl of rice with the sum and perhaps even a spoonful of sugar to go with his rice. These are riches.

What has the white world brought, or what may it bring, to the Orient, that can add to the life satisfaction of this man who is inwardly content? The white man has never asked this of himself. He has taken it for granted that his is the superior civilization and that therefore it cannot fail to impress the inferior Oriental. He does not realize that the Oriental is convinced that his is the superior civilization. The Oriental's is based upon belief in the soul; the Occidental's on material things.

This is the source of the greatest misunderstanding between East and West. There are smaller sources, equally important to peoples who must share the same country while living in different worlds.

The Oriental is hypersensitive and thin-skinned, courteous to the point of appearing to fawn. His very courtesy makes him out a liar to the white man. And his reluctance to rush against eternity is a trait the Occidental mistakes for laziness.

The Occidental says, "Good-by," and the Oriental, "God be with you." The Occidental says, "Thank you," and the Oriental, "God repay you." These are minor differences. In the Oriental they hark back to his inner trust, his placing of even small matters in the hands of the infinite.

Even in the Philippines we use the common Tagalog expression, *Bahala na!*

*Bahala na*—leave it to God! It is an expression that covers many needs. The pest of grasshoppers arrives, and the Filipino does not throw up his hands in despair. He collects the pests in baskets and roasts them; they are as delectable as shrimps. *Bahala na!*

The river rises and flood washes away the houses of the village. The people do not wail and despair. Houses can be rebuilt. The people take to their bancas, the river is bobbing with river boats, the swains row their girls, and as they push on the long bamboo poles they all sing. It is like a festival, but an unexpected one. *Bahala na!*

*Bahala na*—the Filipino's *mañana*, his selah, and so what!

This is not indolence but faith and a placing of ill luck in the lap of providence. But the white man frowns upon such Oriental resignation to fate. He thinks it a symptom of laziness and a lack of respect for the material values.

In his way, he is right. The Oriental does not have a vast respect for material values. To him the soul is paramount—the soul is all that matters. His entire civilization is based upon this concept. Feelings to him are sacred, to be hidden and not expressed, because they are revelations of the soul. He wants to make you happy, he tries not to make you unhappy, because he is careful not to hurt your feelings, which are your soul. This consideration results in great confusion between the Oriental and the white man.

To make matters more puzzling to the Occidental, there are certain Oriental languages which do not possess the negative. Even if there is a negative, the Oriental is very likely to dislike using it. This is a form of reticence the white man can never understand. Why, he demands, doesn't the Oriental say no when he means no? He does not realize that the Oriental believes a direct no can be unkind.

The Oriental always prefers avoiding pain of the moment. So, instead of telling you he cannot meet you on the morrow, he says, "I may see you tomorrow."

For the moment he has spared your feelings. He has protected your soul.

If he is in your employ and for some reason desires to leave you, he will not come out with a reason that might be embarrassing to you both. Therefore, his mother is sick, or he is going to visit his cousin, or he needs a vacation. You part with kind words and plans for a speedy reunion. But you both know, if you, too, are versed in the ways of the Orient, that he will not return. Something has gone wrong between you. But since it would hurt your feelings to explain, why should he explain?

These shadings of truth are for purposes of courtesy. They are the equivalents of Mrs. Jones ordering her maid to tell the unwelcome visitor she is not at home, or her pallid and suffering friend that she is looking unusually well today!

I do not know why the average white man demands more in the way of truth from John Chang than from Mrs. Jones.

Mutual misunderstandings born of word usage have been largely overcome in the Philippines, where the Filipino has captured the American point of view with its speech and even its slang, and the American, in turn, has acquired a good-natured understanding of our Oriental side, for even among the Filipinos there are holdover traits of Orientalism.

For example, many a Filipino who was a firm believer in independence for the Philippines would not admit this to his American guest out of courtesy to the American point of view. The American believed the Philippines should remain subservient to America; since that was his belief, the Filipino host would not dream of offering him the discourtesy of an argument. So he would agree politely with all the American said and felt on the subject, and later the American, seeing his Filipino friend's name on a list of citizens favoring independence, would be indignant and conclude that the Filipino was a dissembler. But the American had merely failed to fathom his friend's inner conviction. Oriental consideration was to blame, as in so many such misunderstandings.

The Filipino could not bring himself to condemn the opinions of a guest. He had placed consideration for his guest's feelings above his own. This the white man can never understand. There are many things he fails to comprehend about the Orient. One of his blindest spots is the white man himself.

The foundation of misunderstandings between East and West is built upon the fact that Oriental and Occidental each believes his to be the highest type of civilization.

The Occidental is very sure his is the superior type of civilization. To prove his contention he conquers entire nations and introduces into them governments, business methods, automobiles, airplanes, electric refrigerators, and radios.

The Oriental has nothing to show but his soul. But the Oriental, rightly or not, believes that his civilization is based upon the eternal spirit and the Occidental's upon transient materialism. He holds the physical to be incidental and the spirit supreme.

Behind him innumerable ages of Oriental logic uphold his faith in the supremacy of the soul. Therefore, the Oriental concludes, his is the superior civilization.

The white man, not knowing this, and positive in his belief in his own civilized superiority, is willing, if need be, to enforce that claim with violence. This has been done many times in the Orient. And this has given rise to many misunderstandings and much suspicion and even hatred.

Why, the Oriental wishes to know, should the Occidental insist upon the superiority of his civilization and try to force it upon the Oriental, when their values are so different?

There are two precepts the Oriental never fails to emphasize: first, that there can be no friendship without mutual respect, and that there can be no mutual respect where one person feels himself the superior of the other.

The invariable attitude of the white man toward the Oriental is that of a superior to an inferior.

The white man may have the friendliest and most democratic of intentions, but he is a rare man if he does not unconsciously assume a superior attitude toward a member of a colored race. He may not be aware of this mental attitude, but he betrays it without knowing. He may be overly effusive—the Oriental senses and is hurt by his attempt to "talk down."

The Oriental is too easily hurt in all his dealings with the Occidental. He is hurt because he expects to be hurt, because for centuries the white man has lorded it over him. He waits, inwardly trembling, outwardly calm, for the slight he is certain the most amiable Occidental will sooner or later offer. The slight may be unintentional, but the Oriental is quick to interpret it as such, because of this background of inconsiderate lordliness by other white men.

The long history of petty and personal, major and national hurt in the Orient goes back for many centuries. It is not to be easily forgotten.

I realize I am being unpleasantly frank and upon occasion am dropping to the level of a petty resentment I myself do not feel; but such resentments, large and small, have given birth to the cataclysm in the Far East. They stem from the very soul of more than half the people in this world of ours; they have been too long hidden and are better brought out into the open.

The major sins of the white man in the Orient, as the Oriental sees them, are well known. Conferences have been held about them, and wars fought over them. These larger difficulties will adjust as men progress and democracy evens up the level of mankind. But it is the little gestures that bring on wars and also have frequently been able to avert wars. It was not the important gifts of democracy that brought us close to America in the Philippines. The smaller gifts held greater, more lasting power.

The major arrogances of the white man in the Orient, aided by his pettier sins, served to turn the Orient against him. Let us be open about these matters and survey them frankly from both sides, from East and West, and try to understand.

It is only too easy for the white man in the Orient to misunderstand—and to be misunderstood.

# X. THE WHITE MAN IN THE ORIENT

I HAVE ADMITTED, perhaps too frankly, the average white man's blanket opinion of the Oriental. It is only fair to state that the Oriental's opinion of the white man, from the Oriental's point of view, is equally damning.

The Oriental, exploited, overworked, ashamed, and afraid, gives as his verdict: "The white man is a drunkard." And, even worse by Oriental standards: "He has no soul."

Before examining these charges it might be well to consider the strange effect of the Far East upon white women and men.

Again I have no desire to condemn either nations or individuals. I realize that thousands of colonizers with the kindliest of intentions have come to the Orient from England, Holland, and France. I am convinced that many of these arrive with the conviction that they are destined to be of service to benighted natives in great need of the civilizing example they are about to set. But they find a long-established system in the Orient. They become part of it and they cannot escape.

If a white man does undertake to take the part of that underdog which is the native he is immediately regarded with suspicion by his white neighbors. If he opens the eyes of the natives or tries to elevate them in any way from their "place," he is promptly ostracized.

Even as America has been berated by certain white nations for granting independence to the Filipino!

The white man, being human, finds it easier to follow the line of least resistance and ride in the established and comfortable groove worn by centuries of superior white beings in the Orient.

And how comfortable, that groove, to the Occidental in the Far East! No matter how liberal or humanitarian a man may be in his own country, in the Orient he finds himself slipping into its slothful luxuriance.

This white man—this democrat, let us say, disembarks at Manila, Singapore, or Hong Kong. He is perhaps a man of medium salary, kindly, alert, moderate in tastes and habits. Up to this time he has lived in a small servantless apartment. His social activities have been limited by his small income. He has never been regarded as of much importance to anyone but himself and his wife. Overnight this changes.

He finds himself in a fine home that is his for a song, staffed by servants who foresee his slightest whims, and at unbelievably low wages. Furniture, clothing, food, amusement—everything is cheap. He finds himself part of a superior and princely world. He belongs in the white upper stratum—he can look down upon a darker-skinned, unimportant world of men set below him in the social scale. Overnight this plain citizen has become a superior being.

His wife, who perhaps worked in an office before marriage and prided herself upon being an expert cook and housekeeper, now finds herself enjoying comfort and a commanding place in the community. Prestige is hers such as she has never known before. Her house and garden run like clockwork. She never enters the kitchen. She entertains without effort or worry. Amahs and other servants care for the children, and she herself is bathed, massaged, and dressed by personal maids and driven by her own native chauffeur on a ceaseless round of cocktail parties and evening affairs.

Is it any wonder that within a few years this once efficient woman is unable to don her own stockings?

In this paradise of inertia it is easier to give in and float on the surface with the superior race.

The white man and his wife give in. They like the life led by white people in the Orient. They like the rich living of the representatives of power, the extravagant hospitality of their beautiful homes, their comfortable and exclusive clubs. And they learn to overlook the sufferings of the Oriental watching from the dust, and they never see the contempt on the faces of their Oriental drivers bringing them home at the end of besotted evenings.

The heat and the proximity of the fewer members of one's own race in this great strange sea of brown humanity tend to make heavy drinkers of men and women who never drank before arriving in the Orient.

To the Oriental, who, with the exception of the Japanese, is not a drinker, drunkenness is the ugliest of the venial sins. And it cannot be denied that from the Oriental point of view much of the white man's life in the Orient reveals him as an inconsiderate drinker. The white man is to be seen, as are his women, carried in a bewildered and babbling condition out of night clubs and bars by silent natives. Even in that condition they do not fail to remember their superiority. It usually reveals itself in abuse of the nearest native.

Clark Lee in his book, *They Call It Pacific*, tells of an incident in Manila just before the invasion. He saw a Filipino constabulary soldier attempting to steer a drunken American woman out of a bar. She slapped his face, saying, "You Filipinos are dirt!"

A week later Clark saw that same soldier lying on a heap of dead at Bataan.

I wonder where that American woman was then!

Persistent examples of drunkenness among white men in the Far East have brought the Oriental to his damning conclusion that "all white men are drunkards."

Then, even worse, he adds, "The white man has no soul."

The white man has done much to make himself hated in the Orient. Even more, to make himself disliked by the touchy Oriental, who is touchy because he has been under white domination for centuries and has never failed to resent that domination.

Comfortable, well fed, well cared for, the white man looks from automobile or rickshaw upon the wretched native, in scenes of unbelievable humiliation.

The Oriental, watching from the dust, sees the unmoved interest of this sightseer. He thinks, "He has no soul." He sees the white man's trained police beating helpless natives with clubs, and concludes that the white masters who order such brutalities are without soul.

Imagine the feelings of the Chinese—that proud and sensitive race whose civilization is the oldest in the world—who read, posted in Chinese characters before parks in their own native land, the order:

"Dogs and Chinese Not Allowed!"

Let John Doe picture to himself such signs posted in his own Central Park, denying entry to Americans!

It is worth mentioning here that in the Philippines, during the early days of the American occupation, it was punishable by imprisonment for the Filipinos to play their national anthem or display the Filipino flag. This insult to us as a nation was deeply resented and loudly protested. But this was not a personal indignity. And we were not only permitted to protest, we were not thrown into jail for protesting; and we were eventually permitted to display our own red, white, and blue flag with its golden rayed sun and three stars beside the American Stars and Stripes.

I shall not dwell here upon the economic and social wrongs done the native everywhere else in the Orient under the guise of civilization. I am only trying to translate his attitude toward the white man.

We have, in Tagalog, another saying: "His face is money!"

That is the way the average Oriental looks upon the white man. To him the white face expresses greed, cunning—a soulless desire to bleed him, the helpless native, of his last drop of blood.

It cannot be denied that the majority of white men in the Orient are there in their desire to make money.

This fact bolsters the Oriental opinion that while his civilization is based upon the spirit, the white man's is concerned only with material gain.

This substantiates the Oriental verdict that the white man has no soul.

So these are the things that have made the white man the loser in the Orient—his patronizing ways, his almost universal greed, his exploitation of the native, and his refusal to let the native speak.

This last omission could and should be corrected if the East and West are ever to have clear pictures of each other.

I have told elsewhere and at length my adventures with the censors in the Far East, and with what *savoir faire* my articles were tossed aside, deleted, or made to change meaning by clever transference of words. I was threatened with imprisonment for writing the truth in imperialistic countries, and in each case I simply moved on to the next country and cabled my story from there. It made no difference that each time I had abundant proof to uphold my statements.

The truth must not leak out under a crown.

The stories the natives wanted told could not be told.

For example, I chanced to be in Burma three weeks after the question was asked on the floor of the Burmese Legislature:

"Does the Atlantic Charter apply to Burma?"

Not one of the white correspondents had flashed that question and its answer over the wires. Yet it was of vital importance to Burma. I had to fly to Bangkok in order to cable the story to America.

The Oriental in the Orient has never been given a chance to express his views through the press services.

What chance has the Occident to learn the Oriental's side of the story, when news is poisoned at the source? His side is never told. He has neither representation nor voice. Much misinformation and mistrust have spread to other countries because of this lack of fair news representation.

I have no wish to indict the news bureaus by this statement, but certain individual correspondents who find it more comfortable and relaxing to fall into the rich way of living with the exponents of power. The newspaperman likes that life, and his wife likes it. They drink at the rich white clubs, dine at the homes of the rich white men, and write, for their newspapers, the imperialistic point of view of their powerful friends.

Yes, as a general rule, even the newspaperman, that exponent of liberalism, finds it impossible to escape the point of view of the imperialistic pattern.

I am not saying that all the white correspondents are unfair. There have been many who refused to fall into the imperialistic point of view.

But it is easy—in the Orient—to fall into the "gin-sling routine." If the contacts are with the luxuriously living white men, as a result the newspaperman reflects only their point of view. This is a continual source of irritation to the Oriental. He knows that not only is he voiceless, but that he is frequently misrepresented.

Even in the Philippines, to cite one recurrent source of annoyance, stories were frequently sent to America concerning our wild tribes, the Igorots, in which they were represented as Filipinos. These primitive black people are no more Filipino than the American Indian is representative of the United States citizen. They hold exactly the same position—they are our aborigines.

This small percentage—not more than 100,000 of his tribe exist in our mountains—was in the Philippines long before the Malayans, our ancestors, came from the southerly tip of Asia. Doubtless the Igorot has a better claim to the Philippines than we—as the American Indian has prior claims on America.

The fact remains that the Igorot is not Filipino and we are not related, and it hurts our feelings to see him pictured in American newspapers under such captions as, "Typical Filipino Tribesman."

We passed laws in the Philippine Legislature forbidding pictures under such captions to be taken out of the Philippines.

We are sensitive in such matters, because the Filipino is as yet an unknown quantity to the world. It is easy to misrepresent an unknown quantity. A known one cannot be misrepresented.

The unknown and unproven Filipino is anxious to lift his head. Every such misrepresentation the Filipino regards as an attempt to push him back into obscurity.

The Oriental has always been a submerged individual, trying very hard to assert his personality. Each time an Occidental, without perhaps meaning to, assumes a patronizing attitude toward an Oriental, the Oriental feels himself pushed back and down.

More than all else, the Oriental has come to resent patronizing manners and condescension.

One of the greatest needs of the future will be the establishment of information centers in the world capitals insuring the dissemination of accurate news of each country.

What is true of the white man in the Orient holds for the white man in the Philippines. But there the attitude of the white man—

who in the Philippines is an American—toward the native is different.

I shall not pretend that all was sheer beauty between the Filipino and the American. Neither is saintly in character. I am not saying that the American is above retaining a sense of superiority, nor the Filipino above holding certain lurking vestiges of suspicion. Little wounds are kept open by the best intentioned of Americans.

Even with us—Westernized though we are and able to give and take in the latest American idiom and usages—even with us the hurt is awaited and expected. The white man does not intend to drop barbs in his speech. He does not intend to assume a superior attitude. Often he does not know he regards himself as superior. But despite his most democratic concept of himself he is very likely to make manifest his sense of superiority.

He leaves the boat at Manila and a Filipino doctor examines him at quarantine. Immediately he asks, "Isn't there a white doctor here?" He may be speaking to a surgeon who was trained at Johns Hopkins and is holding a high rank in the United States Navy. He intends no personal slur against a man who has attained his position through merit and hard study. But with the question, unconsciously, he has put an entire race "in its place."

When he learns the doctor is adequate, even impressively learned, he is frank in his astonishment.

On the pier he asks the taxi driver, "Where is the white man's hotel?" He does not know that in Manila Americans and Filipinos have always shared the same districts and hotels, even homes. He forgets he is in a democracy, under his own American flag. And he tells the driver to "chop-chop," or hurry, as he would speak to a Chinese coolie, not realizing that our taxi drivers are organized, speak English learned in American schools, and have the sharp awareness of what is going on in the world peculiar to taxi drivers in all Americanized cities.

In the Manila hotel he asks the desk clerk, "Isn't there a white manager here?" He is speaking to a man who has studied hotel management in the world's leading hotels and has entertained the heads of countries and the notables of the world.

No matter how frequently he may stress that term "white man," it never fails to find its barbed way home! Through centuries of unkindness it has come to have an unkind meaning to the Oriental. It has ever been used by the imperialists to prove their superiority in the brown man's world.

The white man, not knowing this, proceeds to give the elevator boy and room boy orders in pidgin English—"chop-chop," and "topside" or "bottomside," meaning upstairs and downstairs. Probably he has picked up such terms in traveling in the Orient. Since his dealings while traveling are mostly with the servant class, he adopts the terms of their idiom, and uses them for the world at large. But in the hotel he may be speaking to young students who are working their way through college and speak English as well as he. And he will use the same "coolie talk" to all he meets of Oriental blood—including people of good position who have legions of servants of their own. He does not understand the subtle insult conveyed by addressing these people in such terms. Nor does he understand, in his efforts to pick up what he considers a smattering of the native idiom, that he is insulting them by his ignorance of the terms "thee" and "you," which in nearly every language, with the exception of English, are used to mark the difference between the upper and lower classes.

The Oriental, not realizing the white man does not know this difference, fiercely resents being addressed as a servant. He feels humiliated. He is also humiliated when the Occidental, wishing to summon him, beckons with his finger. This is also a gesture reserved for servants. The Oriental has no way of knowing that the American summons everyone by this gesture, even members of his family and his closest friends.

In Filipino homes where he is a guest even the American is likely to ask questions, in his ignorance, without stopping to think of the hurt they can convey. He shows his astonishment constantly at the evidences of culture he finds in these homes. He is astonished by the appearance of manhattans and canapés on silver trays. He stares at modern paintings in rooms moderne, and is amazed when the hostess sits down at the grand piano to produce Bach or boogie-woogie. In little ways he betrays his condescension.

One of the most cultured and gracious Filipinas I know, a graduate of the Sorbonne in Paris, who has made a hobby of collecting fine pieces of French porcelain, has grown accustomed to having her American guests exclaim, "You have such things?"

Even in Manila I have frequently seen white men in elevators with hats clamped to their heads in the presence of Filipinas—when an American woman entered, they would remove their hats.

I realize only too well that these are petty wounds. They are small in comparison to the actions of white men in other sections of the Orient. In the Philippines both the American and the Filipino have learned to understand much and forgive much in one another.

We have learned to give and take—but not without much mutual astonishment.

For example, it was difficult for us in the beginning to understand the lure club life holds for the American. No white man feels at home in the Orient until he joins a club. Since the Oriental, with the exception of the Japanese, does not drink, is a family man, and likes to stay home, clubs hold no fascination for him. But the Filipino, through his American friends, learned to enjoy the social exchanges of club life, and in turn built handsome clubhouses to share with his American friends. He could not understand, nor has he ever understood, why the Occidental in the tropics should regard it as strictly *de rigueur* to wear black tuxedos and stiff shirts and collars to formal parties. No matter how sweltering the night may be, that is the ordained costume.

This is the style set by the Occidental, and the Oriental must follow or commit a social error. When one of our first American high commissioners announced that even the photographers must wear tails to one of his first formal parties the Manila undertakers reaped a small harvest renting out their formal garments. Incidentally, it was one of the hottest nights of the season!

This is the white man's way, and I am not saying it is not best— for him. It is not my way, but I respect it. For myself I shall never be able to see the advantage to morale of a high collar, black shoes, and thick clothing on a hot tropical night. I prefer my way of ending the day, when, after long hours at the office, I can appear at the dinner table in my woven slippers, thin slacks, and silk *camisa*.

The first Americans in the Philippines used to laugh at these camisas, which we wear with the tail out over the trousers. The American did not understand that they were cooler worn that way. But now nearly every teen-age boy and girl in America wears these brightly colored shirts out over their slacks. Hollywood set that fashion for Americans after taking it from the Orient.

Another fashion upon which I need not comment—our women were smoking cigarettes when the first Americans came to the Philippines.

The Americans looked down their noses on the habit. "How native!"

These are small differences. I cite them to show how small are the hurts that create differences. Despite them the American changed our opinion of the white race. He was our friend. In turn, our attitude toward him has changed the opinion of the entire Orient.

The rest of the Orient came to understand how matters stood between us in the Philippines. They realized that the American was one white man "whose face was not money." Where other men exploited, he spent too freely. In fact, he was disliked and condemned for his free spending by other white men, for it raised living standards wherever he might be.

A white man who did not live for money was a paradox to the Oriental. The Oriental in his own fashion said of the American, "He is a queer fellow!"

The American talked to natives wherever he traveled and did not expect them to kowtow. This, too, made him queer—different from other white men.

The Orientals of other countries knew that Filipino leaders who were for independence were not shot or imprisoned by the Americans. Instead, they were honored. They knew, when war broke out between Japan and China, that American sympathies were with China. They knew, when Stimson wished to show a firm hand in Manchukuo, that other white men, not Americans, refused to uphold this American protest against the criminal invasion by the Japanese.

The American was for the underdog.

The Oriental from elsewhere in the Orient who visited us in the Philippines found us dining and dancing with the Americans in clubs and hotels and homes, and returned to his home in the Far East filled with wonder. This, to him, was the final realization of democracy. For while the Occidental may judge the progress of colonization by tall buildings and economic advantages, the Oriental sees it in the simple term—how well do the white race and the brown regard each other?

So the Oriental returning to his native country, where white men looked down upon him, reported, "It is true. The Americans are different from other white men."

Democracy in its complete analysis means both economic and social equality. The Oriental saw it nowhere else in the Orient, only in the Philippines.

John Chang's language, as a rule, held no actual word for "democracy." The very concept of democracy was too new in the Orient. But he knew it existed—in the social and economic equality granted the Filipino he saw at last the manifestation of that word—democracy. And to the Oriental it translated into a simpler word—"America."

The Filipino stands closest to America—closest to the white world—on the bridge between East and West.

On the farthest end, vengeful and dangerous, stands that lone wolf of the Orient, the Japanese.

# XI. THE JAPANESE MIND

THE JAPANESE IS A PROBLEM as a personality and as a nation he is a menace.

While the Oriental mind is generally perplexing to the white man, the Japanese point of view is incomprehensible. Of late the white man has closed his thoughts to any attempt at understanding. Pearl Harbor sacrificed to the Japanese all pretensions to the human equalities.

No man has more reason to distrust and hate the Japanese than his fellow Oriental, the Filipino. Long before America felt the heat of the Rising Sun we feared for our lives in the Philippines. And yet I believe we are able to trace through the labyrinth of Japanese pride that led up to the concurrent treacheries of Honolulu and Manila! It is well that the entire world make an attempt, not to forgive, but to understand.

Pearl Harbor was no manifestation of the Orient, but solely of the Japanese mind. Only the Japanese could be capable of a Pearl Harbor.

We of the Philippines recognized Japan's capacity for treachery. China knew it well. The entire Orient knew—and hated and distrusted Japan, the enemy in the Orient.

Why, then, did the entire Orient—with the sole exception of the Philippines—take the path of the Rising Sun?

Why did the Philippines alone stand with white men against Japan?

For the future of East and West it is well to understand how such things came about and how Japan was able to make them come to pass. It is well to know why some followed through fear and others through choice a country as universally hated as Japan.

For many years and in many ways the Japan that was capable of Pearl Harbor had made itself manifest in the Orient. Japan had no part in the hoped-for "Brown Democracy." Where white men hold together in the belief that all white people should be protected and the average colored man believes in protection for all the colored, the Japanese cared for no one, but remained apart, resentful of and resented by, both East and West.

China's reasons for hating Japan have been universally known. China has long held Japan her greatest enemy. China, recognizing the conflict of interests in the Far East between Japan and America, looked to America for help. America's unconcealed sympathy for China brought her in turn the hatred of Japan, and as a side issue left the Filipino in the Philippines to face the direct enmity of Japan.

The Japanese hated us because we represented American democracy in the Far East.

This resentment was not noticeable from the West, but to us it was made pointedly apparent, and long before December 9, 1941, we were the victims of Japanese treachery. Long before the Japanese planes came over Manila we knew they were out to get us.

We were painfully close to Japan. Across the narrow strip of sea between our countries they had kept close watch on us for nearly half a century. They watched also from within, by the same unprincipled methods of infiltration that make the Japanese in war the most unscrupulous fighters in the world. It was their business infiltration we resented in the beginning.

The first Japanese to invade the Philippines were the apa vendors, who sold rice-flour cakes for ice cream in the streets and were generally ridiculed. Then, about 1916, we noticed for the first time in the Walled City small Japanese shops that specialized in a sweet mixture of seeds or fruits mixed with shaved ice, sugar, and cream, *mongo con hielo*. These shops multiplied until they were on every corner of Calle Real.

Japanese barbershops began making their appearance in the capital. Japanese massage parlors opened. These spread through other sections.

We became aware that in Davao great areas of houses were occupied by Japanese. Japanese schools opened there. Davao was a Japanese town by the time Japan attacked.

Almost immediately we were made to realize that the Japanese were in the Philippines to undermine our economic security.

Slowly an entire section of Manila filled with Japanese bazaars. A district of Japanese shops developed and grew rich in Baguio. Japanese fishermen with fleets of well-equipped boats gradually took over the fishing industry on our coasts. While doing this, they accomplished a thorough job of sounding Philippine waters—an invaluable aid to the Japanese invaders who were to land on our shores!

Meanwhile vast hemp plantations were being acquired by Japanese. Japanese textiles undermined our textile trade. Immense forest concessions in the Philippines poured wealth into Japanese hands.

As foreigners, the Japanese were not permitted to own land, fishing boats, or forest concessions. Also, to prevent the amassing of the too-large estates that once had held the poor in bondage, Philippine law forbids the ownership of more than 1,041 hectares of land.

The Japanese got around this impasse by hiring ignorant Filipinos to serve as dummies, buying boats, securing fishing permits, and acquiring, in groups, great forest concessions, plantations, homes, and stores. Ostensibly owners and employers, they were in reality robots of Tokyo.

By 1930 it was apparent that the Philippines were being bled to death from within by Japan.

The same infiltration methods were projected into our social life. Japanese living in the Philippines tried in every way to flatter and bribe the Filipinos into friendship. Prominent Filipinos, passing through Japan on their way to the United States, were showered with all manner of attentions and gifts. A consistent campaign of flattery accompanied the more vicious infiltration methods for nearly half a century.

In Manila the Japanese chamber of commerce, the Japanese tourist bureau, and leading Japanese carried out a program of social activity subsidized and directed by Tokyo. They gave parties, made lavish gifts, stressed constantly their admiration for Filipino customs and ways. They appeared at social affairs wearing the embroidered Filipino costumes. Their conversations with Filipinos invariably held hints calculated to turn them from the American point of view. These were part of long-planned propaganda.

In this way, as early as 1928, we learned of Japanese plans for a federation of Far Eastern countries. This has been brutally implanted on the Philippines since the invasion as the "Co-Prosperity Sphere of East Asia."

The Japanese persistently stressed in many subtle ways the fact that the Filipinos and Japanese should stand together as "fellow Orientals." But the Filipino had no sympathy with Japanese ideology and the Japanese point of view. The Japanese was no closer to us than he was to the American. In every way we were different.

To begin with, there is the matter of pride which the Oriental, with the exception of the Filipino, terms "face."

The term "face" is not in the Filipino's vocabulary. To other Orientals it is honor. To the Japanese it is the difference between life and death—a means for treachery and an excuse for every human crime. It makes him deceitful in his relations with all other people and a sadist in war. "Face" is honor and honor is life, and the Japanese who loses "face" takes his life by hara-kiri, the bloodiest way imaginable, slashing his abdomen crisscross with a sharp sword.

In view of this belief, butchery and torment of others seem fair enough to the Japanese. He himself is not afraid of suffering or death. Why shrink from torturing or murdering another?

History takes the kindly view, and in the long current of events much will be expiated and forgotten. But it will not be easy for this generation to forget. It will not be easy to wash away the memory of one clear and unforgettable Japanese etching—of two frock-coated Nipponese emissaries hissing peace words in Washington while Nipponese bombs wiped out American pride at Honolulu. A knife to the heart and a pat on the shoulder—no other country in history has presented such a "face" to the world as has Japan.

We cannot forget blood-printed pictures of Nanking—so terrible they have never been shown in detail.

It will be difficult for the people of the Philippines to forgive as long as Manila streets exist that saw the crucifixion of Filipinos over pools of their own blood, for standing by America in defiance of Japan.

☆          ☆          ☆

Beneath such demonstrations of swaggering cruelty and treachery skulks the lowliest inferiority sense in the Orient.

The Japanese, awkward in appearance, speech, and social graces, masks these deficiencies with a bristling air of superiority which serves to uphold "face." He develops an exaggerated politeness outwardly and an inner dream of becoming master of the world. Although he is hypersensitive, this does not make him sensitive to the sufferings of others. He is too far above the ordinary run for such weaknesses. He is the family, the State, and the son of God, for the Emperor himself, who is God, is his father!

With such responsibilities of dynasty and divinity, who would dare smile, weep, or sink to levity?

Therefore the Japanese stresses the importance of "face." His face must be inscrutable, for if he betrays emotion upon his face he has broken Japanese tradition.

To other peoples the face is the mirror of the soul, but to the Japanese it is a concealing mask. His pride is in his stoicism. From childhood he trains himself not to betray any emotion by facial expression. To lose "face" is to lose caste among the Japanese. This explains his being a poor sport. He plays games, not for fun, but to win. If he loses he loses "face." I have seen Japanese athletes, in the Far Eastern games, go into stadium corners after defeat and hide their faces in shame.

The outstanding swimming champion of Japan, defeated by a Filipino, refused to come out of the water and had to be forcibly pulled out of the pool.

During one of our Rotary international conventions a prominent Japanese delegate came to me in anguish. He had been delegated to advocate a certain measure and had discovered the measure would not pass. "Please, you must help me. I cannot return to Japan unless that resolution passes. I would lose 'face.' "

It was to gain "face" that Japan invaded her supposedly weak neighbor, China.

When that attack failed something had to be done to save the "face" of the Japanese military clique.

Pearl Harbor was the answer. Therefore Pearl Harbor was both necessary and honorable—from the Japanese point of view. But Pearl Harbor did not stem directly from Japan's failure to conquer

China and America's frank admission of being on China's side. Japanese psychology is not so simple and direct as that.

Pearl Harbor was the actual result of a loss of "face" in 1923 that was the greatest Japan had ever known. And yet, Japan said little at the time concerning what it regarded as crushing insult from America. This was the passage of the Oriental Exclusion Act by the United States Congress. By this act, the small, proud country that had defeated gigantic Russia was "slapped in the face" by America.

I have been told this in many ways by Japanese.

Only war with America could restore this terrible loss of "face." This resolve was fed by additional "insults," on the part of America —prohibition of the sale of oil to Japan and the freezing of Japanese credit. Even the Disarmament Conference, which failed to allow Japan the naval ratio asked for, was a loss of "face" for which Japan blamed America.

These, following in the wake of the Exclusion Act, fed the flames of Japanese war preparation through two decades.

There is no questioning the wisdom of the Exclusion Act. The Japanese were practicing infiltration on the Western coast of North America. But the protective move might have been brought about in another manner compatible with the Japanese concept of national honor. By treaty, perhaps, instead of the humiliating method of congressional enactment.

The Japanese pursuing their business and social infiltration tactics in the Philippines used the Exclusion Act as propaganda in their attempts to turn the Filipinos against the Americans.

"Doesn't exclusion infuriate you, as an Oriental?" they have asked me many times.

I had one unvarying answer.

"It does not infuriate me because the Americans evidently found the Exclusion Act necessary. Nor do I see why it should infuriate you as a Japanese, for the Japanese themselves laid the grounds for the act by excluding foreigners from Japan. No foreigner can own land in Japan.

"America also has an immigration quota for Europeans. She means no insult to Orientals. She is only trying to protect herself."

As a Filipino my only recourse was to defend the Exclusion Act. We were desperately hunting some measure that would stop the

Japanese infiltration in our country. They continued to spread everywhere and our distrust of them deepened. Personally and nationally, we disliked and distrusted them. While Filipinos intermarried with Spaniards and Chinese, there was little intermarriage with the Japanese. Between the two races there was little feeling except lack of trust.

A few individual Japanese were well liked. Of these, we learned after war began that not a few were in the Philippines as spies. These who were closest to us betrayed us.

I am not saying that the Japanese is not to be trusted. He can be trusted to the death—by his Emperor. He may be your friend, he may in fact love you, but stronger than that friendship and the man himself is "face," which is the honor he owes his Emperor.

In all my visits to Japan I never laid eyes on his Imperial Majesty Hirohito, and, as a matter of fact, few Japanese have seen him. We know him to be cultured, courtly, and given to writing poems dealing with hopes for peace. To every true Japanese he is Japan, the Son of Heaven, and God.

"Face" holds the Japanese ready to live or die for that God.

Friendship, love, family, home, and life are poor tributes to lay at the feet of the Emperor.

Before that shining majesty Pearl Harbor was a minor trophy. The world belongs at the feet of the Emperor, and any Japanese would gladly die to give the Emperor his world. Any trick, any treachery, is justifiable under the bloody and relentless warrior code of the Samurai if it yields tribute worthy of the Rising Sun.

This faith in himself as part of the God-Emperor provided the Japanese with his "face."

It gave America Pearl Harbor, Wake, Guam, the Aleutians.

It gave the Philippines—America's representative in the Far East—Bataan and Corregidor.

# XII. OUR THIRD FIGHT FOR FREEDOM

WITH the single exception of the Philippines, Japan's demand for recognition of "face" crystallized opinion in the Orient. Millions of colored peoples who resented white authority listened to Japan. Only the Filipino refused to listen. Despite years of Japanese propaganda urging "the Orient for the Orientals," the Oriental Filipino struggled to retain his position in the white man's world.

The teeth of the Japanese propaganda arguments had been removed, for Filipinos, forty years before by William Howard Taft with the simple promise: "The Philippines for the Filipinos." That promise had been kept. No Japanese arguments that we should stand by our "fellow Orientals" could lessen this fact.

Mother America had kept this promise despite long and powerful opposition from representatives of American vested interests who were not willing to yield in the Philippines without a struggle.

Vested interests followed the American soldier into the Philippines shortly after the turn of the century. I have told before how many of the soldiers remained after the occupation was accomplished, to earn livings as civilians and make the country their home. These were joined by businessmen from America.

Eventually many grew rich through introducing American enterprise and initiative in the virgin territory. These men, while maintaining a friendly relationship with the Filipinos, naturally arrived at the conclusion that their business affairs would be aided by the continuation of American sovereignty. These, the vested interests, were the leaders in opposing the carrying out of America's promise of independence.

This point of view of local businessmen was shared by certain business interests representing larger companies in America.

The opinions of certain vested interests in America came in time to be impressed upon the Philippines and to hinder our movement toward independence.

Added to the money-weighted arguments of men like these were the opinions of some of the American officials who had been sent from America to train Filipinos in official duties. Mother America had sent these officials in preparation for the time when Filipinos would live as Americans, under self-rule. The majority of these officials carried out their assignment with missionary zeal and showed pride as their pupils mastered the working details of a democracy. Such men gladly stepped aside, when the native understudy was prepared, yielding his place to the Filipino. But there were other officials who looked upon politics as a vested interest and who had no intention of stepping aside voluntarily. They knew the advance of Filipinization would eventually cost them their jobs. These men sided with big business and opposed the policy of the Philippines for the Filipinos.

Then came the press services. As I have said before they reflected the point of view of the vested interests.

I am not questioning the honesty of these men who came to the conclusion that it would be bad business to grant independence to the Philippines, and opposed America's original plan with all their considerable might.

Only, in future dealings with Far Eastern problems, it will be well to consider the case of the Philippines, where the policy of democracy was not permitted to swerve from its main course by any considerations of selfishness and greed. Powerful attempts were made to swerve the democratic policy. They were made by Americans who were turned into imperialists by the metamorphosis that so often overtakes the white man in the Orient.

These Americans, who had come to the Philippines as sane, clear-thinking, loyal Americans, did not realize that their views toward democracy were changed by rich and easeful living, finer homes, elevated social position, and a plenitude of servants. So, via the luxury route, they arrived at a concept of imperialism.

But the process of rationalization began. All flaws in the local government were picked up and magnified. All aspirations and ideals of Filipinos were opposed.

Without perhaps realizing it they were inwardly saying: "This is a rich country. Why not keep it for ourselves?"

"The Philippines for Americans" policy would protect the American vested interests in mining, sugar, hemp, embroideries, exports, and imports of all kinds.

Outwardly they quoted Kipling's "Little brown brother." The poor Filipino was in need of guidance and it was the American's duty to take care of him.

But in the meantime the Filipino was grasping the working details of democracy. The Filipino who had fought Spain, then America, had no intention of becoming the little brown brother of this newly born imperialist. He was willing to be the brown brother of a white democrat. Working from this premise he staged his third fight for freedom.

This was the fight for Philippine independence.

His fight was contested through many years—not by America—but by the American imperialist in the Philippines. The American imperialist was not only contesting every progressive step made by Filipinos under the benevolent policy of America; he was also opposing America.

This type of American, despite the metamorphosis he had undergone, was loudest in his complaints against America and its failure to protect him and his business interests in the Philippines.

I have heard this American imperialist all over the Far East voicing the same complaints against America. It was a leading topic of conversation in certain wealthy American circles in Manila and Shanghai.

Often I have heard such Americans say bitterly: "Washington doesn't care what happens to us out here. No matter where the Dutch or English go, they have the full support of their government behind them."

They did not realize that their complaint, to the Far East, was one of the soundest arguments in favor of democracy.

America, an isolationist nation, made it clear to every businessman who left America that he was on his own as an individual. As a citizen he was entitled to all the protection that was his due. As a colonizer, exploiter, or profiteer he had no recognition from America.

This was in contrast with other powers, where imperialism invariably accompanied the commercial interests on their march to power. An Englishman or Dutchman who set up a business in the Far East was regarded as part of the advance guard of government.

This refusal on the part of America to protect the business interests of her citizens in the Far East, while a source of much indignation to the moneyed Americans, was of great satisfaction to the natives all over the Orient. It did much to turn the trust of the Orient toward America. It was first made apparent in the Philippines during our fight for independence. That struggle for independence grew as we gained in wisdom under the tutelage of America. It was from America that we learned what we actually wanted.

In the beginning our struggle was one of fighting resentment. This died as friendship developed between American and Filipino. Filipino leaders, trained by Americans, took over the reins in the race toward democracy.

We were dealing with Americans, who, beyond all other people, were most capable of understanding our desire to be free. The Philippine struggle for independence was not unlike the one America herself had staged against England in 1776.

We knew this, and America knew it, from the beginning.

We were upholding the American principle that any government without the full consent of the governed was tyranny.

Every arrow in our destiny had pointed toward democracy. We had resented imperialism and set up our own Philippine Republic before the arrival of the Americans. In many ways the democratic pattern of the Republic had been similar to America's.

The constitution approved by that Republic had been inspired by Apolinario Mabini, "the sublime paralytic," who had fought the occupation with his pen and brains as adviser to Aguinaldo. He was a great admirer of the American Constitution and the Philippine Constitution as approved by the Republic[1] has been cited by American constitutional authorities as one of the most democratic ever drafted.

It established separation between Church and State and in its every provision made for government "for, by, and of the people, and deriving all powers from the consent of the governed."

The Americans, powerful with conquest, might have made short

[1] See Appendix.

shrift of the cripple Mabini. In another subject country he would probably have been shot. Instead, they called him into conference with their own political leaders and heard his opinions with deference.

We remained convinced that we were capable of working out our own destiny.

We asked only what America had asked in 1776—freedom.

We were awarded that freedom over the protests of the American imperialists in the Philippines, whose voices were heard loudly in America. But America listened also to the protesting Filipinos.

In the end, America herself decided, and moved steadily toward the goal set down by Taft: "The Philippines for the Filipinos."

The American principle remained sound.

Many times Americans in the Philippines, opposing measures passed by the Philippine Legislature, openly advocated their veto by the President in Washington. Often their suggestions were turned down.

Then there was the case of Nicholas Roosevelt, whose appointment as vice-governor of the Philippines had been made and announced. Such a storm of protest was raised by Filipinos who had read his articles declaring he believed us incapable of self-government that his appointment was withdrawn.

An outstanding example of American fair play was the controversy over Governor General Leonard Wood. No American ever arrived in the Philippines carrying more prestige and general power of respect. General Wood had practically the unanimous support of the American people. But the Filipinos came to the conclusion that he was reactionary and that backward steps in our autonomy were being taken under him. In the political crisis that followed he was actively fought by the Filipinos led by Manuel L. Quezon.

Many Americans in the Philippines advocated that the American Government in Washington adopt an iron policy to support Wood's views. But Washington, while it neither disowned nor disauthorized Wood, failed to sanction the steps he had taken.

This failure to uphold Wood, in view of his prestige, made a great impression upon the Filipinos. Impossible to imagine an imperialistic Governor General or Viceroy fighting native leaders without the full support of the Crown!

The principle of Americanism was with the Filipino all the way.
There were many cases of vested interests in conflict which
proved to be a help, instead of hindrance, to the side for independence.

For example, while it was true that Philippine sugar was competing against large sugar interests in the United States and our Philippine hemp against American cordage interests by entering the
United States duty free, this was not looked on with disfavor by the
Philippine vested interests, nearly all of which were American. The
sugar and cordage interests in America wanted us free, so the Philippine interests would have to pay tariff. The American-Philippine
interests naturally wanted us to remain dependent and duty free.

In the end those who wanted our independence overbalanced
those who did not.

The ancient imperialistic saw, *divide et impera*, divide and rule—
which summarizes the technique of colonization—found no welcome
in the Philippines. There were cases where Americans of the vested-
interest type—incidentally, we learned early to call them "carpetbaggers"—tried to emphasize cleavages among the natives.

There are many tribes and dialects in the Philippines, and it is
not generally known in America that one dialect is understood by
all. This is Tagalog, a dialect of Malayan origin. But the difference
in peoples was cited by the carpetbaggers as a reason for keeping
the Philippines dependent. "The tribes will spring at each other's
throats if granted independence."

Part of the "divide-and-rule" campaign was the introduction of a
bill to separate the island of Mindanao from the rest of the Philippines—a bill which never went through. It was an attempt to alienate the Moros, or Mohammedan Filipinos, living on that island from
the Christian Filipinos.

The measure failed, partly because it did not have the support of
the American people and partly because the Filipinos knew how to
get along with the Moros. In the long run the Moros came to attend
the public schools and became very friendly. They co-operated
with the Christian Filipinos in many matters, the last and most important, in fighting the Japanese.

The introduction of English as the language of instruction in
all schools did much toward giving the country a sense of oneness.

This was the exact opposite of the usual pattern, "divide and rule."

American history as taught in the public schools told the stories of American leaders who had been heroes and rebels—who had been fighters for freedom. Pictures on schoolroom walls—Washington, Lincoln, Jefferson—held before the young Filipino the ideal of America's fight for freedom. Beside those pictures, on the same schoolroom walls, was the picture of the rebel-hero of the Philippines—José Rizal.

Filipino pupils were encouraged to debate the subject of independence in the schools, some taking the negative and others the affirmative. The teachers took no active part in these debates, beyond saying at times that the Philippines were not yet ready for self-rule and for that reason should prepare. As a result the Filipino heart, already flaming with desire for freedom, was constantly being fed on America's own story of struggle for independence.

Despite the hindrances set in our path by the retroactive, the Philippines were led step by step, by America, toward independence.

It is for the benefit of both sovereign and subject nations that we outline the basic principles of this movement of a subject people toward freedom. It would be well for such countries as India and Java to study the Filipino's technique of asking for independence without sacrificing loyalty, and to see how we brought about the dovetailing of loyalty with the struggle for freedom.

The Filipino fight for independence is important because it shows that the unflagging determination of a people and their willingness to undergo any sacrifice are essential to their being free. It must never be forgotten that America's democratic policy was a beacon in the Philippine fight for freedom.

It is of importance to note that the fight for freedom was waged without personal or racial bitterness. In all fairness it must be said that the great majority of those Americans living in the Philippines who opposed independence did so, not for reasons of cupidity, but because they sincerely believed it was for the best interests of the Filipinos that they remain under the American flag. Most of these Americans were sincere friends of the Filipinos and their names were always foremost in the lists of all movements calculated to aid and improve the lot of the Filipinos.

For this reason it was less a fight for freedom than an assertion for the rights of liberty. As Quezon once said, it was not that we "loved America less, but freedom more."

It is necessary for the sovereign nations to realize that a subject nation can fight for freedom and still be loyal, as was the case between the Philippines and America.

It should be a lesson, to such a country as India, to remember that our fight for independence was at its hottest when America entered World War I. Immediately the independence movement stopped: in America's hour of need we were with America. Manuel L. Quezon, in a stirring speech on the floor of the Philippine Senate, offered all the Philippines possessed to America; offered 25,000 Filipino members of the Philippine National Guard. These men were in training and eager to fight, in Europe, for America.

The guard was left in the Philippines, but the offer made possible the removal of every American soldier in the Philippines to Europe.

When the war ended, the fight for independence began again with renewed vigor.

It will be well for the sovereign nations to realize, as in this example set by America, that dividends are earned by recognizing the self-respect of a people.

Loyalty cannot be expected where self-respect has been destroyed, for only self-respecting people can know what loyalty means.

Sovereign and subject nations alike can profit by understanding how the principles of democracy were put on a working basis, while the struggle for independence went on in the Philippines.

# XIII. DETAILS OF DEMOCRACY

WHILE American schoolteachers laid the foundations for democracy in the Philippines, American politicians were completing the structure in its final triumphant spire.

These men, politicians in the finer sense of the word, built carefully and with infinite patience. Their work had been outlined for them in the unprecedented charge of President McKinley:

"The Philippines are ours, not to exploit but to develop, to civilize, to educate, to train in the science of self-government."

These words carried the Philippines through the changes that followed.

The simplicity of the democratic structure aided Filipinos and Americans alike in its building.

The Philippine pattern followed the American pattern that began in 1776. The transformation of the Philippine Government of 1901 to civil government was political science personalized; and the principles of political science, neither abstruse nor abstract, were applied in the personal and human way.

The American put himself in the place of the Filipino. He studied the degree of training in the Filipino and the preparations he had made for self-government. He realized that what he had asked of England in 1776 the Filipino had asked in 1898 from Spain and in 1899 from America.

The Americans said of the Filipinos in effect: "These people have wanted freedom as we once wanted freedom. How did we achieve ours? Through oneness!

"The Filipinos have the same solidarity, born of their need to be free. What can we do to help them?"

And the first decision was: "The Filipinos must learn to read and write!"

So schools were opened throughout the Philippines. But the important part of their building was that they were not built with American money taken from American taxes. The schools were built with taxes imposed upon the Filipino. The American schoolteachers' salaries were paid out of Philippine taxes. The Filipino realized he was paying for benefits received and that he was no object of charity. This meant much to his self-respect.

The Americans found the sanitary conditions primitive, and the first American soldiers in their barracks and quarters set examples that served to teach sanitation to the people of the towns. They boiled the drinking water—a process hitherto unknown in the cholera- and typhoid-infested country. They installed sewers and cisterns. The Filipinos were glad to follow these innovations.

American schoolteachers urged sanitation upon the children: encouraged them to wash their hands and brush their teeth. The precepts of cleanliness were carried into the homes by the children. Classes in domestic science taught dietary values to the girls.

American physical directors developed the health standards of the new generation. The value of athletics to the Filipino people cannot be overemphasized. Provincial athletic meets were held everywhere and aided in developing the network of community feeling and good sportsmanship that is so typical of America. For these privileges, the Filipino was paying, and with his own money. It was a matter of great satisfaction to him to know that these schools, teachers, and athletic instructors were provided for out of the taxes he paid.

The passion for paying one's way is the mark of the independent. Even in small matters, the Filipino is an independent soul.

The Americans, themselves the acme of independence, recognized this spirit from the beginning and fostered it. They knew the Filipino spirit would never rest short of freedom. The movement toward self-government was plain from the beginning. It began, as self-government began in America, in the towns.

But democracy is a slow process. Its complete acceptance was disputed long, even in the Philippines. The Americans, taking into consideration the receptivity of the Filipino, moved with care. They laid the groundwork first. They began their experiment in democracy in the towns, because in America the town is the important unit of government.

It was experimental, and the Filipinos knew it as such. The fact was put to them frankly. If they succeeded in the first steps, the experiment would be carried further.

This was begun while the country was still under military rule.

Many Filipinos had come to trust the Americans and were willing to co-operate with the American rule. The American commanding officer in a town would select certain Filipinos he knew to be loyal, and the first municipal councils were made up of such men, selected from the barrios, or villages, surrounding the town. The councils varied in size according to the town's population—there were perhaps from six to two dozen. These Filipinos elected the town president, or mayor, and mayor and council together governed the town under the supervision and control of the American commanding officer.

This was no puppet system. The officer interfered only if he felt the native government was in error. The system was functioning ably by the time the government passed from the military to the civil. Due to its success, the Americans decided to allow the people of the towns to elect the council and mayor by secret ballot. This direct vote was extended to the entire Philippines with the exception of the non-Christian tribes. And again it was understood that if this democratic means of town government proved successful, the experiment would be widened.

The Filipinos responded with enthusiasm to the voting. The same means of government was then extended from the town to the province.

The American Governor General, who, with his Civil Commission, held the reins of the national, or insular, government, appointed Filipinos to replace the first provincial governors, who were Americans. These appointives were replaced by Filipinos elected by the municipal councils of the towns. This system proved successful, whereupon the provincial governor was elected by the direct vote of the people of the province.

Each American provincial governor had been assisted by a provincial board consisting of a superintendent of schools, a treasurer, and a third member, known as the elective, who was the only Filipino. It was in this board that the elimination process known as Filipinization of government service began.

The Americans eliminated one appointive member of the board and made two elective. Naturally, by the elimination process, and as the Filipino members showed their grasp of the details involved, these elective members were Filipinos.

Filipinization was actually Americanism put on a workable basis for the Philippines.

The slow process of democracy moved upward, through the towns, through the provinces, to the national government.

To show how gradually this came about, Filipinization did not actually commence in the government until 1916. This was an important year for the Filipinos. It was important because a man with a tremendous vision of world security, Woodrow Wilson, was President of the United States.

The failure of that vision to materialize in Wilson's lifetime would not shake the Filipino's opinion of him as a great man. He would remain one of the greatest of our heroes.

Wilson, in this important year 1916, signed the Jones Act, which was of vital importance in our struggle for independence, and the longest step we had taken along the road to freedom.

☆ ☆ ☆

It is interesting to note the way the struggle for independence, our third fight for freedom, was keeping step with the advance of democracy in the Philippines. In fact, the movements dovetailed so completely and were so similar in pattern that it is difficult to say where Americanization left off and actual independence began.

If, from the very beginning, American policy was divided as to American rights in the Philippines, it is only fair to say that the opinions of the Filipinos were also at odds. There were not a few Filipinos who considered American occupation an advantage and felt that the Philippines would benefit by remaining part of the American Union.

Upon the end of the revolution, at the start of the century, these pro-American advocates formed the Federal party, sponsoring

Americanism in toto, and receiving encouragement and abetment from the American Government.

But there were other Filipinos unwilling to accept the complete authority of America. They arrived at this conclusion, fairly enough, through American teachings. Many of them were the recipients of one of the first and most interesting acts of the Philippine Commission, that had selected two hundred young students from the entire Philippines by competitive examination. These bright young men had been sent to schools and colleges in the United States. Now, back in the Philippines, they became political and educational leaders. Several were appointed presidents of universities.

These were the men imbued with American ideals from the very fount of Americanism, who founded the Philippine Columbian Association, composed of Filipino graduates of American universities, which would become the bulwark of Filipino nationalism.

Then the nationalist party was organized with two outstanding young leaders.

One, Sergio Osmeña, was the governor of the southern island of Cebu. As an editorialist he had been uncompromising in his campaign for independence, first against Spain, then America. The other, Manuel Luis Quezon, had served as a major in the revolutionary army of Aguinaldo. He was governor of the province of Tayabas. These two began—and carried out to victory—the fight for independence.

The first contest between the young nationalist party and the staid Federal party began over the chairmanship of a convention of provincial governors that had been called in Manila.

Osmeña was elected.

Then the National Assembly, elected by the people, was created in 1908. Its importance in the gradual evolution of the Filipino toward self-government cannot be overestimated. If it failed, our struggle for independence might end with it. It was the Filipino's first real test in self-government.

The Filipinos revealed themselves as overwhelmingly behind the young nationalists by electing them to the largest number of seats. Osmeña, elected Speaker, assumed the leadership of the Filipino people in the government, taking the place of Aguinaldo, who had laid down his leadership with his arms when war ended.

Osmeña laid the grounds for the fight for independence in the Philippines.

Manuel Luis Quezon would carry that fight into the stronghold of America.

Quezon was elected floor leader of the majority part of the house, then sent as Resident Commissioner to Washington. Fiery, sincere, and a brilliant speaker, he continued to wage his long and uncompromising battle for independence from the floor of the American Congress.

The Filipinos were behind him all the way. Each year the municipal councils prepared and approved resolutions asking for independence for the Philippines, and each year Quezon in Washington presented these demands of a people to America. In every way the Filipinos could devise the struggle for freedom was carried on, both in America and in the Philippines.

Quezon set up a Philippine press bureau in Washington so that the truth about the Philippines might be fairly presented to America. He published his own magazine there, the *Filipino People*, and copies were sent to every publication and person of influence in the United States.

By 1916—that all-important year—the Filipinos had achieved the National Assembly, elected by the people, and the Upper House, composed of the Philippine Civil Commission, appointed by the President of the United States.

But legislative power was not in Filipino hands. It was this the nationalists asked and were given with the passage of the Jones Act.[1]

The Jones Act accomplished many things. It carried the first congressional promise of independence. Before this promises had been made in the form of statements issued by American officials, unverified by the American Congress. We had been given many such unauthorized promises since the beginning of American rule.

The Jones Act, by providing for the creation of a Philippine Senate elected by the people and the abolishment of the Philippine Commission, placed legislative powers completely in Filipino hands.

With the creation of the Senate the National Assembly assumed

[1]See Appendix.

a minor role. But the success of the assembly had been the sternest test in the great American experiment.

The Filipinos had passed with credit the tests set by their American leaders. For this much credit should be given to the statesmanship, tact, and patriotism of Sergio Osmeña, who steered the first legislative body, composed entirely of Filipinos, to success under American rule.

Quezon, as president of the Senate, became leader of the nationalist party, which split into two wings, the Collectivist under Quezon and the Unipersonal under Osmeña.

This division in sentiment was carried in traditional American fashion to the Filipino people. The resultant election gave the majority to Quezon. The triumph of the Jones Act had made him first president of the Senate. The two parties fused and the temporary rift healed over. The struggle for independence went on. This fusion reveals the high degree of patriotism of these two leaders. They might have continued the cleavage. But their aim was mutual—Philippine independence—and because of that aim they united. Their example might have been followed, thereby changing the shape of history, in such countries as Burma, Java, and India, where nationalistic leaders failed to submerge personal differences in favor of patriotism.

The nationalists of the Philippines won much through presenting a united front.

But the two greatest desires of the Filipinos, the assumption of executive and judiciary powers, were still beyond reach of their hands.

Governor General Francis Burton Harrison, appointee of President Wilson, directly upon his arrival in the Philippines, in 1916, announced his policy of Filipinization, or placing government power in the hands of the Filipinos. He was the first of the democratic governors, and his announced policies made a great impression upon the Filipinos. He inaugurated what was known as the New Era, greatly resembling what would later be known as the New Deal. The Filipinos came to speak of the pre-Harrison period as "Empire Days."

Harrison's announced policy neither went unnoticed nor unprotested by those American imperialists who were growing richer hour by hour in the Philippines, nor by the few Americans in government service who had hoped their positions would be lifelong sinecures. These protested loudly, and their protests were heard in America. But they were not heeded. The majority of the Americans in the government conscientiously trained Filipino understudies in the methods of public service, and, when they found them ready, voluntarily stepped aside. Their sacrifice was made pleasanter for them by the passage of the Retirement Act Bill as drafted by Osmeña.

Once Harrison had announced the Filipinization policy it forged ahead rapidly.

At this time the national government, consisting of the Governor General and his Cabinet and the directors of bureaus, with one or two exceptions, were Americans. In the civil departments all heads were Americans with the exception of two Filipino members of the commission. Under these departments were bureaus, the heads of which were Americans.

Harrison proceeded to Filipinize all bureaus and departments.

As complete a reversal followed in the judiciary. There were, in the lower courts, the unit Justices of the Peace, then the Courts of First Instance; lastly the Supreme Court.

The Justices of the Peace were all Filipinos, but the Courts of First Instance were at one time composed almost entirely of American judges, holding jurisdiction, in places, over as many as four provinces. Gradually these American judges were replaced until all the courts were presided over by Filipinos.

The Supreme Court was made up of an American majority—nine Americans and two Filipinos. But it is illustrative of American fairness that despite the American majority they had made a Filipino, Cayetano Arellano, the first Filipino chief justice under American rule.

After 1916, as the American justices retired, Filipinos were appointed in their places, until the majority were Filipino. The chief justice was always a Filipino.

After the passage of the Tydings-McDuffie Independence Act in 1934[2] the Supreme Court became entirely Filipino.

This act was the result of the unflagging continuance of the fight for freedom. The Filipinos continued to send missions to America

[2]See Appendix.

demanding full independence. Halfway measures were not enough, any more than they had been for America under British rule.

In 1933 a mission arrived in America headed by Sergio Osmeña, president pro tempore of the Senate, and Manuel Roxas, Speaker of the House. The result of this mission was the approval by the Lower House of the Hawes Bill, granting independence to the Philippines.

Quezon succeeded in having this bill modified with the completion of the Tydings-McDuffie Act, which was signed by President Roosevelt in 1934.

The long struggle for independence was over. The fighters for freedom had won. It is of the greatest importance, to subject and sovereign nations alike, to note that every step of the way the Filipinos had co-operated with America, and that their loyalty to America had never been questioned.

It is true that the fight for independence was encouraged by American interests whose products were competing with ours, and whose assistance carried the selfish desire that independence would eliminate Philippine hemp, sugar, tobacco, and other products from the free market of America. But, precisely because their interests were tinged with selfishness, they could not have won the fight for us if we had not presented our united front in convincing America we wanted freedom. They could not have won, because they were lobbyists, and the lobbyist, while in many instances powerful, is still regarded with wholesome suspicion in Washington.

We accepted their aid, because they offered aid in our struggle to be free.

But credit must be given to such unprejudiced American statesmen as Congressman William Atkinson Jones, of Virginia, author of the Jones Act; Senator Harry B. Hawes, of Missouri, joint author of the Hawes-Cutting Bill; and Senator Millard E. Tydings, of Maryland, who authored and fought for the passing of the Tydings-McDuffie Act.

Through the passage of the Tydings-McDuffie Act the Commonwealth Government of the Philippines was inaugurated in 1935, a commonwealth of autonomous status with complete independence promised in 1946. Manuel Luis Quezon was elected first president of the Philippine Commonwealth and Sergio Osmeña his vice-president.

To honor the new government leading representatives of America's civil government, Army and Navy, made the long trip to the Philippines. Among them were Vice-President John Garner and Secretary of War George Dern.

On the afternoon of his inauguration Quezon reviewed the American Army in the Philippines—the army that had made his country subject a quarter of a century before!

Now the hierarchy of that sovereign country was there to pay tribute to the once-captive nation—a tribute that has never been duplicated in the long history of colonization.

We of the Philippines were grateful. At our backs, in the vast regions of Asia, other Oriental people learned that we of the Philippines had found our status beside the Americans as men equal and free.

America had set the standards of democracy in the Far East.

The Americans who journeyed to the Philippines to honor the new Commonwealth found that the Filipinos had added new heroes to their own lists during the struggle for independence. Pinned to the schoolroom walls were the historic figures that had led the way —Lincoln, Washington, Jefferson.

But there were newer American figures honored in the Philippines. Among these the two leading figures were Woodrow Wilson, because he had signed the Jones Act and given impetus to the process of Filipinization, and Franklin Delano Roosevelt, because his signing of the Tydings-McDuffie Act promised freedom for the Philippines.

These visiting Americans discovered that the finest boulevards in Manila had been named by the Filipinos in honor of Americans who had won their respect—Harrison Boulevard in honor of that Governor General who introduced the New Era; Dewey Boulevard for the admiral who had symbolized the advent of America by bringing his fleet into Manila Bay; Taft Boulevard for the President who had first made the promise so ably fulfilled: "The Philippines for the Filipinos."

These were Filipino tributes to Americans who had served in leading the Filipinos, step by step, to democracy.

In 1898, shaking free of Spanish imperialism, the Philippines had established the fledgling Philippine Republic.

In 1946 it would again be the Philippine Republic.

We were returning to our starting point, but with the advantage of wider experience and a practical knowledge of working democracy we might not have acquired in centuries if left to our own devices.

That we were better prepared to absorb democratic principles than any other Oriental nation was due to our Spanish heritage and our Christian training. But it is inconceivable that we might have worked out a practical system of democracy in forty-two years.

America had led us along the short way.

In forty-two years America led the Filipino nation to the point where it was willing to fight to the death in defense of democracy.

Imperialistic nations always say of the subject people they refuse to set free: "They are not yet prepared!"

America prepared the Philippines in forty-two years.

How many centuries, may I ask, have other white races occupied other sections of the Orient?

# XIV. PROBLEMS OF OTHER PEOPLE

It was a shocking experience for an Americanized Filipino to travel through other sections of the Orient before the outbreak of the present war.

The Filipino who has grown to manhood under Americanism is likely to take democracy for granted, as does his contemporary the American. His right to speak freely, to meet all peoples on equal terms, to argue, criticize, debate, and cast his vote on the side he believes to be right has never been questioned.

As a Filipino I was proud of my nationality. As a nationalist I had faith in the genius of my people. I set out to visit the other countries of the Far East; to gather the opinions of fellow Orientals whose languages I could not speak and whose ways I did not share. But I expected them to show pride in their nationality. I waited their saying with Oriental dignity and pride: I am Burmese, or Indonesian, or Malay!

Instead, I found them ashamed to speak. The very mention of nationalism was taboo. It was disgraceful to be a native in Asiatic countries controlled by Holland, France, or England.

These people were living in such misery as I had never known existed. My travels heretofore had been many and long, but they had been luxurious tours circling the earth, or concentrated on the gayer places of America and Europe and even Asia. Now I realized I had flashed by Clipper or private car past many of the sore places of the earth.

How could such misery exist, I found myself wondering constantly, under the vast powers and wealth of the white imperialisms? How could they suffer such hideous injustices to peoples in their charge?

Without criticizing or justifying any individual country, let us come hastily to the conclusion that the imperialist believes people can be contented without being free. It is true that many subject countries in the Far East wore the outward mien of content.

Let us give credit to the imperialists by concluding that they did work toward the contentment of their subjects, and in many places apparently succeeded. But their success resembled that of the dairy farmer who has taken the best of care of his cattle.

Physical content is not enough. In every normal man is the urge that has expressed itself finally in the democratic belief that there can be no contentment without freedom.

Even in Far Eastern countries outwardly peaceful and contented the listener with his ear to the ground heard the ferment of unrest. Only the imperialist would not disturb his position of superiority by placing his ear to that troubled earth. The white man had no heed for the murmured protests of brown men. When at last he heard them his day was over in Asia—it was too late. The submerged tide had risen and swept him from his proud position in the Orient.

But for those willing to hear, a billion whispering voices gave testimony that Burma, Thailand, French Indo-China, British Malaya, Singapore, Hong Kong, and the Dutch East Indies were willing to bend before a yellow totalitarianism—anything to escape the white despotism!

These countries would yield one by one to Japan, letting fall into Nipponese hands the richest empire in all history.

The Oriental nations, before Pearl Harbor, watched Japan. They had watched it with dread since the first Nipponese invaders swarmed over helpless China. Each knew, if Japan turned its awful face their way, that they might well be another China.

And yet, when the time came, they were with Japan!

I traveled through these countries in their most critical moments, when they were deliberating which route to follow when crisis came. Everywhere I found a sense of betrayal at white hands.

The Atlantic Charter had summed up the long suspicions of one billion colored peoples. All Asia, in the beginning, had thought itself included under the Atlantic Charter that promised freedom, at war's end, to "men of all lands!" Each Far Eastern country had taken the Atlantic Charter as a pledge for self-government to the subject nations of the world. To them, the failure of the pledge to include the Asiatics seemed the final clinching proof of white perfidy.

The Charter promised freedom—but not to them. Freedom was for the white peoples who had been crushed under the Nazi yoke. It was not for the brown man. It was not for Asia.

They, the one billion betrayed, as they considered themselves, had been fought over and shuffled about in the white man's scramble for colonies, and nothing had come of their tragic struggles to throw off the domination of their white masters. And of those struggles little that was favorable was known, thanks to the prejudiced white press bureaus, by the outer white man's world.

Only one of the Asiatic nations had the strength, the daring, and the assurance to utter defiance to the white world.

This was Japan.

Japan, the least liked among them, the lone wolf of Asia, held, despite its dangerousness to them, a wild hope to this billion that felt betrayed. The Asiatics had long felt the need of some powerful colored race to which they could hook the wagons of their destiny.

Had they found it in Japan? Could they trust Japan?

They had pondered these questions in Asia, and reached a despairing conclusion. They could not trust Japan. They had no faith in Japan as a world force.

But any yellow imperialism, they argued bitterly, was better for them than the white imperialisms that had checked so long their genius as nations.

It was primarily a cry for revenge.

Even Japan would serve—if it would yield them the chance to get even!

This was the conclusion, even before war started, of such countries as Burma, Thailand, Java, and French Indo-China.

This the white men did not know.

Even now it is difficult for white men to understand why, in seemingly peaceful Asiatic countries, they were obliged to fight for their lives against not only the incoming Japanese, but also the apparently servile natives they had looked down upon so contemptuously for so many years.

How did this revenge-urge develop, let us ask, in a country as seemingly peaceful and serene as Burma?

The Western world had never troubled to heed the cries of this subject country on the other side of the earth. But Burma was well aware of its importance. In wealth and position it was important. It was not only the largest rice-exporting nation in the world, but it was rich in every commodity an ambitious nation, such as Japan, could possibly need to carry out plans for conquering the world.

Burma was the gateway to India and, before the outbreak of war, the last remaining route of supply into China. Its Burma Road was the aorta leading into the heart of the Orient. It was in political ferment. Its inner unrest and its agitation for freedom were indicative of the turbulence in its next-door neighbor, India.

The Burmese are a gentle, cleanly, friendly people. They are faithful adherents to their religion, which is Buddhism. They are more like the Filipinos in their racial characteristics than any other people in Asia. Their inherent nationalism resembled the Filipino; they share our passion for being free.

Knowing this, I entered Burma with the fervent hope that the country was preparing to side with the democracies, with the assurance that democracy was to be their reward. I talked with the people and their leaders, the newspapermen who could not write what they really thought because under the English rule there was no free press, and the nationalist leaders who could not say all they wanted to say for fear of imprisonment under the English. Rather, I talked with those who remained after Burma's long and bitter fight for self-determination. The majority of them were under arrest for having voiced the discontent of Burma.

One leader was arrested while I was in Rangoon. The Burmese capital is a jewel city well planned and cared for; its citizens apparently peaceful and content. This man was placed in jail—no one knew where.

The entire story of the Burmese move toward nationalism reminded me forcibly of the history of our own Katipunan, that had fought for Philippine liberty in the days of Spanish rule.

I had hoped to talk with Dr. Ba Maw, former Premier and leading voice in Burmese nationalism. But I did not have the opportunity of interviewing him. He was in jail for "non-co-operation" with the British. As Premier he had demanded certain constitutional reforms and changes. His party platform was based upon an old Burmese axiom:

"Two acres of land and a cow for every person."

For this and similar radical demands Dr. Ba was in jail.

How different is that criminal expression from Mr. Hoover's oft-quoted: "A chicken in every pot!"

Ba Maw was jailed in 1940, while Burma was preparing to defend itself against the threatened Japanese invasion. His successor, Premier U Saw, went to London in 1941 to ask dominion status for Burma. Needless to say it was not granted. While returning from this fruitless errand he was arrested by the British under the charge of having conspired with the Japanese.

Over other Burmese leaders lay the unmistakable hand of Japan. Over all Burma lay the shadow of advancing Nippon. This was not apparent to the casual onlooker. Only those who looked below the surface could see that Burma, in the very face of war, was discontented and resentful. The rising tide of nationalism, grown deeper and stronger under oppression, was directed against sovereign England.

The British rulers saw none of this. They were immensely pleased with the war preparations going ahead in Burma. Everything, they said, was ready, and invasion could be successfully repelled. The impregnable jungles would serve as bulwarks against Japanese invasion by land. Large-scale army maneuvers were being held. More and more troops were massing. All Burma was bristling with preparation for war.

I talked with many British officials in Burma—who, incidentally, were more considerate than any other British officials I had met on my travels—and asked them if the situation did not make them jittery.

"Not in the least," they replied unconcernedly to a man. "Burma is so thoroughly armed for defense, it is perfectly safe."

Armed in every point save its chink in the armor—the loyalty of the Burmese people.

The gentle faces of the Burmese were sullen and secretive. Let the white masters make their plans for defense. They would not aid them when the time came. They were preparing to receive Japan.

I asked them why.

They had many reasons. They were eager to tell them to a fellow Oriental who in their eyes represented America. They were the old, familiar reasons inevitable under white authority—lack of freedom, lack of speech, of pride, honor, all that made life worth while.

"You would be no better off under Japanese domination," I warned them.

Again the familiar argument: "No change could be for the worse."

The Burmese wave of nationalism had fitted perfectly into the plans of Japan. For years Japanese propagandists had been at work in Burma, fanning race prejudice—the opening wedge of Nazism— in this case brown resentment of white oppression. This Hitlerian form of propaganda was the most convenient torch to touch against the brands of hatred. It was simple to paint a picture of Japan as the champion of the oppressed colored peoples of Asia before a people sick at heart of white autocracy.

Burmans who visited Japan were flattered and fawned upon, banquets were given in their honor, and in every way the Japanese spared no expense to show that they considered them honored guests. How different from the way these people were treated by white people in their own country!

Of course these visitors were impressed. Who wouldn't be?

Japanese plans in Burma had received their biggest impetus by the disappointment that followed Churchill's speech excluding Burma and all other Asiatic countries from the war aims of the democracies. To the Burmese, this was the ultimate in white betrayal.

But the resentment, so universal in this small and lovely country, went deeper than speeches and political impasses. It reached far back into the social exclusions, to the snubs and wounded pride, to the gesture, so familiar in India, Indo-China, Java, and every Asiatic country under white rule, of a native woman or man making way on the sidewalk at the approach of the white master—the ungraceful, frightened movement of the mouse before the cat. Yes, even in peaceful Burma one saw the gentle Burmese women shrink back to their "proper place" before white majesty in a business suit and a straw hat.

In these dangerous days, when white men and brown most needed to hold together against the menace of Japan in the Far East, every act of racial discrimination was being remembered and enlarged upon by the wily advance workers for the enemy. For every act of snobbery or cruelty to natives in the Far East the white man was to pay a humiliating price under the advancing heel of Japan.

These were the inner reasons that led to the fall of the white man in Burma.

The outer reasons should have been apparent to the most prejudiced eyes. The Burmese poured them out to those willing to listen. Their resentments were many.

In rich, important Burma the white men occupying the country were getting steadily richer, while the native as consistently grew poorer.

The Burmese were not being trained in self-government, as the Filipinos had been trained by the Americans. They were not being educated.

Formerly eight promising young Burmese students had been selected from the country every year and sent to study in England. Now only two were being sent. These young men, upon their return to Burma, were not given the positions their training and talents deserved. They were placed in positions of no consequence, or offered none at all.

The fact that of Burma's struggles toward freedom nothing was known in the white world had long been resented. Their protests never reached the countries they wished to hear them, notably, America.

It was to America the Burmese hoped to appeal when England, made jittery by war, and as an appeasement gesture, closed the Burma Road for three months.

Then England, with her back to the wall, declared Burma a participant in its war against Germany.

The Burmese House of Representatives overwhelmingly passed a resolution expressing regret "that the British Government has made Burma a participant in the war between Britain and Germany without the consent of the people of Burma, and have further, in complete disregard of Burmese opinion, passed laws and adopted measures curtailing the powers and activities of the Burma Government."

It stated further:

"This house is of the opinion that the Government should convey to the British Government that, in consonance with the avowed aims of the present war, it is essential, in order to secure the co-operation of the Burmese people, that the principles of democracy, together with adequate safeguards for the preservation of the rights and interests of the minorities, be immediately applied to Burma, and that Burma be recognized as an independent nation entitled to frame her own constitution."

Needless to say, no word of this appeared in the white presses of the world.

Then came the signing of the Atlantic Charter, firing Burma with new hope. Burmese leaders rejoiced at the glorious words signed by President Roosevelt and Winston Churchill:

". . . respect the right of all peoples to choose the form of government under which they will live; and they wish to see sovereign rights and self-government restored to those who have been forcibly deprived of them."

The leaders promptly issued statements that Burma, certainly among the oppressed countries, would be among those set free.

But Prime Minister Churchill in England promptly clarified this pledge in his historic address to the House of Commons:

"At the Atlantic meeting we had in mind primarily the restoration of the sovereignty, self-government, and national life of states and nations of Europe now under the Nazi yoke, and of principles which would govern any alteration in territorial boundaries of these countries which will have to be made.

"That is quite a separate problem from the progressive evolution of self-governing institutions in regions whose peoples owe allegiance to the British Crown."

None of the resultant indignation in Burma was permitted to escape in print to the outer world. Right or wrong, the Burmese considered the failure of the Atlantic Charter to include them as the greatest double cross in their history. Every word of Churchill's address seemed a blow aimed directly at them.

What allegiance, they asked, did they owe the British? What right had England to ask their lives, now England was in the crisis?

These were the questions rampant in Burma before the outbreak of war. Resentment against Britain was summed up by U Chit Hlaing, Speaker of the Burmese House of Representatives. This Cambridge-educated, fiery, and salient leader told me he was retiring from political life.

"It is useless for me to remain in a position where I am unable to do anything for my country," he said. "Everything of importance is decided for us by our masters, and they do not explain anything they do."

The accumulative resentments were tinder to the flame of Japanese propaganda. I wrote at the time pleas, addressed to Englishmen and Americans together, that countries like Burma needed assurance given them that they would not be pressed into oblivion when the day of adjustment came. And I wrote for the benefit of the Burmese that despite all the wrongs done them their place was with us, by the side of the democracies:

"It is a cruel thing to say, but it must be said: The hope of Burma and India today is still with imperial Britain, and, after the war, with an England grown vastly more democratic than it is today and in a world become more free."

It was a matter of days before Japan moved into Burma, through fallen Thailand. Weary of white exploitation, superiority, and what it considered perfidy, and softened by years of subtle Japanese propaganda, Burma fell.

☆　　　☆　　　☆

And what of Singapore—that fortress—capital of British Malaya, guardian of the imperial British life line from Manila to Batavia, sentinel of the Burma Road, India, Burma, the Netherlands East Indies, Australia, Thailand, New Zealand?

Singapore, already impregnable, was arming more than ever before the break of war.

I wrote of it then as the key that would unlock the gates of Empire—a tragic and terrible prophecy.

The faint lines that divide content from satisfaction were apparent in Singapore. Outwardly, the natives seemed unambitious and peaceful. The Malayan is not nationalistic. Living in an incredibly rich country, he did not seem to mind the fact that all its wealth was pouring into the coffers of white men. His needs were modest and easily supplied by the largesse of the land. I saw few signs of poverty among the British Malays. But I saw, in Singapore, the terrible arrogance of the white man toward the native.

When crisis came, the Malayan would find no reason for allegiance to his white masters. He would not stand beside them, a man among men, and fight their battle. The British Malayans had a passive dislike of white mastery. They saw no reason for disliking their fellow Orientals, the Japanese.

Singapore fell in reprisal for white arrogance.

Under the Dutch the East Indies held riches—rubber, quinine, tin, oil, sugar, rice, tea, coffee, metals, copra—everything a power-mad Japan could desire to assist it in conquering the world.

The Indies under Dutch rule, in comparison to India under British rule, were liberal and even independent. There was a certain amount of autonomy permitted under the Dutch, and natives were holding offices of no little authority.

And yet, all over Indonesia I found duplicated our own Philippine struggle for independence, as it had been at the beginning of the century. Over many decades revolt had flared and threatened, and had always been stamped out by the Dutch masters. But the nationalist movement had continued to grow among the Indonesians. I attended secret meetings of the groups in Java. Rather, I talked with the leaders who remained, for nearly all were dead or in exile. Two of their greatest leaders, Dr. Soetomo and Thamrim, had died one after the other, after receiving injections. The natives regarded their deaths with grave suspicion. Mohammed Hatta and Engineer Soekarno, other leaders, were in exile. Tan Malacca, a leading spirit in the movement, had been exiled, and died, a hunted man, somewhere in Hong Kong.

How different the fate of these men who dared to believe in freedom from the treatment awarded our Filipino leaders by America!

Those who were left impressed me with their nationalism, their patriotism, and their belief in America. They could not ask questions enough regarding America and her work in the Philippines. They knew every move of the struggle for independence waged by the Filipinos and our victory of the Tydings-McDuffie Act. Their talk was all for democracy. But they were with Japan.

How could this be, I demanded, this paradox of ideals? Japan represented everything America most hated.

Patiently they explained. Holland, they said, had gutted the riches of the East Indies. Holland ran the East Indies, the life blood of Holland, solely for its own profit.

By deliberately starving the educational system, political reform, and true representation, the Dutch were keeping the natives a subject race.

"We have only 5 per cent literacy under the 'enlightened Dutch,'" these leaders told me. "We have asked for a more representative parliament. And what are we told? That 'assigned' persons will be called to the conferences. It is clear enough that if our people are not assigned, our people will not be represented. The native will, as usual, be left out of the picture."

The disappointment over the Atlantic Charter had given impetus to the nationalistic movement. Despite Churchill's explanation it had first brought a surge of hope through Burma and Java.

Twenty-eight Indonesian members took the floor of the Volksraad, the People's Council, and asked in a formally submitted petition if the Roosevelt-Churchill declaration applied to the Indonesian people. Was it intended for all races, the colored as well as the white?

The issue was side-stepped by the Dutch.

The Dutch press explained that the declaration had been primarily meant for that large group of people in the United States which was as yet unconvinced of the interest America might have in the final outcome of the war. Also, for the German people and those subjects of Hitler's slave states, "who, in as far as they have not yet lost all taste for freedom and righteousness, are bound to be impressed by the prospects of a better future which these principles also open for them. . . .

"With this ideal of a better world in view, the idealistic and young American people will more easily be willing to take its share in the realization of this future than was the case when America was still uncertain about it."

A few weeks later the conscription bill was under discussion and a number of members took the floor of the Volksraad to oppose the passing of the bill. "A conscription bill," they held, "can only be passed by a parliament truly representative of the people. The Volksraad is not such a parliament."

Its president, they pointed out, was appointed by the Netherlands Crown. It was apparent that the Indonesians had no intention of fighting in allegiance to that Crown.

Queen Wilhelmina issued her statement over Radio Orange—an implied promise of constitutional reforms to go into effect "after the war." The answer to her promise was given in the stubborn insistence of the nationalist leaders:

"Any rule would be better for us than life under the Dutch."

The Dutch in the East Indies were making their preparations for the expected invasion by the Japanese.

The Indonesians—weary of white rule, white evasions, and white demands for loyalty that had never been fostered by human kindness—were secretly letting down the gates to the oncoming hordes of the Rising Sun.

I did not see French Indo-China under French rule, for upon my arrival there before the outbreak of war the Japanese were already in power. But I had been told by native Annamites: "The French have two rules for dealing with natives—the boot and the riding crop."

The universal cry against the white man was repeated in French Indo-China: any change would be better! That cry of unrest had been answered in person by the Japanese. They were everywhere—swarming in parks and streets, occupying the best hotels and finest villas—the men marching by thousands, the officers strutting in groups and rattling their sabers even in public dining rooms.

"They even wear them into the bathroom," one disgruntled French official told me.

But the French were saying very little in those nerve-racking days. They had suffered a terrible loss of "face" in Oriental eyes. The natives, ruled so long by the boot and crop, were sensing the quite human pleasure of seeing the superior white men cringe before the swaggering Japanese as they, the natives, had so often cringed before the white men.

With awe the Annamites regarded the spectacle of streets where they had walked so humbly bristling now with armed Oriental forces. Oriental soldiers marched all day long in those streets—it did not matter to the Annamites that these Orientals were Japanese. They were Orientals, and they had made the Frenchman lose "face" in French Indo-China.

The Japanese soldiers made arrests or committed depredations, and the French authorities stood watching helplessly, not daring to protest. They had not protested from the first day the Japanese moved into French Indo-China, using the same methods they had carried out in Manchukuo. Japan needed the country's air bases for aerial offensives against the Burma Road. French Indo-China would be a strategic point for the invasion of other countries.

The Japanese had stressed the fact that this move was not for territorial gain. As in China, they were in French Indo-China to maintain "peace and order." Japanese economic penetration had arrived ahead of the military. Vichy had approved an immense loan to Japan. This, in effect, left the people of Indo-China paying the expenses of their own invasion—a fact they had yet to realize.

Japanese propaganda stressed the argument that French Indo-China was part of the "Co-Prosperity Sphere," and their fellow Orientals, the Annamites, would prosper under the guidance of the Japanese.

The natives, in the beginning, were prospering. They had not been so well off under the French. For some time the Frenchmen and natives alike had been growing poorer in this undeveloped and improperly colonized country. For many reasons the Frenchman has long been considered a poor colonizer, the principal one being that he is too fond of urban pleasures and the companionship of his own kind.

The natives, hired by the Japanese to build military barracks, were being well paid—with their own money. They were enjoying

a prosperity they had not known before, and they watched the
Japanese soldiers parading in the streets where they had once
cringed before white men who now were cringing in turn in their
homes, afraid to come out.

In every city the Japanese soldiers marched and marched. They
did nothing but march. But it was terrifying. They chose public
parks and playgrounds for their maneuvers, especially bayonet practice. They left nothing undone that might impress the simple Annamites. Wild whoops and yells accompanied every thrust of the bayonet.

The natives watched in terror—and in pride. What did it matter
to them if these marching men were Japanese—a people they had
long distrusted and feared? They were fellow Orientals—and the
first Orientals to rub the white face in the dust of Asia.

☆      ☆      ☆

Why did Thailand capitulate in five hours to Japan?

Thailand, once Siam, was the last of the absolute monarchies, the
last of the independent countries, the last neutral country, and the
last medieval kingdom in the Far East.

My first impressions of Thailand were reassuring. The Siamese,
or Thais, are doll-like, gentle, almost timid, subsisting mainly on rice
and given to artistry, music, and dancing that are strange to Occidental ears and eyes. It was a country that appealed to the imagination, like an antique scroll. But its principles, the Thai leaders assured me, were soundly democratic. At first appearance I thought
this to be true. The natives apparently were masters in their own
country. The country seemed content and at peace. Officials attended to matters with dispatch and courtesy, unlike those in other
Oriental countries I had visited.

"Thailand means 'land of free people,' and the government of
Thailand is fully determined to defend the freedom of the Thai
people," Nai Direck Jayanam, Minister of Foreign Affairs in Bangkok, the capital, told me by way of analyzing Thailand's position
in the coming war crisis.

We were conversing in the Saranromya Palace in Bangkok, a
cathedral-like place of deep-red velvet hangings, high ceilings,

thick rugs, and glittering chandeliers. There was a medieval quality to the setting, as there was to all Thailand. The Minister told me that Thailand believed in and practiced the democratic form of government.

I asked him what he thought of the totalitarian form of government and he parried the question.

"A form of government that is good for certain peoples may not be good for others, and while we think democracy best for Thailand, we cannot presume to believe that it is necessarily good for other people."

I demanded bluntly, "If Japan invades, will Thailand fight Japan?"

Again he evaded the direct question.

"Thailand is democratic. We are pro-Thailand and pro no other country. We are friendly to all countries. We are neutral."

I left that splendid setting knowing that Thailand was neither democratic nor dreamlike.

I knew then, and prophesied almost to the hour, that Thailand would accept Japan.

The Japanese were all over Thailand, pushing their way in everywhere, spreading among the Siamese their propaganda of "The Orient for the Orientals."

In the leading hotel in Bangkok, where I was staying, more than three fourths of the guests were Japanese. There were more Japanese newspaper correspondents there than I had seen in Washington, D.C. The majority of these guests were mysterious. They were "technical men," who left the hotel early, to work all day—no one knew where. No one questioned what they were doing in Thailand. But it was this type of Japanese that urged Nippon into unsuspecting Thailand with loans, technical work, propaganda, and flattering gestures.

As in the Phillipines, the Japanese had carried on an extensive campaign to "foster cultural relations." Staffs of Japanese photographers and motion-picture operators, acting upon the theory that they were making "travel pictures," had succeeded in photographing every inch of Thailand, as had also been done by the Japanese in the Philippines.

The Nichi-Nichi and Mainichi press was popular in Thailand.

All the radio programs came from Berlin. Totalitarianism was in the very air of the country.

There had been half-hearted attempts to stem the tide of incoming fifth columnists. A bill to bar entry of foreigners into Thailand had been promptly pigeonholed.

The Japanese had made secret treaties with the Thai Government. The Japanese technicians had completed their surveys for naval bases, landing fields, and wharves.

The power of diplomatic pressure was brought home to me at a reception given by the Thailand Foreign Minister to the diplomatic corps. It was an affair glittering with gold braid, splendid uniforms, and rainbow sashes—reflecting the color and pageantry dear to the heart of this small and exquisite kingdom.

Brightest of all amid the glitter shone the splendid person of the Japanese Ambassador—the only representative of an embassy in Thailand. All the other countries saw fit to be represented by mere legations.

No other country but Japan was taking the trouble to woo the friendly Thais.

Thailand was a buffer state, pressed on all sides, by the British in Burma and Malaya, the French in Indo-China, and, from within, the fawning, propaganda-spreading, farsighted Japanese.

The white rulers in adjoining countries saw no reason for going out of their way to treat the Siamese with courtesy. Thailand was fertile ground for the Japanese urge to restore the lost dignity of the Oriental.

I begged then for expressions of support from England and America to bolster the wavering status of Thailand. I wrote a few weeks before the invasion: "Tomorrow may be too late!"

Tomorrow was too late for the white neighbors of Thailand to offer friendship.

Thailand, the only sovereign and independent people in all Malaysia, would yield, as other Asiatic countries yielded, to Japanese diplomatic pressure and Japanese fifth-column propaganda.

But long before this Thailand had yielded to resentment against white arrogance and white domination.

# XV. COUNTRIES IN JEOPARDY

My impressions of India, as I saw it for the third time in 1939, were those of an enormous, teeming country straining at the leash. That is the only word that can describe India—leashed. It seemed that all India felt itself on the brink of some terrible cataclysm. It was only a question of time before we would hear the snap of the leash. And yet it would have taken very little to have settled the problem of India. Less by far than what was done for the Philippines by America. The people of India are accustomed to little and have asked for little. They were refused the smallest request. The denial was resented in the blazing, humiliated faces of three hundred million Hindus.

It was less what is seen in India than the things one does not see that had fed this national indignation.

In Calcutta, Bombay, Delhi, wherever I traveled, the panorama of filth and incredible misery continued. Wherever one turned there were skinny bodies in filthy sarongs, sores encrusted upon the bodies of the starving people and their starving animals, eyes whitened with cataract. The faces of the people, made ugly and inhuman by misery, were terrible to see.

I saw no children in India. The wretched little creatures that never laughed, never flung arms and legs about in the wild abandon peculiar to young creatures well tended and unafraid, could not be called children.

I asked: "Where are the schools?" and found there were few schools worth mentioning for the youth of India.

As now in China and in Japan, as in the Philippines before the Americans came, Indian children are sold into economic slavery by their starving parents.

I tried to avoid entering the native districts. One can see enough in a single tour to make India a lasting horror in the memory. But I was a frequent guest in the separated districts, carefully screened from sight, sound, or smell of the native districts, where stood the handsome residences of the British.

Nowhere else in the world have I seen as magnificent and luxurious a way of life as that of the Englishman in India.

I was constantly recalling our own way of life in the Philippines, where there were no separate districts for white and native and where a native woman, meeting a white man on the street, did not instinctively cringe and step aside—again I repeat, with the gesture of the mouse before the cat. Why should such misery exist under so great a power?

When I asked such questions of the Englishmen I met they stared at me. Impossible, they explained, to lift the Hindu above the status set by his caste and religion. Ridiculous to imagine so helpless and decadent a race capable of self-government such as we Filipinos were practicing in the Philippines.

Were we, the Filipinos, a race more intelligent than the Indians, I persisted?

But whatever I asked, I was given the same reply: "They are not ready!"

It was foolish to ask: "Then where are the schools, the civil-service privileges, the tutors in self-government, that will help them prepare?"

One did not ask such questions in India before the war.

But if the English treated the matter in an offhand manner, the natives did not. I talked with every native I met in India and found none who disguised his feelings toward the English Crown. Their protests and resentments and hatreds were poured out, but they summed up, as always, to the composite resentment: they were not free!

Their grievances were voiced more ably by the nationalist leaders of India, beginning with Gandhi.

Foremost of all their demands was the right to be free. The leaders gave many specific reasons for the need for freedom. Britain, they said, has drained the wealth of India. White men have grown rich where the natives undergo famine.

The native is taxed to the point of beggary to pay the exorbitant salaries of the English officials. Tariffs imposed upon India have aided in keeping the native in peonage.

The cultured Indian who would be welcomed in other parts of the world cannot enter certain august portals in India sacred to the white masters.

The average Indian is ignorant and backward, but again, where are the schools that might have alleviated his ignorance?

The Indian has asked for freedom and his white masters have assured him he is not prepared for freedom.

But the Indian knows the whole story of the Philippines. He knows that the Filipinos were likewise ignorant and unprepared—forty-two years before.

How long ago, may I ask, did the white man enter India?

England in travail asked India to stand by her.

America asked no such fealty from the Philippines. But the morning of Pearl Harbor our campi were wiped clean of Filipino youth—they had dropped their books to stand in line for enlistment under the American flag.

Granted that this was in self-defense, born of a long-nursed hatred against the wiles and mechanisms of the threatening Japanese.

Granted, too, that the Filipinos fought to hold their native land against the Japanese. But that land was under the American flag—under the Stars and Stripes set there by white men. The Filipinos did not question the presence of that flag. They stood in line below it to enlist in a white man's army, to offer up their youth and their hopes and their lives beside white men. They died with white men—as they had lived—on equal terms with white men on Bataan and Corregidor.

Can you comprehend their sacrifice, Mother India?

India and China, equally tremendous, teeming, hungry, are countries in jeopardy. Their destinies hang in the balance of the future. India needs assurance. China, certain of the path before her, needs aid. She has always been certain of that way. It is marked in the soul of every citizen of China. It is the way of peace and good will to all men.

The Chinese, a reasonable person, is willing to abide by whatever laws may be, to live by them but not die for them, like his fanatical neighbor—the Japanese. He has his flaws. The most handicapping of these, for him, is his unfailing courtesy. His patience and forbearance do not desert him even under abuse. If he is knocked down, he dusts himself off and apologizes for having been in the way. He is living up to the ancient Confucian principle, which antedated the Christian precept, of turning the other cheek.

This principle, while humiliating to him in individual instances, has saved him in the main. The white powers wrangled and tore at one another's throats over the possession of this vast and helpless country. China's Asiatic neighbors nibbled at the edges of her domain. Like some protoplasmic creature, China has wrested from her living portions of her body and very entrails, but the centuries always found her reassembled again and living out her vast and introspective destiny.

The city of Kunming in China when I saw it last was in ruins, but in the center of its destroyed areas I came upon a little park that had escaped by a miracle the devastation of the Japanese bombs. Swans still lifted their proud throats over a crystal lake that was rimmed with dahlias red as blood. It seemed to me that this exquisite place was representative of the soul of China—beauty and peace in the core of desolation.

That is China. That is the secret of its indestructibility as a country and a people.

The Chinese are like the Filipinos in their love of life, their fondness of gaiety, and their fundamental urge for democracy. They are friendly, curious, kindly, and interested, and no matter how meager their lot they retain the gift for happiness. They enjoy everything, down to their last chopstickful of rice. They are not ridden by the caste system that has retarded the progress of the native of India. The Chinese put their faith in wisdom. They have their aristocracies, but they are those of intelligence and merit. If angered, they can be cruel. If badgered long enough, they fight like lions. We have seen their capacity as fighters during the four years China bore alone the brunt of Japan's determination to conquer the world.

The Chinese struggle against Japan had been long in inception. They had feared and dreaded Japan. They had asked help of the white world against the enemy.

Only America listened.

And yet fortunes that defy the imagination had been taken out of China by white men who were not Americans. These white men made no move to protect China. They had never protected China, not even from their greediest representatives, some of whom had founded great fortunes on opium that aided in keeping the Chinese docile.

Against the white man's debit to the Asiatic is the shame of Shanghai—where white men lived in unbelievable luxury and grew steadily richer; where Chinese babies were left on the streets by their starving mothers; and where every day in the streets one saw the stiff, twisted bodies of those Chinese who had died of hunger.

Along the water front at Hong Kong I have seen the Chinese people who live in sampans picking out of the water bits of garbage tossed from the luxury liners towering above their boats, and putting the waste food directly into their mouths.

It has been computed that the contents of an average American garbage can would feed ten Chinese families.

We weep now for Greece and Poland and other starving nations of Europe, but there is not an hour in her entire history when we might not have shed such tears for China. She has survived misery such as no other country has known; she, the world's supreme lover of peace, has had to struggle through centuries to push back the pressing invaders—Mongols, Manchus, Japanese. She showed less resistance in fighting the white exploiters who devoured her resources from within.

In China I talked with rickshaw men, street cleaners, waiters, clerks, professors, and the native representatives of government—these last miserably paid officials who worked without complaint eighteen hours a day in their bombed offices to aid in restoring the face of ruined China.

What did China want, I asked them?

Their first answer was always: "Peace!" And in almost the same breath they added: "To be free."

What did they mean by freedom? The freedom all men ask for—from want, oppression, exploitation, fear. The freedom of China for the Chinese.

In view of the tragedy that has overtaken white people in Hong Kong—a blow to white "face" in the Orient that will never be forgotten by Orientals—it is cruel to recall these reasons for the slow accumulation of resentment against white men in China. Much has been done there by white men that was self-sacrificing and good. Let us remember these things as China herself remembers. And let us remember also the trust China never failed to show toward America. How anxiously, before Pearl Harbor, she laid her case before America, voiced her protests, told her story, not to the world of white men—for what reason had she to trust that world? —but to America.

Everywhere in China one found that simple trust in "A-mell-ica." It was a word the humblest Chinese knew.

It was a word that signified to them another they had perhaps never heard—the word "democracy."

The year 1899 that saw the entry of America into the Philippines to alter their destiny along surer and quicker ways to democracy also saw America's entry into the destiny of China.

When in that year America, by voicing her Open-Door policy, held open the ports of trade in the Far East, she inadvertently moved into place as the ally of China in her slow struggle toward independence.

The white man has taken much out of China. The American, who of all white men had acquired the least, alone came to the aid of China in her troubled hour.

Centuries of white exploitation have made the Chinese slow to trust members of the Occidental races. But everywhere in China, long before Madame Chiang Kai-shek carried to the hearts of Americans the tears and prayers of China, one saw on Chinese faces the dawn of interest and hope, and heard the note of friendship and trust in Chinese voices as they spoke the word:

"A-mell-ica!"

☆     ☆     ☆

This is the Orient, and these are its people.

Among them the Filipino, until Pearl Harbor, was most fortunate of all. He knew it, and the rest of Asia knew it. In all that benighted and unredeemed world of colored peoples he alone stood free.

In other countries in Asia one saw the mark of white colonial greed and imperialistic exploitation. In other countries one might seek fruitlessly among the white authorities for any other reason why the native should not be granted the rights of independence than the customary: "He is not ready for freedom."

There was never any use to ask why other peoples are not prepared, when America had prepared the Filipino and promised him freedom in the space of forty-two years.

America, with small economic interests in Asia and without proselyting, had been able to demonstrate through the Philippines the value of democracy to the satisfaction of the entire Far East.

America had done this by example alone, setting her people, arms, and interests behind a principle—that of democracy.

If the purpose of government is to protect and provide for the human interests of the governed, then other white governments have failed in miserably large areas in the Orient. Only under pressure have these governments taken progressive steps, and never generously and voluntarily, as did America in the Philippines.

Is it strange, wherever one traveled in the Orient before the war, that to all these inarticulate peoples the court of last appeals seemed to be America?

# XVI. VOICES OF THE FAR EAST

BEHIND the little peoples of the Far East are great leaders whose voices have been too long unheeded by the white world.

It is unfortunate that imperialistic propaganda has made Mohandas Gandhi a figure of ridicule to the West. To the average American the mention of Gandhi conjures up the memory of a diaper pin and a belly laugh.

In all fairness, the mention of a politician to the same American brings up the picture of a fat man with loud checks and a large cigar.

But the imperialist has obscured the image of Gandhi to Western minds. Behind that cartoon is a light that will shine more splendidly a hundred years from now than it does today.

More than that of any other man on earth Gandhi's is the voice of the inarticulate millions. Only when East and West draw closer together will the Occidental understand what it is Gandhi has asked for India.

Teeming, enormous, pitiable India, harried by oppressive riches and incredible poverty, is not like any other country and its leader is not like any other man.

India presents a solitary and a tragic problem.

Gandhi is a man alone.

I met India's greatest leader unexpectedly and under the strangest of circumstances. In a barren native hut in an Indian village there was Gandhi! He was exactly as I had seen him in pictures, wearing the loincloth and working deftly at the traditional spinning wheel. Our mutual astonishment deepened on my side. There was nothing ghostlike or ridiculous about this gentle, friendly man, whose smile is so unexpectedly human and whose luminous eyes are both twinkling and kind. Kindliness radiates from Gandhi—one feels at first meeting to have known him lifelong.

After five minutes' conversation I knew Gandhi to be different from other famous men. There is no bitterness, greed, or need for personal aggrandizement in him. Here was a man who had divested himself of every base human impulse. If ever a man has been a saint on earth—Gandhi is that man. He has lived and struggled with malice toward none. This shy, gentle, and sensitive man tied together India's pitiful millions—divided in hundreds of ways by caste and dialect, and by thousands of religions—and held them close in a belief that was as simple and strong and spiritual as Gandhi himself.

It was strange and somehow terrible to remember that Gandhi, descended from a long and proud race of Prime Ministers, as a young attorney was kicked and spat upon by white men and has known every indignity the powerful feel it their privilege to visit upon the undefended. He spoke without bitterness of the British. He accepted their point of view.

"They exploit India because the British Empire must survive," he explained.

"The question is, should it live?"

"I say it should not."

I said: "It is natural that a Britisher should believe in exploitation. If you were British, would you?"

How gently he answered: "No. Being Gandhi, I know what it is like to be underneath the wheel."

He was made Gandhi the patriot by the tragedy of Amritsar in 1919, when a British general ordered his soldiers to open fire upon Hindus, mostly undefended. Men, women, and children died in that holocaust. He turned back the awards and honors that had been presented him by England to make a fighting force of passive resistance in India. He had been against the worst in British rule and Hindu tradition—untouchability, child marriage, purdah—everything that had kept the Hindu shackled in ignorance.

Gandhi might have been the richest man in India. He might have possessed high office, power, and glory. Instead, he was sharing the life of the poorest Hindu—that of the Indian farmer who toils for eight cents a day and returns four cents back in taxes to the English Crown!

I asked the reason for the regimentation and barrenness of his life, the vegetarianism, fasting, and divesting himself of all worldly pleasures.

Gandhi explained that these things were in his creed, and added that it was time mankind realized there was happiness in depriving oneself of known pleasures, if by that sacrifice one contributed to a greater cause.

"What is the greater cause?" I persisted.

He answered, "India."

It was not apparent to me, nor in fact to many others, how his Spartan way of life aided India. I told Gandhi as much. He smiled.

"I am the leader of a cause. Leaders are always supposed to be out after something for themselves. Men have always attributed to those who sponsor a cause the desire for money or power."

Gandhi indicated his surroundings, that were stripped of every comfort.

"Can I be accused of such desires—living as I do?"

He explained his fasting on the same terms. His self-starvation is not a means for threatening the white rulers. Fasting is part of his religion. He utilizes it as a means of expressing faith in that religion and his political beliefs. To Gandhi, religion and politics serve the same end, the resurrection of the soul.

Food is of paramount importance to mankind. When a man is willing to go hungry for a cause, that cause becomes sacred.

Gandhi has suffered for India. What has he asked for India?

The answer was in the questions he asked concerning the American policy in the Philippines. In his gentle voice, using the most beautifully enunciated English I have ever heard, Gandhi asked intelligent questions that showed his awareness of every step taken by the Filipinos toward democracy. No man is more aware of the story of the Philippines. He wanted minute details of the Jones Act, promising independence to the Philippines.

"There was no date to that, was there," he stated, rather than asked.

"None," I answered.

"But the date was fixed later, in 1946, was it not?"

I agreed that the Tydings-McDuffie Act had made the date of independence definite.

He leaned forward a little.

"You Filipinos—did you insist upon that date being set?"

"Yes."

Gandhi smiled once more. There were many meanings in his quiet satisfaction. He was approving something he knew to be important and good.

I understood that by these questions he was revealing his belief in American sincerity.

He said at last: "That is what we want in India. We are entitled to exactly what you were given by America. It is our birthright."

I was reminded of this conversation with Gandhi during a meeting between the Chinese author Lin Yutang, the American editor from Shanghai, J. B. Powell, and myself, in a New York hospital early in 1943. Lin and I were visiting at the bedside of Powell, who lost both feet while a prisoner of the Japanese. With true Chinese humor Lin told of an Englishman with whom he had discussed America's grant of independence to the Philippines.

"The Englishman told me," said Lin, with a twinkle in his eye, "that the promise of independence had been quite all right—until the Americans set a date!"

☆          ☆          ☆

Freedom, in Gandhi's vision for India, is democracy.

It is the same hope of democratic freedom Chiang Kai-shek holds for China.

They understood one another, the non-resistant Gandhi who unified India and the gentle warrior Chiang who has unified China. Gandhi tied together a country split a myriad ways by ignorance, dialects, and caste. Chiang Kai-shek unified a country equally shattered by lack of a shared language, poverty, and civil war. Gandhi's power was in resistance to white autocracy; Chiang Kai-shek's to Japanese imperialism.

Physically, spiritually, and mentally these great leaders are not unlike. Both are spare, esthetic, delicately built, sensitive, and abstemious, even to the point of refusing the mildest of stimulants.

Both are deeply religious, Gandhi in the faith of his ancestors, Chiang Kai-shek as a Methodist convert. Both, as the Oriental must to attain the widest measure of his existence, have given this spiritual urge to nationalism—they have shared their faith and their lives, with the attempt to revive the genius of their people.

This, too, is the Orient, which subsists upon the soul.

I have talked twice with Chiang Kai-shek and each time while his country was in crisis. The first interview was held in the Military Academy at Nanking, in August 1937, when in calm and controlled tones he announced for the first time that China had only one course left open—to fight Japan.

It would be war, he said, that could not end in compromise. It would mean either victory or the annihilation of the Chinese race. "China will never accept the humiliation of surrendering to demands which would make the Chinese virtually foreigners in their own land."

How reminiscent that was of the universal complaint of the Orient: "Strangers—in our own land!"

He had hoped until the last moment to avoid the war. "As a people we understand and realize our national position. We know our weakness. We want to live in peace, and there is nothing we covet more than peace. . . .

"Weak as we are, we have reached the end of human endurance compatible with national self-respect and dignity.

"We are ready to throw the last ounce of our nation's energy into the struggle for national existence."

Only twelve hours later I saw the Japanese warships anchored in the river beside Shanghai.

The war began that would pour Japanese hordes into every inlet of the Pacific.

Four years later, in September 1941, I talked again with Chiang Kai-shek in his unpretentious villa near bomb-shattered Chung-king. He had lost one city after another. He had watched for four years the pushing back of his starving lines. He was the leader of a country in extremity. Now the fate of China hung on the question: Would the democracies come to the aid of democratic China?

He was even more heroic, more austere. He said, "I have implicit faith in President Roosevelt and the American people and in their sincere desire to assist my country in her fight for freedom." His grasp of world affairs was direct and sure. When he spoke for democracy it was in no terms of cant, but in words spoken from the heart.

"China's victory will be victory for the Philippines as well as for China," he warned. "We are fighting against aggression and for democracy, and the beneficiaries of our sacrifices will be all those likely victims of future aggression who believe in a democratic destiny for Asia. China's struggle is not ours alone, but the struggle of all the democracies."

He gave warning that the Philippines and then America would be in the list of Japan's victims. All nations bordering upon the Pacific, he said, should band together to isolate Japan, "for only by uniting and isolating Japan can the security and integrity of those nations be assured.

"Our aim is to procure for China free and equal enjoyment of rights under an order in the Orient and throughout the world that shall deserve the name of a just peace. We want every nation in Asia and throughout the world to enjoy freedom, self-government, and the manifold blessings of democracy."

Yes, he was very like Gandhi, this Chiang Kai-shek. He was also strangely like Lincoln.

That day in ruined Chungking that had been bombed for four years by the Japanese I felt myself standing upon the Asiatic ramparts of democracy.

☆ ☆ ☆

Madame Chiang Kai-shek, pleading before the American Congress in February 1943, spoke for Chiang Kai-shek and for all China.

Hers was the voice of Asia, asking America to lead the way in a postwar world where all nations will be members of "one corporate body."

Let us listen again to that wise and gentle voice speaking to the heart of America:

"The hundred sixty years of traditional friendship between our two great peoples, China and America, which has never been marred by misunderstandings, is unsurpassed in the annals of the world. I can also assure you that China is eager and ready to co-operate with you and other peoples to lay a true and lasting foundation for a sane and progressive world society which would make it impossible for any arrogant or predatory neighbor to plunge future generations into another orgy of blood.

"In the past China has not computed the cost to her man power in her fight against aggression, although she well realized that man power is the real wealth of a nation and it takes generations to grow it. She has been soberly conscious of her responsibilities and has not concerned herself with privileges and gains which she might have obtained through compromise of principles. Nor will she demean herself and all she holds dear to the practice of the market place.

"We in China, like you, want a better world, not for ourselves alone, but for all mankind, and we must have it. It is not enough, however, to proclaim our ideals or even to be convinced that we have them. In order to preserve, uphold, and maintain them, there are times when we should throw all we cherish into our effort to fulfill these ideals even at the risk of failure.

"The teachings drawn from our late leader, Dr. Sun Yat-sen, have given our people the fortitude to carry on. From five and a half years of experience we in China are convinced that it is the better part of wisdom not to accept failure ignominiously, but to risk it gloriously.

"We shall have faith that, at the writing of peace, America and our gallant allies will not be obtunded by the mirage of contingent reasons of expediency."[1]

One by one the other great leaders of Asia have turned with the same trust to America.

U Chit Hlaing, the leader of the House of Representatives in Burma, told me that the mass awakening of nationalism in Burma, that would be interrupted by Japan invading, had been stimulated by the signing of the Tydings-McDuffie Act.

[1]From the New York *Times*, February 19, 1943.

"Why have the British not given us the opportunity to show what we can do about governing ourselves—since America has put such trust in the Filipinos?" he demanded. He added with a touch of Oriental imagery, "Who knows whether the boy can swim, if he is not permitted to enter the water?"

He spoke in terms of personal need as well as for his country. This cultured and dynamic leader had passed through the usual experiences of a member of a colored race under imperialistic masters.

U Chit Hlaing was educated in Cambridge and returned to Burma fired with enthusiasm for England, its institutions and freedoms. He found disillusionment waiting for him in his own country. An ambitious native was given no opportunity to rise in Burma. He was not free. His growth as an individual was stunted by white imperialism.

U Chit Hlaing had risen to the place of Speaker, but he knew it was an empty honor.

He said bitterly, "This part of the world is still ruled by three words: Might makes right."

His bitterness was shared by all Burma. It served to turn Burma from the white imperialism of England to the yellow imperialism of Japan.

Burma had asked of England only what America had voluntarily offered in the Philippines—home rule under supervision with the ultimate hope of self-rule.

Home rule, such leaders as U Chit Hlaing assured me, would have lashed Burma in an unbreakable fealty to the side of England.

The bitterness of the Burmese leaders was echoed in Java by nationalists whose names could not be revealed at the time and must not be now. Then, they were afraid of Dutch authority. Now, of Japanese reprisal.

There were very few of these nationalist leaders left in Java. Nearly all were in jail, or dead, or living in exile. Dutch mastery held a strict hand over Java. Yet these leaders represented the will of seventy million Indonesians.

What had they asked, that prison, exile, and death were their punishment?

"We have asked for specific reforms," these men who must be nameless told me. "We have asked for the right to assert the genius of our race. No matter how weak and undeveloped that genius may be, it is ours, and we want it to live.

"We have been given many promises. They always lie vaguely in the future. We want that future now.

"We have asked for a representative government. What is our parliament, the Volksraad, but an instrument of the Netherlands? Our seventy million people have only thirty representatives, and of these twenty are appointed by the Dutch Governor General. But the seventy thousand Netherlanders in Java have twenty-four representatives to speak for them in the Volksraad! What sort of representation is that for the people of Java?"

What, indeed! The Javanese Government was as unreal to the native as one of its own shadow plays. Any thrust toward actuality on the part of a courageous leader might carry him into prison, under the Crown of the Netherlands.

☆        ☆        ☆

These are the voices of the great Asiatic leaders, questioning the white imperialisms and the white democracies as to their rights in the world of the future.

They have asked fair treatment and the reinstatement of their heritage of human dignity.

How can their voices be answered to the satisfaction of both East and West at the end of war?

# XVII. PATTERN FOR THE PACIFIC

THE PEACE CONFERENCE that will be held at the end of this war will be the real battlefield of imperialism versus the principles for which the democracies are supposed to be fighting. The principle of democratic freedom will be the main issue.

The representatives of the United Nations and the conquered nations must agree upon an acceptable pattern for the future if another cataclysm is to be avoided. That will be a racial war. The seeds of that war will be planted in the peace conference unless statesmanship, tolerance, and wisdom are permitted in major roles. The problem of the Pacific represents the race problem of the world.

What pattern, then, for the Pacific?

We have heard the demands of the Orient. We also know what is being asked by the imperialisms.

Churchill has already announced in a formal speech that he is not Prime Minister of England so that he may preside over the liquidation of the British Empire.

This can mean only that India, Burma, British Malaya, and Hong Kong will remain under England.

Queen Wilhelmina has openly stated that there is to be "progressive representation for the Indonesians"—which is by way of indirectly announcing that the Dutch will remain in the Netherlands.

Under these circumstances there is no reason to suppose that France will want to do otherwise than regain hold of French Indo-China, despite its loss of "face" in that country.

Let us start from the premise that these imperialistic countries want to stay where they are in the Orient.

Why, then, are the democracies fighting?

In all fairness, the pattern for the future must be considered from every point of view. It must be admitted that Britain needs her empire in the Far East. Britain, an industrial island nation, requires her far-flung empire in the Orient to feed the vital needs of her industrialism.

The same argument holds true for the dependence of the Netherlands upon the Dutch East Indies.

It will be put forward that America, who will hold such tremendous responsibility at the peace conference, will be weak in arguments against imperialisms because she herself does not need the Philippines.

It is true that America does not need the Philippines for her existence. But in fairness to England and the Netherlands, America will be open to their arguments as coming from the other side.

The statesmen and postwar planners of the past have always smothered peace aims with technicalities. This need not happen at the peace conference that should determine the peace pattern for the future. It can be simply broached in the democratic American way.

America, at that future conference, need only point to the Philippines.

There must be a human approach to this problem of the Pacific upon which is balanced the future of the world. It cannot be a British approach or a Dutch approach. It must be a human approach. We must review the past with all its errors and rectify them.

Only America can convince the Asiatic nations that those errors will be rectified. Only America's word will be believed. The pledges of the crowned heads to atone for their mistakes in the Orient came too late—after the Asiatics had been proffered revenge and atonement from another source, Japan.

But the Asiatic countries would have believed America, for long before any competing nation, such as Japan, came to outbid her in the Philippines, she had given the Filipinos the Jones Act and the Tydings-McDuffie Act.

If the Atlantic Charter had been more specific it would have made a great deal of difference in Asia. It would have greatly minimized the alacrity of the subject nations in helping Japan.

The Charter and faith in America would have carried much weight with the Orientals. That faith, that will be carried to the peace conference, can be the most important medium for the promulgation of a lasting peace.

To convince allies and subject nations alike of democratic soundness America can point to the Philippines. She can point to shrines of loyalty where no Pacific or Atlantic charters were needed— Bataan and Corregidor.

The pattern that applied to the Philippines can apply to every country in the Far East. The success of that American plan has been the greatest in the history of colonization. By following that pattern, by investing spiritually as well as economically in countries under their rule, and by gaining the loyalty and gratitude of the natives, England and the Netherlands will be the gainers in the Far East.

What America accomplished in the Philippines was no utopian project. It was sound business all the way.

The Philippine pattern as set by America may vary in other sections of the Orient. The embroidery may be different, the color of the threads changed to suit the conditions of country or people, but as attested to by actual results in the Philippines, that basic pattern is the only one that will serve through to the final test.

The Orientals will be receptive to that pattern because they trust America, due to America's treatment of the Philippines. They are convinced America will not let them down.

Their problems, in nearly all the Asiatic countries, are the same problems the Filipinos knew at the beginning of this century when America first entered the Philippines. Economically and mentally these problems are similar all over the Far East. The most vital of their problems is their distrust of and hatred toward the white race.

I emphasize this fact unwillingly and from no desire to rake up past errors. If I recall too often the wrongs done by white men in the Orient it is because those wrongs are paramount now in the universal mind of Asia. They are not to be lightly regarded. They will lurk under every argument toward peace and understanding. Brought into the light, they can be forgiven and forgotten. Because Occidental and Oriental are in this hell together, these resentments must be abolished and forgotten. This will take time. But it can be brought about. It was brought about in the Philippines by America.

The Filipinos also hated and distrusted white men when this century began. Three hundred thousand Filipinos died before America succeeded in entering the Philippines. That sacrifice of life required strong erasure on the part of American good will. But America did erase that misunderstanding and successfully imprinted her American pattern upon an Oriental nation. Her policy can be applied anywhere.

England—and by England I mean that democratic postwar England that undoubtedly will hew closely to the democratic ideal—will lose nothing by applying that pattern in Burma, Java, British Malaya, and India.

By following the American example in British Malaya alone, England will be able to retain for her own use the greatest rubber- and tin-production areas in the world.

The French lost their pretense to authority in French Indo-China when they permitted the Japanese to move into their subject realm. If the French desire to re-establish credit in the Orient they have the American pattern to show how it may be done.

The Dutch, English, and French will have a great handicap of distrust to overcome in the Far East before they will be permitted to apply the groundwork of this pattern. It can only be brought about on peaceful terms if the people of the Orient are made to realize, upon the word of America, that the white men are not in Asia this time to exploit, but to aid them in becoming important working factors in a postwar world.

Their distrust will vanish, as ours vanished in the Philippines. This can be brought about, not by resonant promises, but by actions.

The first move, as was America's in the Philippines, must be the opening of schools in every part of the subject countries.

Teachers, scattered among the people to teach them English, or Dutch, will develop the same medium of human exchange our American teachers developed in the Philippines.

As in the Philippines, local government can be given first to the people, then the provincial, and finally the national.

There is nothing involved or complicated in this pattern. Brought about gradually through education and training in self-government, it will, in the end, be equally advantageous to both teacher and pupil.

The first adjustment must be in the minds of those Dutch or English officials in government service who regard their offices as a vested interest to cling to all their lives. Let them, as a few doubting American officials did before them, learn to train their native understudies with good will and relinquish their places with grace—and adequate compensation—when the native is ready for service. Gradually, as was done in the Philippines, let executive power slip into his trained hands.

Let justice be applied by the native, not only to his own people, but to those who are foreigners in his country.

In other words, give the native a chance to show what he can do, let him be master in his own castle, and a unit in the upbuilding of his own race.

If a government is an instrument to further the happiness and welfare of the individual, any government that serves that purpose should be given the opportunity to thrive.

In this interim of development the sovereign nations can supervise the foreign relations of these countries as America did by placing an American High Commissioner in the Philippines.

This policy, if carried out in the Dutch East Indies, would redeem the face of Holland in the Orient.

The Dutch have promised home rule and their willingness to make amends for their harsh dealings in the past with the Indonesians.

With America's example before them they can find the way. They can permit the natives of the Dutch East Indies to legislate for themselves, so that their native industries may be protected by their own legislature. Such legislation should be supported in Holland, as our Philippine legislation was in America, and not, as in the past in imperialistic blindness, taken to Holland and there vetoed.

There is no problem in the Pacific that cannot be solved by the American pattern.

President Roosevelt outlined this when he suggested that the history of America in the Philippines had provided "a pattern for the future of other small nations and peoples of the world."

The President of the United States said in part:

"It is a pattern of what men of good will look forward to in the future—a pattern of a global civilization which recognizes no limitations of religion, of creed, or of race.

"But we must remember that such a pattern is based on two important factors. The first is that there shall be a period of preparation, through the dissemination of education and the recognition and fulfillment of physical and social and economic needs.

"The second is that there be a period of training for ultimate independent sovereignty, through the practice of more and more self-government, beginning with local government and passing on through the various steps to complete statehood.

"Even we in the United States did not arrive at full national independence until we had gone through the preliminary stages. The town meetings in the New England colonies, and the similar local organizations in other colonies, gradually led to county government and then to state government. That whole process of political training and development preceded the final formation of our permanent Federal government in 1789.

"Such training for independence is essential to the stability of independence in almost every part of the world. Some peoples need more intensive training and longer years of it; others require far less training and shorter periods of time.

"The recent history of the Philippines has been one of national co-operation and adjustment and development. We are sure now, if ever we doubted, that our government in the United States chose the right and the honorable course."

There are countries in Asia that present problems out of the usual Asiatic category and that will require special means of adjustment. Caste-ridden Burma and India share virtually the same problems. But in India the results of the caste and religious problems have made deeper marks than on any other country in the Orient.

In no country does religion have such a firm and terrifying grip upon a race as in India.

The problem of caste will be solved slowly through the progress of education. The establishment of schools is of primary necessity in India, as in any other country beginning under the independent pattern.

The problem of religion goes more deeply.

This, then, is where we must strike, at the very root of India, which is its religion.

Education will in time eradicate caste, but it cannot serve to approach and improve upon the religious beliefs of India. They are too devious and too deeply rooted. Education might upheave them in time, but it would take generations. Religions, while they have sapped the lifeblood of India, are still its soul.

Therefore, why attempt to eradicate them? Why not adopt Indian faith as an ally and direct it into a means of service?

This can be done if the problem is approached in a respectful way. The approach to India's problem is by way of studying India's religions and through a sane use of those religions direct the Hindu's national life into more constructive ways.

The salvaging of religion for utilitarian ends was the secret of Gandhi's power. Ignorance of this has cost the white man in India the friendship of its people. It has been an unfortunate error on the part of the West to regard with contempt the religions of the Orient. The Westerner may not know this is the greatest hurt he can offer an Oriental.

Particularly does this insult strike deep to the soul of the Hindu, whose every breath is drawn by religious impulse. Whether his religion contributes to his benefit or his degradation, it is his—it is his soul. Because of this, religion can be made the greatest influence for good in India.

Since, to the Hindu, his religion is paramount, in any regenerative movement in India his creed must play the leading part. To reduce this to practical terms, progress can be made by directing this religion, or rather the spirit that governs it, into the human and practical relationships. This is done by all the successful religions.

There is basic good in the Indian faith, or faiths. But as in the case of all religions that degenerate, India's has been dragged in the dirt through improper teachers. It can be rejuvenated and redeemed. It can be made to serve the original good for which it was ordained. Intelligent religious teachers, resurrecting the basic principles of the

Indian religion which in truth holds the foundations of all world religions, can lead the way in the human and spiritual redemption of India.

Much in Oriental belief can dovetail into and improve upon modern trends of thought in an India that has need of both. Take, for example, the belief in Nirvana, which to the Oriental mind expresses the inner placidity of the soul, but to the Occidental is the outer expression of physical sluggishness. That principle, if applied in the realm of politics, might give a spiritual aspect to politics, which, even to the enlightened Westerner, is a prosaic and mercenary business.

Whereas the Oriental who learns politics according to Western methods is likely to be regarded by the Westerner as a glib and even sly individual, the same Oriental, regarding politics from a religious point of view, might develop into a great influence for advancement, by combining spiritual force with Western practicability. The resultant brand of politics, the essence of which would be made up of human relationships and spiritual farsightedness, might eventually set a world example.

It would be interesting if the universal politician of the future, who dedicates his political genius to the interests of his country, his people, and his God, should develop through the contemplative medium of the Orient!

In the long run the Oriental approach may be of as much value to the Occidental as Western advantages will be of benefit to the Oriental.

China presents only economic problems to be solved by the pattern of the future. Through her leaders she has been made articulate; she has bared her heart to the world. We know her to be democratic, honest, aspiring, and sane. China has long been intellectually close to the political shore lines of America, even as the Philippines are part of the past ambitions and future ideals of America. She has shown what she wants and what she can do, and she has no problem that cannot be solved by the spreading of educational facilities, protected trade, and good will. This is because

China is spiritually sound. She has been harried outwardly and from within, but as a country she has maintained her integrity.

There is democratic understanding between this great Asiatic country and America.

China has already found her place in the democratic pattern of the Pacific.

The problem of Japan will not end with her defeat. Her excuse, at the peace conference of the future, will be based upon her crying need for expansion. It is for land she has murdered millions of innocent neighbors; it is due to her need for expansion that she has cast greedy looks across the entire Pacific! The same excuse has ever served for all despotic countries.

In all fairness, excessive population is one of the most fundamental problems of Japan.

Japan is overcrowded. She is looking for means of expansion. But this is a problem Japan has ever magnified beyond its true proportions.

Japan is overpopulated, but, on the other hand, she has strict immigration laws, and as no foreigners are permitted, there is no problem of foreign labor versus Japanese labor.

America, with all her vastness, has had the problem of foreign labor.

Therefore, an explanation must be sought elsewhere.

The Japanese have always claimed that because they are an island nation they have had additional problems of national defense. These dangers they also magnified. When they took Korea and Formosa and Manchukuo they said by way of explanation that these adjacent countries had been daggers pointing toward the national integrity of Japan. Following that argument to its logical conclusion, and taking into account the shrinking of distances by airplanes and submarines, every nation on earth was a danger to the security of Japan!

No, the real source of the Japanese problem does not lie in the island of Japan or in the Japanese as an individual. It is due to that quirk in the Japanese national mentality—an individual quirk enlarged to national scale—which the Occidental finds impossible to understand. It is the accentuated inferiority complex which the Japanese must cover by a display of swaggering superiority.

It was this that built up his gigantic propaganda machine which in the parlance of today is called imperialism, but which in Japan is termed militarism. It is responsible for the development of the Shinto and Bushido.

These two beliefs are the greatest evils of Japan. They dovetail neatly, with deadly results. Shinto holds all Japanese together in the blood brotherhood of family; as one believes the other must. So closely knit is this family tie that while spies were scattered all over the world by the Japanese after the passage of the Immigration Act in 1924, not one of these, if captured, ever betrayed a secret of Japan's.

Their Bushido, the warrior faith based upon the traditions of the Samurai, has bolstered imperialism and militarism in Japan. Here are beliefs dangerous to a people and their neighbors alike. Shinto and Bushido must be eradicated.

How can this be done?

Let us review history. Let us go back to 1918 and a defeated Germany—a Germany that has long held the same troublesome position in the West as Japan holds in the Orient.

The world had a beautiful opportunity to start afresh when Germany was defeated. The victorious nations muffed their opportunity. Spiritually, they deserted a broken Germany.

Only one man saw ahead into the future. That was Hitler. He took hold of that future by taking charge of the youth. He indoctrinated the youth of Germany with his idea of building up an imperialistic Germany.

Imagine the difference it would have made to the world if the winning nations had held the far vision of a Hitler—if, instead of permitting ruin to overwhelm all countries, they had developed the youth of Germany along democratic lines!

It was their great opportunity. It was permitted to pass.

We will have the German fiasco repeated in Japan if—knowing her ills and weaknesses as a nation—we do not undertake its cure in the new generation of Japan. This can be no one-nation task. It can be done by the co-ordinated effort of all nations interested in maintaining the peace of the world.

In this plan to humanize Japan while holding it in leash the Far East should have a part, because Japan, while a danger to the entire world, is essentially a problem of the Far East. Let the Far East take part in regaining the advantage lost by the Western nations after the first *world* war. To accomplish this, Japan must be properly policed. China will need all her man power. She will be in no position to police Japan. She will need the help of the Western nations.

A practical solution of the problem might be the policing of Japan by the Western nations, by force of arms if necessary, to hold the Japanese in proper restraint, while the problems of the spirit are taken care of by China and the other nations of the Far East.

China should be awarded the opportunity to direct the democratic policies that will govern Japan. Democratic schooling will eradicate the evils of Shintoism and the Bushido. It will allow the youth of Japan the opportunity to develop a true Japanese genius, based upon democratic soundness, which the German youth was not given after the defeat of Germany.

This democratic pattern for the new Japan, to be successful, must retain the Oriental approach. China is best qualified to direct that approach. It should be based on the principle set down by Madame Chiang Kai-shek in her address in Madison Square Garden in New York:

"We must eliminate hatred."

That is the Orient speaking.

# XVIII. POSITION OF THE PHILIPPINES

AT THE PEACE CONFERENCE that will decide the future pattern of the Pacific the position of the Philippines should command attention.

The place of the Philippines in the Far East has been and must remain unique. From that position, granted him by America, the Filipino who will represent the Philippines can speak with a full heart, not only for himself but for the Far East. As the only Christian in the Far East, the Filipino can interpret the Orient to the Western world.

As an Americanized Oriental he has already played his part in interpreting the West in the Orient.

The Filipino at the peace table can demonstrate to East and West alike the success of the American pattern in his own country.

"Here," he can say, "is a policy where hatred was turned to suspicion, suspicion to confidence, confidence to loyalty.

"Shall we, if Occidentals, try out this plan that bore such fruitful results? If Orientals, shall we accept this pattern?

"Or shall we—as nations—continue in the old and dangerous way? The way that leads to ill will, hatred, distrust, and misunderstanding! The way that led to the bloody revolution of Hong Kong and Singapore—and Java and Burma—whereas ours led to the fealty of Bataan and Corregidor!

"The pattern of America worked in the Philippines. It will work again."

Any person who has known the Orient in recent years and felt its repercussions of resentment and unrest will feel assured of the receptivity of the Orient to this pattern if the suggestion is made by America with the Philippine example as argument.

The West should be no harder to convince.

We in the Philippines and the rest of the Far East are well aware that America is not in the Philippines merely through love of us.

The Occidental is equally well aware that seventeen million Filipinos did not stand by the American flag in the Philippines only through a sense of personal devotion to America.

But Americans and Filipinos alike were willing to die together for a principle. That principle, democracy, was never presented more magnificently as an ideal for men to live by than within this century in the Philippines.

As an argument in salesmanship let us sum up the dividends received by America in return for her outlay in altruism.

Americans in the Philippines profited in business, gold mining, export and import of all kinds. Big business was practically all in American hands. All American products entered the Philippines duty free, and Philippine products were sent to America duty free. Every American-developed need of the modernized Filipino—from automobiles to chewing gum—entered our country duty free. Steamship travel, clipper service, American Express, banks, and oil companies were American.

America, an industrial and manufacturing country, broadened her market by developing the standards of living in the Philippines. The Filipino trained in American ways found that all his needs were American. The Philippine market became completely American.

In turn, Philippine products depended upon their American market.

This alone should silence the last argument of the imperialists in favor of the native being kept in an abased, undemanding position.

But there is more to the argument than that of economic advantage.

America as a world power must have prestige in the Far East. The Philippines were America's bulwark in the Orient. There her army and navy headquarters were, there her clippers were based, and there stood her aerial bases.

If America is to continue her hold on Far Eastern trade in the future she will continue to need the Philippines as a base. Our country stands at the crossroads of the air lanes and sea lanes that will be important to her future.

The Philippines are the natural center from which American influence must radiate.

Beyond the market-hungry Philippines stretches the great Far Eastern trade of the future. Yes, America will need in the Orient her bastion of American democracy which is the Philippines!

A frequent question asked in America these days is: "After the war, will the Filipinos still want their independence?"

To ask that question is to divest America of its greatest triumph in the Philippines. Certainly we will want the independence promised us by America in 1946! It is because of that promised independence, because the need for it was implanted in Filipino hearts by America, that we fought on Bataan. We fought as Americans fight, not for ourselves alone, but for others as well, for democracy.

With the conquest of Japan, the only stumbling block to our independence will be removed. The best-intentioned of Americans could say, in the past: "Why give up the Philippines that they may be gobbled up by Japan?"

That, too, was the fate we most feared.

America and the Philippines held together in fear of Japan. That fear will be ended when Nipponese fangs are drawn. But the two countries will continue to stand together. The American-Filipino conference planned for 1946 upon the granting of our independence was to have decided the gradual rise of American tariff rates upon Philippine products. We hope that that conference will still be held, and in a country where the gory flag of Japan may never lift again. Is it a wild dream, perhaps, that such a conference will also be for the determination of peace?

Speaking as a Filipino with no official authority but with love of country to uphold him, I cannot see the Philippines in the position of refusing to America any bases she might need to maintain her position in the Orient, for she owes everything she is and may become to America.

Nor can I imagine America refusing the Philippines anything they may ask for within reason.

Because of Bataan and Corregidor, America's interest in the Philippines can never disappear. American blood has made the Philippines a shrine to democracy and a world symbol of its strength.

It is America's masterpiece.

We may feel serene about the future of the Philippines and America.

Our differences were adjusted long before Bataan.

The great danger, and one that might easily be brought to pass, is the domination of the Far East by one powerful country.

Any practical world program for the future will guard against such a contingency. It might come about, because the United States is making great sacrifices and expected to make greater sacrifices in behalf of the Far East. In politics, if not in spiritualities, the good Samaritan generally comes to look for some delayed form of compensation. Naturally a samaritan country might be expected to accept and favor a plan that would take into account future benefits for present sacrifices.

One has only to review the American story in the Philippines to doubt such a contingency arising. But its mere possibility brings to mind a bit of Filipino folklore, still pertinent, if centuries old.

A prince, hunting in the forests of Luzon, came upon a poorly dressed but beautiful peasant girl. She led him through the jungle to the nipa-thatched shack where her family were living in poverty.

The prince returned to his palace but continued to visit the girl in the forest. His retinue carried presents—food for the family, farm implements for the father, cattle for the farm, silks and ornaments for the girl. Each time the family fell on their knees to thank him. To them, he was a god. But the prince's eyes were always on the girl. He coveted her beauty. As she bloomed under the good treatment and wore her new clothing with grace, she became more beautiful in his eyes and more desirable.

She told him, as did her family: "You must indeed be a god!"

The young prince pondered. He had come to desire the young beauty of the forest more than he had ever before desired any woman. She was innocent and unprotected—she was his for the taking. Was he not a prince?

But she looked upon him as a god. If he took her, as any mortal might, she and her people would know him for no celestial being, but mere man. And the prince let the girl remain in the forest, retaining the illusion of his godship.

To one billion Orientals in the Far East the word "America" has come to hold much of the magic aura that surrounded that legendary prince.

America will not break that illusion!

The pattern for the Pacific will be one for the world to work by if peace is to be achieved throughout the world. For victory, to be true victory, must be for all the peoples of the earth. It must be victory for all men—for the brutalized Japanese and the oppressed Germans—benighted, deluded, and degenerated below the level of any Borneo savage because their viciousness operates under the mask of "civilization."

Has the defeated ever recognized a peace as just? No, because the victor always demands his pound of flesh, and whoever pays that pound can never be made to feel he has not been cheated. He does not feel in the wrong, for what loser ever feels himself in the wrong? He is defeated and disgraced. His resentment will burn, as he pays, and the longer he pays the greater will be his resentment.

This has ever been the result of peace treaties in the past.

But the democratic pattern, if carried out as it was in the Philippines, can allay these resentments.

Why do men fight?

Why, in the Philippines, did we fight America? Why, forty-two years later, did we fight beside America? For the same purpose—freedom.

The essence of our world struggle is that all men shall be free. The Atlantic Charter laid down the premise of that world freedom, binding its signatories "to respect the rights of all people to choose the form of government under which they will live."

The merits of this principle were proven by America in the Philippines. Through that example we know that educational advantages, fair dealing, good will, and the infiltration of the principles of democracy will end war.

World peace can be achieved through a universal adaptation of this pattern.

We have seen millions die and countries deformed in this war. We have learned that there are no economic or spiritual wastes so great as those made by war. We know—or should know by now—that to create peace we must devote to it the same enthusiasm and industry we have shown in our preparations for war.

If, in paving the way for that peace, stronger nations must give up certain privileges for the purpose of protecting the weaker nations, are these not poor prices to pay for the greater privileges of a lasting peace?

This war to be justifiable must mean freedom for John Chang as well as John Doe—freedom to believe in his own gods, to tend his own bit of land, to believe in the genius of his people in lifting their heads above the dust. It is John Chang and John Doe who are fighting. It is for them this war must be won.

To quote again from the Orient, in the words of Chiang Kai-shek:

"There will be neither peace, nor hope, nor future for any of us unless we honestly aim at political, social, and economic justice for all peoples of the world, great and small."

# XIX. SPIRITUAL PATTERN

Economic advantages alone will not serve to sell the democratic pattern to the Far East. Underlying its more apparent advantages must be a pattern of understanding and human recognition approaching that America granted in the Philippines.

We may discuss the Atlantic and the Pacific charters, but the one that will be most needed when this war ends will be the human charter based upon the needs and longings of mankind.

It was the spiritual pattern underwriting the materialistic that succeeded in the Philippines. It is the only pattern that has worked so far; it is the only pattern that can be adapted to general satisfaction.

The greatest dividends paid by Mother America's experiments in the Philippines have been in spiritual gain. America can point out to the world the returns on her benevolent and libertarian policy. They are Bataan and Corregidor. She can quote statements made by the great leaders of the Orient:

"In view of her record in the Philippines, America is the only nation we can turn to and trust."

It is a spiritual dividend to be proud of when the sullen and secretive East will tell her story and bare her heart to a white nation!

It has often been said that the white man was blind in the Orient. His weakness was less blindness than astigmatism. The only corrective for it will be human sympathy—the treatment of others as one would be done by.

This is a simple Galilean solution. But it worked! It worked in the Philippines, where the basic fundamental of the American policy was a respect for the dignity of the human soul.

Fusion of policies, strengthening of trust, the development of a protected trade—these units in the machinery of smoothly functioning governments can be founded only upon a basis of respect between nations.

Its need is as great between nations as between individuals. Human and spiritual adjustments must accompany the national adjustments necessary to the cure of a war-sick world.

The world has shriveled space, and in no spot in the world are we more than two days away from home. In this closely knit world of the future there will be no room for misunderstandings. Under new circumstances, where the very heavens will come under the jurisdiction of the state, every American, for example, must realize that the Far East is not far away, it is only a step from his own door.

In this new world the Filipino stands as the first example of the success of the human charter in the Orient. He is that unit in the Far East who is akin to both East and West, whose country is the fusion point of the two worlds. He is the first man in the Orient to stand in spirit upon the shores of America.

When, to cite an example, the Pan-American movement began in the United States, the Filipino regarded himself as part and parcel of that movement. This movement was the result of the corollary to the Monroe Doctrine establishing the principle of the "two Americas for the Americans," and warning the European nations to avoid encroachment on American shores.

It did not occur to the Christianized and Americanized Filipino that he was geographically removed from the Pan-American project. His understanding and sympathies lay with the West. His politics and economic view were with America. His cultural relations with Mexico and South America had developed through his use of the Spanish language since the days when his government had been ruled through Mexico by Spain. Long before the "good-neighbor" policy became popularized, the Philippines had regarded her relationship with the Americas as more than neighborly. Cultural, religious, and political ties form a closer relationship than those of race.

Considering himself, then, in his position in the Far East, as sharing the Pan-American interest, the Filipino was made increasingly uneasy by the Japanese development of a similar movement in the Orient. The Japanese declared their projected East Asia Co-Prosperity Sphere as the Far Eastern equivalent of the Monroe Doctrine.

The sphere was promulgated as the Japanese began their invasion of Manchukuo, announcing their intention of exercising suzerainty, or influence, throughout the entire East.

The Japanese march toward imperialism began with the annexation of all the countries they had blueprinted as part of the sphere—Burma, British Malaya, Thailand, French Indo-China, the Philippines, Guam, Wake, and the Dutch East Indies.

This was their Monroe Doctrine. This, their untouchable realm.

The Filipino trapped in this alien and enemy movement looked to America for salvation, as before he had turned to her for educational and spiritual understanding.

They were both too late. Japan's version of the Monroe Doctrine had laid ominous hold of the Orient. Its power can be broken by superior force. It can be supplanted only by a stronger doctrine. The only stronger doctrine we know is that charter of human understanding that was given the Philippines. So binding was that charter that under it two of the most dissimilar races on earth, the American and the Filipino, attained a blood brotherhood as attested to by the sacrifice of Bataan.

Good can come from war, terrible though war itself must always be. World War I publicized democracy throughout the world. This present war, that we hope will be the last, may bring about world democracy.

In whatever world the future holds for us the white man and brown will have need for each other. To attain understanding they must listen to each other's voices. They have much to offer each other.

The Westerner can give to the Oriental the comforts of civilization and add to the security and even the length of his worldly existence. In turn the Oriental can contribute that concept of eternal rightness and inward peace that has been his staff throughout the centuries.

The white man will remember words that came to him from the Orient in these troubled years, the voice of Gandhi, "There must be no enmity," and the gentle tones of Madame Chiang Kai-shek, "We must hate no one."

Of great importance for future co-operation between East and

West will be the establishing of press service bureaus, representing all nations, in the principal cities of all countries, that the news of each country may come from fair and unprejudiced sources in the country itself. This will contribute immeasurably toward mutual understanding and good will. And good will is the principal asset of a nation. As in business it is a tangible asset, it can be bartered and sold. The basis of international trade rests upon good will. It is the most profitable investment that can be made by any country. If, for example, England makes a heavy investment of good will in India during the future development of India, will not India prefer to trade with England beyond all other nations?

This must be remembered, that no good will can be established where the shading of one skin demands superior recognition from a skin of another hue.

If, in the Philippines, the American considered the color of his epidermis to be of greater value in the eyes of God, he did not allow his opinion to affect his dealings with the Filipino. It did not alter his fairness. It did not detract from his sense of fair play. And it was not permitted to interfere with the success of the American plan.

This was the most successful plank in the human charter of the Philippines.

The Oriental is given to whetting his arguments upon parables. May I be forgiven for recalling one last fragment of folklore from our native Tagalog?

In the beginning, according to an old Malayan legend, when the God of the Universe decided upon the creation of man, he shaped a small figure carefully and set it in his oven. Since the making of man was a new matter with God, he allowed the dough image to remain too long in the cosmic oven, and burned it black. And God blew upon the cindered shape and put it aside to cool, and this was the Negro.

The next one He removed from the oven too soon and it was a pasty white. This image was likewise set to cool, and it became the white man.

The third image was allowed to remain neither too short a time nor too long, and when God took the new man out of the oven it was neither white nor black but a beautiful warm shade of brown.

And God smiled, because the baking was *just right*.

And that, in Malayan, is how the brown man began.

Under the human charter the superiority of one color over another is waived in favor of the sovereignty of the soul.

The final argument of the imperialistic-minded is always the same:

"What if the natives of these countries are given self-government? They will be no better off. They will probably be more wretched than before."

Granted, that their miseries may be greater and their problems may not be lessened. Self-government will not cure their national illnesses. But there is a psychic difference between being ill in prison and being ill under an open sky. Sick men do not gain strength in the dark.

Already the forces of imperialism are martialing the old arguments. Already they are scheming to seize material advantages from the holocaust of the youthful dead. Imperialism reaches its full flower in Nazism; and as we fight one we must fight the other. Nazism uses force. Imperialism uses cunning and cynical sophistication for the attainment of its material purposes.

Peace terms written for the world by either imperialism or Nazism would be the death certificate of Christian civilization.

The moral rights of nations must be safeguarded and the spiritual rights of the individual must be honored if the victory of peace is to be lastingly won.

The issue in the Pacific is a moral issue.

Whatever the immediate circumstances of the war's beginning, whatever the tactics that precipitated the Japanese aggression, the issue in the Pacific must rest, not upon economics, not upon politics, but upon a moral estimate of the human race. This issue surmounts all partisan considerations of particular nations and all ambitions of governments. Humanity is embroiled in a civil war to determine whether all men or only a selected few shall be free; whether spiritualities or the state shall determine the laws of human conduct.

The Pacific is the paramount issue in our global war. Upon it must rest the basis for world peace.

Unless the new charter for the Pacific is based upon a code of international moralities and human rights, the words of that treaty will once again be written upon water. For that charter a summary specification of national rights and obligations might serve as a criterion:

1. Nations, represented by their constituted governments, acquire a legal equality unaffected by race, religion, or material resources.

2. Nations, properly constituted, acquire by natural processes a condition of sovereignty and a liberty of action consonant with the demands of their own self-preservation and progress, yet regulated in exercise by the precepts of moral conduct, the inalienable rights of others, and the transcendent welfare of that humanity shared by all as members of a world household.

3. Nations, like individuals, enjoy the right to acquire legitimately, and to maintain securely, possession and control of operation of lands and material resources necessary to the maintenance of national and family life and conducive to human progress through an advancing standard of living.

4. Among nations, the political form of legal establishment and the governmental organization and the methods of selecting official personnel are proper objects of private domestic concern, subject only to the moral equities.

5. Political institutions of nations, though diversely fashioned to suit national conditions and temperaments, should be similarly purposed to serve evenly and justly the rights of all citizens, the protection of their domestic security, and the confirmation of their liberty within the limits of the common good, but with the exception of such forfeitures of personal freedom as natural catastrophe may compel or the interests of national defense may judiciously command.

6. The racial origin of nations confers neither a title to unmerited superiority nor an excuse for discrimination.

7. Peace between nations is not acquired by negation of action, but must be won and conserved by moral vigilance, mutual political confidence, and economic toleration, practiced in normal relations and applied through arbitration for a solution of such conflicts as

are inevitable when the activities of growing nations are quickened by ideals of betterment.

The future pattern established in the Pacific will determine the future of the world. In that pattern the paramount issue must be the preservation and vindication of that future, which, by preserving the moral sanctities of the individual, is, to the majority of men on earth, still considered to be the inviolable sanctity of the human soul.

# I. THE CONSTITUTION OF THE PHILIPPINE REPUBLIC

*Approved by the Malolos Congress, January 20, 1899.*

---

WE, the representatives of the Philippine people, lawfully invoked, in order to establish justice, provide for common defense, promote general welfare, and insure the benefits of freedom, imploring the aid of the Sovereign Legislator of the Universe in order to attain these purposes, have voted, decreed, and sanctioned the following—

## POLITICAL CONSTITUTION

### First Title

### THE REPUBLIC

ARTICLE 1. The political association of all the Filipinos constitutes a nation, the estate of which is denominated Philippine Republic.

ART. 2. The Philippine Republic is free and independent.

ART. 3. Sovereignty resides exclusively in the people.

### Second Title

### THE GOVERNMENT

ART. 4. The government of the republic is popular, representative, alternative, and responsible, and is exercised by three distinct powers, which are denominated legislative, executive, and judicial. Two or more of these powers shall never be vested in one person or corporation; neither shall the legislature be vested in one individual alone.

### Third Title

### RELIGION

ART. 5. The state recognizes the equality of all religious worships and the separation of the church and the state.

147

*Fourth Title*

## THE FILIPINOS AND THEIR NATIONAL AND INDIVIDUAL RIGHTS

ART. 6. The following are Filipinos:

1. All persons born in Philippine territory. A vessel flying the Philippine flag shall, for this purpose, be considered a portion of the Philippine territory.

2. The offspring of a Filipino father and mother although born outside the Philippine territory.

3. Foreigners who have obtained certificates of naturalization.

4. Those who, without it, may have gained "vecindad" (residence) in any town of the Philippine territory.

It is understood that residence is gained by staying two years without interruption in one locality of the Philippine territory, having an open abode and known mode of living and contributing to all the charges of the nation.

The nationality of the Filipino is lost in accordance with the laws. (S. C. C., 1st Title, 1st art.; S. C., 1st Title, 1st art.)

ART. 7. No Filipinos nor foreigner shall be arrested nor imprisoned unless on account of crime, and in accordance with the laws. (S. C., 4th art.)

ART. 8. Any person arrested shall be discharged or delivered over to the judicial authority within twenty-four hours following the arrest. (S. C., 4th art.)

Any arrest shall be held without effect or shall be carried to commitment within seventy-two hours after the detained has been delivered over to a competent judge.

The party interested shall receive notice of the order which may be issued within the same time. (S. C., 4th art.)

ART. 9. No Filipino can become a prisoner unless by virtue of the mandate of a competent judge.

The decree by which may be issued the mandate shall be ratified or confirmed, having heard the presumed criminal within seventy-two hours following the act of commitment. (S. C., 5th art.)

ART. 10. No one can enter the domicile of a Filipino or foreign resident in the Philippines without his consent, except in urgent cases of fire, flood, earthquake, or other similar danger, or of unlawful aggression proceeding from within or in order to assist a person within calling for help.

Outside of these cases, the entrance in the domicile of a Filipino or foreign resident of the Philippines and the searching of his papers or effects can only be decreed by a competent judge and executed during the day.

The searching of the papers and effects shall take place always in the presence of the party interested or of an individual of his family, and, in their absence, of two resident witnesses of the same place.

Notwithstanding, when a delinquent may be found, in "flagranti" and pursued by the authority with its agents, may take refuge in his domicile, he may be followed into the same only for the purpose of apprehension.

If he should take refuge in the domicile of another, notification to the owner of the latter shall precede. (S. C., 6th art.)

ART. 11. No Filipino can be compelled to make change of his domicile or residence unless by virtue of an executive sentence. (S. C., 9th art.)

ART. 12. In no case can there be detained nor opened by the governing authority the correspondence confided to the post office, nor can that of the telegraph or telephone be detained.

But, by virtue of a decree of a competent judge, can be detained any correspondence and also opened in the presence of the accused that which may be conveyed by the post office. (S. C., 7th art.)

ART. 13. Any decree of imprisonment, of search of abode, or of detention of the correspondence written, telegraphed, or telephoned, shall be justified.

When the decree may fall short of this requisite, or when the motives in which it may be founded may be judicially declared unlawful or notoriously insufficient, the person who may have been imprisoned, or whose imprisonment may not have been ratified within the term prescribed in art. 9, or whose domicile may be forcibly entered, or whose correspondence may be detained, shall have the right to demand the responsibilities which ensue. (S. C., 8th art.)

ART. 14. No Filipino shall be prosecuted nor sentenced, unless by a judge or tribunal to whom, by virtue of the laws which precede the crime, is delegated its cognizance, and in the form which the latter prescribe. (S. C., 16th art.)

ART. 15. Any person detained or imprisoned, without the legal formalities, unless in the cases provided in this constitution, shall be discharged upon their own petition or that of any Filipino.

The laws shall determine the form of proceeding summarily in this case, as well as the personal and pecuniary penalties incurred by him who may order, execute, or cause to be executed, the illegal detention or imprisonment.

ART. 16. No person shall be deprived temporarily or permanently of his property or rights, nor disturbed in the possession of them, unless by virtue of a judicial sentence. (S. C., 10th art.)

Those functionaries who under any pretext infringe this provision shall be personally responsible for the damage caused.

ART. 17. No person shall be deprived of his property unless through necessity and common welfare, previously justified and declared by the proper authority, providing indemnity to the owner previous to the deprivation. (S. C., 10th art.)

ART. 18. No person shall be obliged to pay contribution which may not have been voted by the assembly or by the popular corporations legally authorized to impose it, and which exaction shall not be made in the form prescribed by law. (S. C., 3d art.)

ART. 19. No Filipino who may be in the full enjoyment of his civil and political rights shall be hindered in the free exercise of the same.

ART. 20. Neither shall any Filipino be deprived of:

1. The right of expressing liberally his ideas and opinions either by word or by writing, availing himself of the press or of any other similar means.

2. The right of associating himself with all the objects of human life which may not be contrary to public morality; and, finally,

3. Of the right to direct petitions, individually or collectively, to the public powers and to the authorities.

The right of petition shall not be exercised by any class of armed force. (S. C., 15th art.)

ART. 21. The exercise of the rights expressed in the preceding article shall be subject to the general provisions which regulate them.

ART. 22. Those crimes which are committed upon the occasion of the exercise of the rights granted in this title shall be punished by the tribunals in accordance with the common laws.

ART. 23. Any Filipino can found and maintain establishments of instruction or of education, in accordance with the provisions which are established.

Popular education shall be obligatory and gratuitous in the schools of the nation. (S. C., 12th art.)

ART. 24. Any foreigner may establish himself liberally in the Philippine territory, subject to the provisions which regulate the matter, exercising therein his industry or devoting himself to any profession in the exercise of which the laws may not require diplomas of fitness issued by the national authorities. (S. C., 12th art.)

ART. 25. No Filipino who is in the full enjoyment of his political and civil rights shall be hindered from going freely from the territory, nor from removing his residence or property to a foreign country, except the obligations of contributing to the military service and the maintenance of the public taxes.

ART. 26. The foreigner who may not have become naturalized shall not exercise in the Philippines any office which may have attached to it authority or jurisdiction.

ART. 27. Every Filipino is obliged to defend the country with arms when he may be called upon by the laws, and to contribute to the expenses of the estate (government) in proportion to his property. (S. C., 13th art.)

ART. 28. The enumeration of the rights granted in this title does not imply the prohibition of any other not expressly delegated.

ART. 29. Previous authorization shall not be necessary in order to prosecute before the ordinary tribunals the public functionaries, whatever may be the crime which they commit.

A superior mandate shall not exempt from responsibility in cases of manifest infraction, clear and determinate, of a constitutional provision. In the other cases it shall exempt only the agents who may not exercise the authority.

ART. 30. The guarantees provided in articles 7, 8, 9, and 10 and 11 and paragraphs 1 and 2 of the 20th article shall not be suspended in the republic nor any part of it, unless temporarily and by means of a law, when the security of the estate shall demand it in extraordinary circumstances.

It being promulgated in the territory to which it may apply, the special law shall govern during the suspension according to the circumstances which demand it.

The latter as well as the former shall be voted in the national assembly, and in case the assembly may be closed the government is authorized to issue it in conjunction with the permanent commission without prejudice to convoking the former within the shortest time and giving them information of what may have been done.

But neither by the one nor the other law can there be suspended any other guarantees than those delegated in the first paragraph of this article nor authorizing the government to banish from the country or transport any Filipino.

In no case can the military or civil chiefs establish any other penalty than that previously prescribed by the law. (S. C., 17th art.)

ART. 31. In the Philippine Republic no one can be tried by private laws nor special tribunals. No person can have privileges nor enjoy emoluments which may not be compensation for public service and which are fixed by law. "El fuero de guerra y mariana" (the jurisdiction, privileges, and powers of army and navy) shall extend solely to the crimes and faults which may have intimate connection with the military and maritime discipline.

ART. 32. No Filipino can establish "mayorazgos" nor institutions, "vinculadoras" (title of perpetual succession by eldest son nor institutions entailed) of property, nor accept honors, "condecoraciones" (insignia or decoration of orders) or titles of honor and nobility from foreign nations without the authorization of the government.

Neither can the government establish the institutions mentioned in the preceding paragraph, nor grant honors "condecoraciones" or titles of honor and nobility to any Filipino.

Notwithstanding the nation may reward by a special law, voted by the assembly, eminent services which may be rendered by the citizens to their country.

*Fifth Title*

## LEGISLATIVE POWER

ART. 33. The legislative power shall be exercised by an assembly of the representatives of the nation.

This assembly shall be organized in the form and under the conditions determined by the law which may be issued to that effect.

ART. 34. The members of the assembly shall represent the entire nation, and not exclusively those who elect them.

ART. 35. No representative shall be subjected to any imperative mandate of his electors.

ART. 36. The assembly shall meet every year. It is the prerogative of the President of the republic to convoke it, suspend and close its sessions, and dissolve it, in concurrence with the same or with the permanent commission in its default, and within legal terms.

ART. 37. The assembly shall be open at least three months each year, not including in this time that which is consumed in its organization.

The President of the republic shall convoke it, at the latest, by the 15th of April.

ART. 38. In an extraordinary case he can convoke it outside of the legal period, with the concurrence of the permanent commission, and prolong the legislature, when the term does not exceed one month nor takes place more than twice in the same legislature.

ART. 39. The national assembly, together with the extraordinary representatives, shall form the constituents in order to proceed to the modification of the constitution and to the election of the new President of the republic, convoked at least one month previous to the termination of the powers of the former.

In the case of the death or of the resignation of the President of the republic, the assembly shall meet immediately by its own right and at the request of its president or of that of the permanent commission.

ART. 40. In the meantime, while the appointment of the new President of the republic proceeds, the president of the supreme court of justice shall exercise his functions, his place being filled by one of the members of this tribunal in accordance with the laws.

ART. 41. Any meeting of the assembly which may be held outside of the ordinary period of the legislature shall be null and void. That which is provided by art. 39 is excepted, and in that the assembly is constituted a tribunal of justice, not being allowed to exercise in such case other than judicial functions.

ART. 42. The sessions of the assembly shall be public. Notwithstanding, they can be secret at the petition of a certain number of its individuals, fixed by the regulations, it being decided afterwards by an absolute majority of the votes of the members present whether the discussion of the same matter be continued in public.

ART. 43. The President of the republic shall communicate with the assembly by means of messages, which shall be read from the rostrum by a secretary of the government.

The secretaries of the government shall have entrance into the assembly, with the right to the floor whenever they ask it, and shall cause themselves to be represented in the discussion of any particular project by commissioners designated by decree of the President of the republic.

ART. 44. The assembly shall constitute itself a tribunal of justice in order to try the crimes committed against the security of the estate by the President of the republic and individuals of the Counsel of Government, by the President of the Supreme Court of Justice, by the Procurer-General of the nation by means of a decree of the same, or of the permanent commission in its absence, or of the President of the republic at the proposal of the Procurer-General, or of the counsel of the government.

The laws shall determine the mode of procedure for the accusation, preparation for trial, and pardon.

ART. 45. No member of the assembly can be prosecuted nor molested for the opinions which he may express nor for the votes which he may cast in the exercise of his office.

ART. 46. No member of an assembly can be prosecuted in a criminal matter without authorization of the same, or of the permanent commission, to whom shall immediately be given information of the act for proper disposition.

The arrest, detention, or apprehension of a member of the assembly cannot take place without previous authorization of the same or of the permanent commission; but having once notified the assembly of the decree of arrest, shall incur responsibility if, within two days following the notification, it may not authorize the arrest or give reasons upon which its refusal is founded.

ART. 47. The national assembly shall have besides the following powers:

1. To frame regulations for its interior government.

2. To examine the legality of the elections and the legal qualifications of the members elected.

3. Upon its organization to appoint its President, Vice-President, and secretaries.

Until the assembly may be dissolved, its President, Vice-President, and secretaries shall continue exercising their offices during the four legislatures; and

4. To accept the resignations presented by its members, and grant leaves of absence subject to the regulations. (S. C., 34th and 35th art.)

ART. 48. No project can become a law before being voted upon by the assembly.

In order to pass the laws there shall be required in the assembly at least a fourth part of the total number of members, whose elections may have been approved and who may have taken the oath of office.

ART. 49. No proposed law can be approved by the assembly without having been voted upon as a whole, and article by article.

ART. 50. The assemblies shall have the right of censure and each one of its members the right to be heard.

ART. 51. The proposal of the laws belongs to the President of the republic and to the assembly.

ART. 52. The representative of the assembly who accepts of the government pension, employment, or commission with a salary, shall be understood to have renounced his office.

The employment of the secretary of the government of the republic and other offices prescribed in special laws are excepted from this provision. (S. C., 31st art.)

ART. 53. The office of representative shall be for a term of four years, and those who may exercise it have the right, by way of indemnity, according to the circumstances, to a sum determined by the law.

Those who may absent themselves during the whole of the legislature shall not be entitled to this indemnity, but will recover this right if they assist in those which follow.

## Sixth Title
## THE PERMANENT COMMISSION

ART. 54. The assembly, before the closing of its sessions, shall elect seven of its members in order to constitute a permanent commission during the period of its being closed, the latter being obliged in its first session to designate a president and secretary.

ART. 55. The following are the functions of the permanent commission in the absence of the assembly:

1. To declare whether or not there is sufficient reason to proceed against the President of the republic, the representatives secretaries of the government, President of the Supreme Court of Justice, and the Procurer-General in the cases provided by this constitution.

2. To convoke the assembly to an extraordinary meeting in those cases in which it should constitute a tribunal of justice.

3. To transact the business which may remain pending for consideration.

4. To convoke the assembly to extraordinary sessions when the exigency of the case may demand; and

5. To substitute the assembly in its functions in accordance with the constitution, exception being made of the right to make and pass the laws.

The permanent commission shall meet whenever it may be convoked by him who presides in accordance with this constitution.

## Seventh Title
## THE EXECUTIVE POWER

ART. 56. The executive power shall reside in the President of the republic, who exercises it through his secretaries.

ART. 57. The conduct of the interests peculiar to the towns, the provinces, and of the estate belonging respectively to the popular assemblies, to the provincial assemblies, and to the active administration, with reference to laws, and upon the basis of the most ample "desceb-trakizacion" (distribution) and administrative autonomy.

## *Eighth Title*
## THE PRESIDENT OF THE REPUBLIC

ART. 58. The president of the republic shall be elected by an absolute majority of votes by the assembly and the representative specially met in constitutive chamber.

His term of office shall be for four years and he will be re-eligible.

ART. 59. The President of the Republic shall have the proposal of the laws as well as the members of the assembly, and shall promulgate the laws when they have been passed and approved by the latter and shall watch over and insure their execution.

ART. 60. The power of causing the laws to be executed extends itself to all that which conduces to the conservation of public order in the interior and the international security.

ART. 61. The President of the Republic shall promulgate the laws within twenty days following the time when they have been transmitted by the assembly definitely approved.

ART. 62. If within this time they may not be promulgated it shall devolve upon the President to return them to the assembly with justification of the causes of their detention, proceeding in such case to their revision, and it shall not be considered that it insists upon them, if it does not reproduce them by a vote of at least two thirds of the members of the assembly present. Reproducing the law in the form indicated the government shall promulgate it within ten days, announcing his nonconformity.

In the same manner the government shall become obligated if he allow to pass the term of twenty days without returning the law to the assembly.

ART. 63. When the promulgation of a law may have been declared urgent by a vote expressed by an absolute majority of the votes of the assembly the President can call upon them by a message, stating his reasons for a new deliberation, which cannot be denied, and the same law being approved anew, shall be promulgated within the legal term, without prejudice to the President's announcing his nonconformity.

ART. 64. The promulgation of the laws shall take place by means of their publication in the official periodical of the republic and shall take effect after thirty days from the date of publication.

ART. 65. The President of the Republic shall have command of the army and navy, making and ratifying treaties of peace, with the previous concurrence of the assembly.

ART. 66. Treaties of peace shall not be binding until passed by the assembly.

ART. 67. In addition to the necessary powers for the execution of the laws, the President of the Republic shall have the following:

1. To confer civil and military employment with reference to the laws.

2. To appoint the secretaries of the government.

3. To direct diplomatic and commercial relations with foreign powers.

4. To see to it that in the entire territory may be administered speedy and complete justice.

5. To pardon delinquents in accordance with the laws, excepting the provision relative to the secretaries of the government.

6. To preside over national assemblies and to receive the envoys and representatives of the foreign powers authorized to meet him.

ART. 68. The President of the Republic shall need to be authorized by a special law:

1. In order to alienate, cede, or exchange any part of the Filipino territory.

2. In order to annex any other territory to that of the Philippines.

3. In order to admit foreign troops into the Philippine territory.

4. In order to ratify treaties of alliance, offensive and defensive; special treaties of commerce—those which stipulate to give subsidy to a foreign power—and all those which may bind individually the Filipinos.

In no case can the secret articles of a treaty derogate those which are public.

5. In order to grant amnesties and general pardons.

6. In order to coin money. (S. C., 55th art.)

ART. 69. To the President of the Republic belongs the power of dictating regulations for compliance and application of the laws in accordance with the requisites which the same prescribe. (S. C., 54th art.)

ART. 70. The President of the Republic can, with the previous concurrence adopted by a majority of the votes of the representatives, dissolve the assembly before the expiration of the legal term of its office.

In this case they shall be convoked for new elections within a term of three months.

ART. 71. The President of the Republic shall only be responsible in cases of high treason.

ART. 72. The compensation of the President of the Republic shall be fixed by a special law, which cannot be changed until the end of the presidential term of office.

## Ninth Title

## THE SECRETARIES OF THE GOVERNMENT

ART. 73. The council of the government shall be composed of a President and seven Secretaries, who shall have charge of the offices of Foreign Affairs, Interior, Treasury, Army and Navy, Public Instruction, Public Communications and Works, Agriculture, Industry, and Commerce.

ART. 74. All that which the President may order or provide in the exercise of his authority shall be signed by the Secretary to whom it belongs. No public functionary shall give compliance to any which lack this requisite.

ART. 75. The secretaries of the government are responsible jointly to the assembly for the general policy of the government and individually for their personal acts.

To the Procurer-General of the nation belongs the accusing of them, and to the assembly their trial.

The laws shall determine the cases of responsibility of the secretaries of the government, the penalties to which they are subject, and the mode of procedure against them.

ART. 76. If they should be condemned by the assembly, in order to pardon them there shall precede the petition of an absolute majority of the representatives.

## Tenth Title

## THE JUDICIAL POWER

ART. 77. To the tribunals belong exclusively the power of applying the laws in the name of the nation in civil and criminal trials.

The same codes shall govern in the entire republic without prejudice to modifications which for particular circumstances the laws may prescribe.

In them shall not be established more than one jurisdiction for all the citizens in common trials, civil and criminal.

ART. 78. The tribunals shall not apply the general and municipal regulations only in so far as they conform with the laws.

ART. 79. The exercise of the judicial power resides in the Supreme

Court of Justice and in the tribunals which are prescribed by the laws.

The composition, organization, and other attributes shall be governed by the organic laws which may be determined.

ART. 80. The President of the Supreme Court of Justice and the "Procurer-General" shall be appointed by the national assembly in concurrence with the President of the Republic and Secretaries of the government, and shall have absolute independence of the executive and legislative powers.

ART. 81. Any citizen can institute a public prosecution against any of the members of the judicial power for the crimes they may commit in the exercise of their office.

### Eleventh Title
## PROVINCIAL AND POPULAR ASSEMBLIES

ART. 82. The organization and powers of the provincial and popular assemblies will be regulated by their respective laws.

The latter shall be regulated according to the following principles:

1. Government and management of the interests peculiar to the provinces or towns, by their respective corporations, the principle of popular and direct election being the basis for the organization of said corporations.

2. Publicity of the sessions within the limits prescribed by the laws.

3. Publicity of the budgets, accounts, and important decisions.

4. Intervention of the government, and in the proper case of the national assembly in order to prevent the provincial and municipal corporations from exceeding their powers, to the prejudice of general and individual interests.

5. Determination of their powers in the matter of taxes, in order that the provincial and municipal taxation may never be antagonistic to the system of taxation of State.

### Twelfth Title
## THE ADMINISTRATION OF STATE

ART. 83. The government shall present yearly to the assembly budgets of income and expenses, setting forth the alterations made in those of the preceding year and enclosing the balance of the last fiscal year in accordance to law.

When the assembly may meet the budgets will be presented to it within ten days following its convening.

ART. 84. No payment shall be made except in accordance with the law of budgets or other special laws, in the form and under the responsibilities fixed thereby.

ART. 85. It is necessary that the government be authorized by law in order to dispose of the goods and properties of State or to secure a loan upon the credit of the nation.

ART. 86. The public debt which is contracted by the government of the republic in accordance with this constitution shall be under the special guaranty of the nation.

No indebtedness shall be created unless at the same time the resources with which to pay it are voted.

ART. 87. All the laws relating to incomes, public expenditures, or public credit shall be considered as a part of those of the budgets, and shall be published as such.

ART. 88. The assembly shall fix each year, at the request of the President of the Republic, the military forces of land and sea.

## Thirteenth Title
## REFORMS IN THE CONSTITUTION

ART. 89. The assembly, upon its own motion or at the proposal of the President of the Republic, can resolve the reform of the constitution, prescribing for that purpose the article or articles which should be modified.

ART. 90. The declaration made, the President of the Republic shall dissolve the assembly and convoke the "constituyente" (constituting power), which shall meet within three months following. In the convocation shall be inserted the resolution referred to in the preceding article.

## Fourteenth Title
## THE OBSERVANCE AND OATH OF THE CONSTITUTION— LANGUAGES

ART. 91. The President of the Republic, the government, the assembly, and all the Filipino citizens, shall faithfully guard the constitution; and the legislative power, immediately after the approval of the law of budgets, shall examine as to whether the constitution has been exactly observed and as to whether its infractions have been corrected, providing that which is most practicable in order that the responsibility of the transgressors may be made effective.

ART. 92. Neither the President of the Republic nor any other public functionary can enter upon the performance of his duty without previously taking the oath.

Such oath shall be taken by the President of the Republic before the national assembly.

The other functionaries of the nation shall take it before the authorities determined by law.

ART. 93. The use of the languages spoken in the Philippines is optional. It can only be regulated by the law, and solely as to the acts of public authority and judicial affairs. For the purpose of these acts shall be used at present the Castillian language.

## TEMPORARY PROVISIONS

ART. 94. In the meantime, and without prejudice to the 48th article and the commissions which may be appointed by the assembly for the preparation of the organic laws for the development and application of the rights granted the Filipino citizens, and for the regime of the public powers determined by the constitution, the laws in force in these islands before their emancipation shall be considered as the laws of the republic.

In like manner shall be considered in force the provisions of the civil code in respect to marriage and civil registry, suspended by the general government of the islands; the instructions of the 26th of April, 1888, in order to carry into effect articles 77, 78, 79, and 82 of said code; the law of civil registry of the 17th of June, 1870, referred to by article 332 of the same, and the regulations of the 13th of December, 1870, for the execution of this law, without prejudice to the local chiefs continuing in charge of the entries in the civil registry and intervening in the celebration of the marriage of Catholics.

ART. 95. Pending the approval and enforcement of the laws referred to in the preceding article the provisions of the Spanish laws temporarily enforced by said article may be modified by special laws.

ART. 96. After promulgating the laws which the assembly may approve in accordance with the 94th article, the government of the republic is authorized to issue the decrees and regulations necessary for the immediate formation of all the organizations of state.

ART. 97. The President of the Revolutionary Government shall at once assume the title of President of the Republic, and shall exercise said office until the constituting assembly meets and elects the person who is to fill said office definitely.

ART. 98. This congress, with the members who compose it, and those who may be returned by election or decree, shall continue four years —that is to say, the whole of the present legislature, beginning the 15th of April of next year.

ART. 99. Notwithstanding the general rule established in the 2d paragraph of the 4th article, during the time the country may have to struggle for its independence the government is hereby authorized to determine, at the close of congress, whatever questions and difficulties, not provided for by law, may arise from unforeseen events, by means of decrees, which may be communicated to the permanent commission and to the assembly on its first meeting.

ART. 100. The execution of the 5th article of title 3 is hereby suspended until the meeting of the constituting assembly.

In the meantime, the municipalities of those places which may require the spiritual offices of a Filipino priest shall provide for his maintenance.

ART. 101. Notwithstanding the provisions of arts. 62 and 63, the laws returned by the President of the Republic to congress cannot be reproduced until the legislature of the following year, the President and his council of government being responsible for the suspension. If the reproduction be made, the promulgation will be compulsory within ten days, the President stating his nonconformity if he so desires.

If the reproduction be made in subsequent legislatures, it will be considered as being voted for the first time.

ADDITIONAL ARTICLE. From the 24th of May last, on which date the dictatorial government was organized in Cavite, all the buildings, properties, and other belongings possessed by the religious corporations in these islands will be understood as restored to the Filipino government.

Barasoain, January 20, 1899.

THE PRESIDENT OF THE CONGRESS.
PEDRO A. PATERNO.

*The secretaries:*
PABLO TECSON.
PABLO OCAMPO.

# II. THE JONES ACT

ACT OF CONGRESS APPROVED AUGUST 29, 1916, TO PRO-
VIDE A MORE AUTONOMOUS GOVERNMENT FOR THE
PHILIPPINE ISLANDS AS AMENDED TO OCTOBER 1, 1931

[PUBLIC—NO. 240—64TH CONGRESS.]
[S. 381.]

*An Act To declare the purpose of the people of the United States as to the
future political status of the people of the Philippine Islands, and to provide a more
autonomous government for those islands.*

Whereas it was never the intention of the people of the United States
in the incipiency of the War with Spain to make it a war of conquest or for territorial aggrandizement; and

Whereas it is, as it has always been, the purpose of the people of
the United States to withdraw their sovereignty over the Philippine
Islands and to recognize their independence as soon as a stable
government can be established therein; and

Whereas for the speedy accomplishment of such purpose it is desirable to place in the hands of the people of the Philippines as large a
control of their domestic affairs as can be given them without, in
the meantime, impairing the exercise of the rights of sovereignty by
the people of the United States, in order that, by the use and exercise
of popular franchise and governmental powers, they may be the
better prepared to fully assume the responsibilities and enjoy all the
privileges of complete independence: Therefore

*Be it enacted by the Senate and House of Representatives of the
United States of America in Congress assembled,* That the provisions
of this Act and the name "The Philippines" as used in this Act shall
apply to and include the Philippine Islands ceded to the United States
Government by the treaty of peace concluded between the United
States and Spain on the eleventh day of April, eighteen hundred and
ninety-nine, the boundaries of which are set forth in Article III of
said treaty, together with those islands embraced in the treaty between

Spain and the United States concluded at Washington on the seventh day of November, nineteen hundred.

SEC. 2. That all inhabitants of the Philippine Islands who were Spanish subjects on the eleventh day of April, eighteen hundred and ninety-nine, and then resided in said islands, and their children born subsequent thereto, shall be deemed and held to be citizens of the Philippine Islands, except such as shall have elected to preserve their allegiance to the Crown of Spain in accordance with the provisions of the treaty of peace between the United States and Spain, signed at Paris December tenth, eighteen hundred and ninety-eight, and except such others as have since become citizens of some other country: *Provided,* That the Philippine Legislature, herein provided for, is hereby authorized to provide by law for the acquisition of Philippine citizenship by those natives of the Philippine Islands who do not come within the foregoing provisions, the natives of the insular possessions of the United States, and such other persons residing in the Philippine Islands who are citizens of the United States, or who could become citizens of the United States under the laws of the United States if residing therein.

SEC. 3. That no law shall be enacted in said islands which shall deprive any person of life, liberty, or property without due process of law, or deny to any person therein the equal protection of the laws. Private property shall not be taken for public use without just compensation.

That in all criminal prosecutions the accused shall enjoy the right to be heard by himself and counsel, to demand the nature and cause of the accusation against him, to have a speedy and public trial, to meet the witnesses face to face, and to have compulsory process to compel the attendance of witnesses in his behalf.

That no person shall be held to answer for a criminal offense without due process of law; and no person for the same offense shall be twice put in jeopardy of punishment, nor shall be compelled in any criminal case to be a witness against himself.

That all persons shall before conviction be bailable by sufficient sureties, except for capital offenses.

That no law impairing the obligation of contracts shall be enacted.

That no person shall be imprisoned for debt.

That the privilege of the writ of habeas corpus shall not be suspended, unless when in cases of rebellion, insurrection, or invasion the public safety may require it, in either of which events the same may be suspended by the President, or by the Governor General, wherever during such period the necessity for such suspension shall exist.

That no ex post facto law or bill of attainder shall be enacted nor shall the law of primogeniture ever be in force in the Philippines.

That no law granting a title of nobility shall be enacted, and no person holding any office of profit or trust in said islands shall, without the consent of the Congress of the United States, accept any present, emolument, office, or title of any kind whatever from any king, queen, prince, or foreign State.

That excessive bail shall not be required, nor excessive fines imposed, nor cruel and unusual punishment inflicted.

That the right to be secure against unreasonable searches and seizures shall not be violated.

That slavery shall not exist in said islands; nor shall involuntary servitude exist therein except as a punishment for crime whereof the party shall have been duly convicted.

That no law shall be passed abridging the freedom of speech or of the press, or the right of the people peaceably to assemble and petition the Government for redress of grievances.

That no law shall be made respecting an establishment of religion or prohibiting the free exercise thereof, and that the free exercise and enjoyment of religious profession and worship, without discrimination or preference, shall forever be allowed; and no religious test shall be required for the exercise of civil or political rights. No public money or property shall ever be appropriated, applied, donated, or used, directly or indirectly, for the use, benefit, or support of any sect, church, denomination, sectarian institution, or system of religion, or for the use, benefit, or support of any priest, preacher, minister, or other religious teacher or dignitary as such. Contracting of polygamous or plural marriages hereafter is prohibited. That no law shall be construed to permit polygamous or plural marriages.

That no money shall be paid out of the treasury except in pursuance of an appropriation by law.

That the rule of taxation in said islands shall be uniform.

That no bill which may be enacted into law shall embrace more than one subject, and that subject shall be expressed in the title of the bill.

That no warrant shall issue but upon probable cause, supported by oath or affirmation, and particularly describing the place to be searched and the person or things to be seized.

That all money collected on any tax levied or assessed for a special purpose shall be treated as a special fund in the treasury and paid out for such purpose only.

SEC. 4. That all expenses that may be incurred on account of the Government of the Philippines for salaries of officials and the conduct of their offices and departments, and all expenses and obligations contracted for the internal improvement or development of the islands, not, however, including defenses, barracks, and other works undertaken by the United States, shall, except as otherwise specifically provided by the Congress, be paid by the Government of the Philippines.

SEC. 5. That the statutory laws of the United States hereafter enacted shall not apply to the Philippine Islands, except when they specifically so provide, or it is so provided in this Act.

SEC. 6. That the laws now in force in the Philippines shall continue in force and effect, except as altered, amended, or modified herein, until altered, amended, or repealed by the legislative authority herein provided or by Act of Congress of the United States.

SEC. 7. That the legislative authority herein provided shall have power, when not inconsistent with this Act, by due enactment to amend, alter, modify, or repeal any law, civil or criminal, continued in force by this Act as it may from time to time see fit.

This power shall specifically extend with the limitation herein provided as to the tariff to all laws relating to revenue and taxation in effect in the Philippines.

SEC. 8. That general legislative power, except as otherwise herein provided, is hereby granted to the Philippine Legislature, authorized by this Act.

SEC. 9. That all the property and rights which may have been acquired in the Philippine Islands by the United States under the treaty of peace with Spain, signed December tenth, eighteen hundred and ninety-eight, except such land or other property as has been or shall be designated by the President of the United States for military and other reservations of the Government of the United States, and all lands which may have been subsequently acquired by the government of the Philippine Islands by purchase under the provisions of sections sixty-three and sixty-four of the Act of Congress approved July first, nineteen hundred and two, except such as may have heretofore been sold and disposed of in accordance with the provisions of said Act of Congress, are hereby placed under the control of the government of said islands to be administered or disposed of for the benefit of the inhabitants thereof, and the Philippine Legislature shall have power to legislate with respect to all such matters as it may deem advisable;

but acts of the Philippine Legislature with reference to land of the public domain, timber, and mining, hereafter enacted, shall not have the force of law until approved by the President of the United States: *Provided*, That upon the approval of such an act by the Governor General, it shall be by him forthwith transmitted to the President of the United States, and he shall approve or disapprove the same within six months from and after its enactment and submission for his approval, and if not disapproved within such time it shall become a law the same as if it had been specifically approved: *Provided further*, That where lands in the Philippine Islands have been or may be reserved for any public purpose of the United States, and, being no longer required for the purpose for which reserved, have been or may be, by order of the President, placed under the control of the government of said islands to be administered for the benefit of the inhabitants thereof, the order of the President shall be regarded as effectual to give the government of said islands full control and power to administer and dispose of such lands for the benefit of the inhabitants of said islands.

Sec. 10. That while this Act provides that the Philippine government shall have the authority to enact a tariff law the trade relations beween the islands and the United States shall continue to be governed exclusively by laws of the Congress of the United States: *Provided*, That tariff acts or acts amendatory to the tariff of the Philippine Islands shall not become law until they shall receive the approval of the President of the United States, nor shall any act of the Philippine Legislature affecting immigration or the currency or coinage laws of the Philippines become a law until it has been approved by the President of the United States: *Provided further*, That the President shall approve or disapprove any act mentioned in the foregoing proviso within six months from and after its enactment and submission for his approval, and if not disapproved within such time it shall become a law the same as if it had been specifically approved.

Sec. 11. (as amended by Acts of Congress of July 21, 1921, and May 31, 1922). That no export duties shall be levied or collected on exports from the Philippine Islands, but taxes and assessments on property and license fees for franchises, and privileges, and internal taxes, direct or indirect, may be imposed for the purposes of the Philippine government and the provincial and municipal governments thereof, respectively, as may be provided and defined by acts of the Philippine Legislature, and, where necessary to anticipate taxes and revenues, bonds and other obligations may be issued by the Philippine government or any provincial or municipal government therein, as may be provided by law and to protect the public credit: *Provided, however,* That the entire indebtedness of the Philippine government created by the authority conferred herein, exclusive of those obligations known as friar land bonds, shall not exceed at any one time 10 per centum of the aggregate tax valuation of its property, nor that of the city of Manila 10 per centum of the aggregate tax valuation of its property, nor that of any Province or municipality, a sum in excess of 7 per centum of the aggregate tax valuation of its property at any one time. In computing the indebtedness of the Philippine government, bonds not to exceed $10,000,000 in amount, issued by that government, secured by an equivalent amount of bonds issued by the Provinces or municipalities thereof, shall not be counted.

SEC. 12. That general legislative powers in the Philippines, except as herein otherwise provided, shall be vested in a legislature which shall consist of two houses, one the senate and the other the house of representatives, and the two houses shall be designated "The Philippine Legislature": *Provided,* That until the Philippine Legislature as herein provided shall have been organized the existing Philippine Legislature shall have all legislative authority herein granted to the government of the Philippine Islands, except such as may now be within the exclusive jurisdiction of the Philippine Commission, which is so continued until the organization of the legislature herein provided for the Philippines. When the Philippine Legislature shall have been organized, the exclusive legislative jurisdiction and authority exercised by the Philippine Commission shall thereafter be exercised by the Philippine Legislature.

SEC. 13. That the members of the senate of the Philippines, except as herein provided, shall be elected for terms of six and three years, as hereinafter provided, by the qualified electors of the Philippines. Each of the senatorial districts defined as hereinafter provided shall have the right to elect two senators. No person shall be an elective member of the senate of the Philippines who is not a qualified elector and over thirty years of age, and who is not able to read and write either the Spanish or English language, and who has not been a resident of the Philippines for at least two consecutive years and an actual resident of the senatorial district from which chosen for a period of at least one year immediately prior to his election.

SEC. 14. That the members of the house of representatives shall, except as herein provided, be elected triennially by the qualified electors of the Philippines. Each of the representative districts hereinafter provided for shall have the right to elect one representative. No person shall be an elective member of the house of representatives who is not a qualified elector and over twenty-five years of age, and who is not able to read and write either the Spanish or English language, and who has not been an actual resident of the district from which elected for at least one year immediately prior to his election: *Provided*, That the members of the present assembly elected on the first Tuesday in June, nineteen hundred and sixteen, shall be the members of the house of representatives from their respective districts for the term expiring in nineteen hundred and nineteen.

SEC. 15. That at the first election held pursuant to this act, the qualified electors shall be those having the qualifications of voters under the present law; thereafter and until otherwise provided by the Philippine Legislature herein provided for the qualifications of voters for senators and representatives in the Philippines and all officers elected by the people shall be as follows:

Every male person who is not a citizen or subject of a foreign power twenty-one years of age or over (except insane and feeble-minded persons and those convicted in a court of competent jurisdiction of an infamous offense since the thirteenth day of August, eighteen hundred and ninety-eight), who shall have been a resident of the Philippines for one year and of the municipality in which he shall offer to vote for six months next preceding the day of voting, and who is comprised within one of the following classes:

(a) Those who under existing law are legal voters and have exercised the right of suffrage.

(b) Those who own real property to the value of 500 pesos, or who annually pay 30 pesos or more of the established taxes.

(c) Those who are able to read and write either Spanish, English, or a native language.

SEC. 16. That the Philippine Islands shall be divided into twelve senate districts, as follows:

First district: Batanes, Cagayan, Isabela, Ilocos Norte, and Ilocos Sur.

Second district: La Union, Pangasinan, and Zambales.

Third district: Tarlac, Nueva Ecija, Pampanga, and Bulacan.

Fourth district: Bataan, Rizal, Manila, and Laguna.

Fifth district: Batangas, Mindoro, Tayabas, and Cavite.

Sixth district: Sorsogon, Albay, and Ambos Camarines.

Seventh district: Iloilo and Capiz.

Eighth district: Negros Occidental, Negros Oriental, Antique, and Palawan.

Ninth district: Leyte and Samar.

Tenth district: Cebu.

Eleventh district: Surigao, Misamis, and Bohol.

Twelfth district: The Mountain Province, Baguio, Nueva Vizcaya, and the Department of Mindanao and Sulu.

The representative districts shall be the eighty-one now provided by law, and three in the Mountain Province, one in Nueva Vizcaya, and five in the Department of Mindanao and Sulu.[1]

The first election under the provisions of this Act shall be held on the first Tuesday of October, nineteen hundred and sixteen, unless the Governor General in his discretion shall fix another date not earlier than thirty nor later than sixty days after the passage of this Act: *Provided*, That the Governor General's proclamation shall be published at least thirty days prior to the date fixed for the election, and there shall be chosen at such election one senator from each senate district for a term of three years and one for six years. Thereafter one senator from each district shall be elected from each senate district for a term of six years: *Provided*, That the Governor General of the Philippine Islands shall appoint, without the consent of the senate and without restriction as to residence, senators and representatives who will, in his opinion, best represent the senate district and those representative districts which may be included in the territory not now represented in the Philippine Assembly: *Provided further*, That thereafter elections shall be held only on such days and under such regulations as to ballots, voting, and qualifications of electors as may be prescribed by the Philippine Legislature,[2] to which is hereby given authority to redistrict the Philippine Islands and modify, amend, or repeal any provision of this section, except such as refer to appointive senators and representatives.

SEC. 17. That the terms of office of elective senators and representatives shall be six and three years, respectively, and shall begin on the date of their election. In case of vacancy among the elective members of the senate or in the house of representatives, special elections may be held in the districts wherein such vacancy occurred under such regulations as may be prescribed by law, but senators or representatives elected in such cases shall hold office only for the unexpired portion of the term wherein the vacancy occurred. Senators and representatives appointed by the Governor General shall hold office until removed by the Governor General.

[1] The number of representative districts has been increased to 94 by the Philippine Legislature.

[2] Act 3387 of the Philippine Legislature, approved December 3, 1927 (election law), provides that general elections shall be held on the first Tuesday in June of the year 1928 and upon the same day every three years thereafter.

SEC. 18. That the senate and house of representatives, respectively, shall be the sole judges of the elections, returns, and qualifications of their elective members, and each house may determine the rules of its proceedings, punish its members for disorderly behavior, and, with the concurrence of two-thirds, expel an elective member. Both houses shall convene at the capital on the sixteenth day of October next following the election and organize by the election of a speaker or a presiding officer, a clerk, and a sergeant at arms for each house, and such other officers and assistants as may be required. A majority of each house shall constitute a quorum to do business, but a smaller number may meet, adjourn from day to day, and compel the attendance of absent members. The legislature shall hold annual sessions, commencing on the sixteenth day of October, or, if the sixteenth day of October be a legal holiday, then on the first day following which is not a legal holiday, in each year. The legislature may be called in special session at any time by the Governor General for general legislation, or for action on such specific subjects as he may designate. No special session shall continue longer than thirty days, and no regular session shall continue longer than one hundred days, exclusive of Sundays. The legislature is hereby given the power and authority to change the date of the commencement of its annual sessions.[3]

The senators and representatives shall receive an annual compensation for their services, to be ascertained by law, and paid out of the treasury of the Philippine Islands. The senators and representatives shall, in all cases except treason, felony, and breach of the peace, be privileged from arrest during their attendance at the session of their respective houses and in going to and returning from the same; and for any speech or debate in either house they shall not be questioned in any other place.

No senator or representative shall, during the time for which he may have been elected, be eligible to any office the election to which is vested in the legislature, nor shall be appointed to any office of trust or profit which shall have been created or the emoluments of which shall have been increased during such term.

SEC. 19. That each house of the legislature shall keep a journal of its proceedings and, from time to time, publish the same; and the yeas and nays of the members of either house, on any question, shall, upon demand of one-fifth of those present, be entered on the journal, and every bill and joint resolution which shall have passed both houses shall, before it becomes a law, be presented to the Governor General. If he approve

[3]Philippine Legislature, by Act 3125, approved February 28, 1924, changed the date of commencement of annual sessions of legislature to July 16 of each year.

the same, he shall sign it; but if not, he shall return it with his objections to that house in which it shall have originated, which shall enter the objections at large on its journal and proceed to reconsider it. If, after such reconsideration, two-thirds of the members elected to that house shall agree to pass the same, it shall be sent, together with the objections, to the other house, by which it shall likewise be reconsidered, and if approved by two-thirds of all the members elected to that house it shall be sent to the Governor General, who, in case he shall then not approve, shall transmit the same to the President of the United States. The vote of each house shall be by the yeas and nays, and the names of the members voting for and against shall be entered on the journal. If the President of the United States approve the same, he shall sign it and it shall become a law. If he shall not approve same, he shall return it to the Governor General, so stating, and it shall not become a law: *Provided*, That if any bill or joint resolution shall not be returned by the Governor General as herein provided within twenty days (Sundays excepted) after it shall have been presented to him the same shall become a law in like manner as if he had signed it, unless the legislature by adjournment prevent its return, in which case it shall become a law unless vetoed by the Governor General within thirty days after adjournment: *Provided further*, That the President of the United States shall approve or disapprove an act submitted to him under the provisions of this section within six months from and after its enactment and submission for his approval; and if not approved within such time, it shall become a law the same as if it had been specifically approved. The Governor General shall have the power to veto any particular item or items of an appropriation bill, but the veto shall not affect the item or items to which he does not object. The item or items objected to shall not take effect except in the manner heretofore provided in this section as to bills and joint resolutions returned to the legislature without his approval.

All laws enacted by the Philippine Legislature shall be reported to the Congress of the United States, which hereby reserves the power and authority to annul the same. If at the termination of any fiscal year the appropriations necessary for the support of government for the ensuing fiscal year shall not have been made, the several sums appropriated in the last appropriation bills for the objects and purposes therein specified, so far as the same may be done, shall be deemed to be reappropriated for the several objects and purposes specified in said last appropriation bill; and until the legislature shall act in such behalf the treasurer shall, when so directed by the Governor General, make the payments necessary for the purposes aforesaid.

SEC. 20. That at the first meeting of the Philippine Legislature created by this Act and triennially thereafter there shall be chosen by the legislature two Resident Commissioners to the United States, who shall hold their office for a term of three years beginning with the fourth day of March following their election, and who shall be entitled to an official recognition as such by all departments upon presentation to the President of a certificate of election by the Governor General of said islands. Each of said Resident Commissioners shall, in addition to the salary[4] and the sum in lieu of mileage now allowed by law, be allowed the same sum for stationery and for the pay of necessary clerk hire as is now allowed to the Members of the House of Representatives of the United States, to be paid out of the Treasury of the United States, and the franking privilege allowed by law to Members of Congress. No person shall be eligible to election as Resident Commissioner who is not a bona fide elector of said islands and who does not owe allegiance to the United States and who is not more than thirty years of age and who does not read and write the English language. The present two Resident Commissioners shall hold office until the fourth of March, nineteen hundred and seventeen. In case of vacancy in the position of Resident Commissioner caused by resignation or otherwise, the Governor General may make temporary appointments until the next meeting of the Philippine Legislature, which shall then fill such vacancy; but the Resident Commissioner thus elected shall hold office only for the unexpired portion of the term wherein the vacancy occurred.

SEC. 21. That the supreme executive power shall be vested in an executive officer, whose official title shall be "The Governor General of the Philippine Islands." He shall be appointed by the President, by and with the advice and consent of the Senate of the United States, and hold his office at the pleasure of the President and until his successor is chosen and qualified. The Governor General shall reside in the Philippine Islands during his official incumbency, and maintain his office at the seat of government. He shall, unless otherwise herein provided, appoint, by and with the consent of the Philippine Senate, such officers as may now be appointed by the Governor General, or such as he is authorized by this Act to appoint, or whom he may hereafter be authorized by law to appoint; but appointments made while the senate is not in session shall be effective either until disapproval or until the next adjournment of the senate. He shall have general supervision and control

[4]Act of Congress approved March 4, 1925 (Public, 624, 68th Cong.), provides that on and after March 4, 1925, the compensation of Resident Commissioners from the Philippine Islands shall be at the rate of $10,000 per annum.

of all of the departments and bureaus of the government in the Philippine Islands as far as is not inconsistent with the provisions of this Act, and shall be commander in chief of all locally created armed forces and militia. He is hereby vested with the exclusive power to grant pardons and reprieves and remit fines and forfeitures, and may veto any legislation enacted as herein provided. He shall submit within ten days of the opening of each regular session of the Philippine Legislature a budget of receipts and expenditures, which shall be the basis of the annual appropriation bill. He shall commission all officers that he may be authorized to appoint. He shall be responsible for the faithful execution of the laws of the Philippine Islands and of the United States operative within the Philippine Islands, and whenever it becomes necessary he may call upon the commanders of the military and naval forces of the United States in the islands, or summon the posse comitatus, or call out the militia or other locally created armed forces, to prevent or suppress lawless violence, invasion, insurrection, or rebellion; and he may, in case of rebellion or invasion, or imminent danger thereof, when the public safety requires it, suspend the privileges of the writ of habeas corpus, or place the islands, or any part thereof, under martial law: *Provided,* That whenever the Governor General shall exercise this authority, he shall at once notify the President of the United States thereof, together with the attending facts and circumstances, and the President shall have power to modify or vacate the action of the Governor General. He shall annually and at such other times as he may be required make such official report of the transactions of the government of the Philippine Islands to an executive department of the United States to be designated by the President, and his said annual report shall be transmitted to the Congress of the United States; and he shall perform such additional duties and functions as may in pursuance of law be delegated or assigned to him by the President.

SEC. 22. That, except as provided otherwise in this Act, the executive departments of the Philippine government shall continue as now authorized by law until otherwise provided by the Philippine Legislature. When the Philippine Legislature herein provided shall convene and organize, the Philippine Commission, as such, shall cease and determine, and the members thereof shall vacate their offices as members of said commission: *Provided,* That the heads of executive departments shall continue to exercise their executive functions until the heads of departments provided by the Philippine Legislature pursuant to the provisions of this Act are appointed and qualified. The Philippine Legislature may thereafter by appropriate legislation increase the number or abolish any of the executive departments, or make such changes in the names and duties thereof as it may see fit, and shall provide for the appointment and removal of the heads of the executive departments by the Governor General: *Provided,* That all executive functions of the government must be directly under the Governor General or within one of the executive departments under the supervision and control of the Governor General. There is hereby established a bureau, to be known as the Bureau of Non-Christian tribes, which said bureau shall be embraced in one of the executive departments to be designated by the Governor General, and shall have general supervision over the public affairs of the inhabitants of the territory represented in the legislature by appointive senators and representatives.

Sec. 23. That there shall be appointed by the President, by and with the advice and consent of the Senate of the United States, a vice governor of the Philippine Islands, who shall have all of the powers of the Governor General in the case of a vacancy or temporary removal, resignation, or disability of the Governor General, or in case of his temporary absence; and the said vice governor shall be the head of the executive department, known as the department of public instruction, which shall include the bureau of education and the bureau of health, and he may be assigned such other executive duties as the Governor General may designate.

Other bureaus now included in the department of public instruction shall, until otherwise provided by the Philippine Legislature, be included in the department of the interior.

The President may designate the head of an executive department of the Philippine government to act as Governor General in the case of a vacancy, the temporary removal, resignation, or disability of the Governor General and the vice governor, or their temporary absence, and the head of the department thus designated shall exercise all the powers and perform all the duties of the Governor General during such vacancy, disability, or absence.

Sec. 24. That there shall be appointed by the President an auditor, who shall examine, audit, and settle all accounts pertaining to the revenues and receipts from whatever source of the Philippine government and of the provincial and municipal governments of the Philippines, including trust funds and funds derived from bond issues; and audit, in accordance with law and administrative regulations, all expenditures of funds or property pertaining to or held in trust by the government or the Provinces or municipalities thereof. He shall perform a like duty with respect to all government branches.

He shall keep the general accounts of the government and preserve the vouchers pertaining thereto.

It shall be the duty of the auditor to bring to the attention of the proper administrative officer expenditures of fund or property which, in his opinion, are irregular, unnecessary, excessive, or extravagant.

There shall be a deputy auditor appointed in the same manner as the auditor. The deputy auditor shall sign such official papers as the auditor may designate and perform such other duties as the auditor may prescribe, and in case of death, resignation, sickness, or other absence of the auditor from his office, from any cause, the deputy auditor shall have charge of such office. In case of the absence from duty, from any cause, of both the auditor and the deputy auditor, the Governor General may designate an assistant, who shall have charge of the office.

The administrative jurisdiction of the auditor over accounts, whether of funds or property, and all vouchers and records pertaining thereto, shall be exclusive. With the approval of the Governor General he shall from time to time make and promulgate general or special rules and regulations not inconsistent with law covering the method of accounting for public funds and property, and funds and property held in trust by the government or any of its branches: *Provided*, That any officer accountable for public funds or property may require such additional reports or returns from his subordinates or others as he may deem necessary for his own information and protection.

The decisions of the auditor shall be final and conclusive upon the executive branches of the government, except that appeal therefrom may be taken by the party aggrieved or the head of the department concerned within one year, in the manner hereinafter prescribed. The auditor shall, except as hereinafter provided, have like authority as that conferred by law upon the several auditors of the United States and the Comptroller of the United States Treasury and is authorized to communicate directly with any person having claims before him for settlement, or with any department, officer, or person having official relations with his office.

As soon after the close of each fiscal year as the accounts of said year may be examined and adjusted the auditor shall submit to the Governor General and the Secretary of War an annual report of the fiscal concerns of the government, showing the receipts and disbursements of the various departments and bureaus of the government and of the various Provinces and municipalities, and make such other reports as may be required of him by the Governor General or the Secretary of War.

In the execution of their duties the auditor and the deputy auditor are authorized to summon witnesses, administer oaths, and to take evidence, and, in the pursuance of these provisions, may issue subpoenas and enforce the attendance of witnesses, as now provided by law.

The office of the auditor shall be under the general supervision of the Governor General and shall consist of the auditor and deputy auditor and such necessary assistants as may be prescribed by law.

SEC. 25. That any person aggrieved by the action or decision of the auditor in the settlement of his account or claim may, within one year, take an appeal in writing to the Governor General, which appeal shall specifically set forth the particular action of the auditor to which exception is taken, with the reason and authorities relied on for reversing such decision.

If the Governor General shall confirm the action of the auditor, he shall so indorse the appeal and transmit it to the auditor, and the action shall thereupon be final and conclusive. Should the Governor General fail to sustain the action of the auditor, he shall forthwith transmit his grounds of disapproval to the Secretary of War, together with the appeal and the papers necessary to a proper understanding of the matter. The decision of the Secretary of War in such case shall be final and conclusive.

SEC. 26. That the supreme court and the courts of first instance of the Philippine Islands shall possess and exercise jurisdiction as heretofore provided and such additional jurisdiction as shall hereafter be prescribed by law. The municipal courts of said islands shall possess and exercise jurisdiction as now provided by law, subject in all matters to such alteration and amendment as may be hereafter enacted by law; and the chief justice and associate justices of the supreme court shall hereafter be appointed by the President, by and with the advice and consent of the Senate of the United States. The judges of the court of first instance shall be appointed by the Governor General, by and with the advice and consent of the Philippine Senate: *Provided*, That the admiralty jurisdiction of the supreme court and courts of first instance shall not be changed except by Act of Congress. That in all cases pending under the operation of existing laws, both criminal and civil, the jurisdiction shall continue until final judgment and determination.

SEC. 27 (repealed and superseded by provisions of Act of Congress approved February 13, 1925, pertinent extracts of which are attached hereto on p. 179).

SEC. 28. That the government of the Philippine Islands may grant franchises and rights, including the authority to exercise the right of eminent domain, for the construction and operation of works of public utility and service, and may authorize said works to be constructed and maintained over and across the public property of the United States, including streets, highways, squares, and reservations, and over similar property of the government of said islands, and may adopt rules and regulations under which the provincial and municipal governments of the islands may grant the right to use and occupy such public property belonging to said Provinces or municipalities: *Provided,* That no private property shall be damaged or taken for any purpose under this section without just compensation, and that such authority to take and occupy land shall not authorize the taking, use, or occupation of any land except such as is required for the actual necessary purposes for which the franchise is granted, and that no franchise or right shall be granted to any individual, firm, or corporation except under the conditions that it shall be subject to amendment, alteration, or repeal by the Congress of the United States, and that lands or right of use and occupation of lands thus granted shall revert to the governments by which they were respectively granted upon the termination of the franchises and rights under which they were granted or upon their revocation or repeal. That all franchises or rights granted under this Act shall forbid the issue of stock or bonds except in exchange for actual cash or for property at a fair valuation equal to the par value of the stock or bonds so issued; shall forbid the declaring of stock or bond dividends, and, in the case of public-service corporations, shall provide for the effective regulation of the charges thereof, for the official inspection and regulation of the books and accounts of such corporations, and for the payment of a reasonable percentage of gross earnings into the treasury of the Philippine Islands or of the Province or municipality within which such franchises are granted and exercised: *Provided further,* That it shall be unlawful for any corporation organized under this Act, or for any person, company, or corporation receiving any grant, franchise, or concession from the government of said islands, to use, employ, or contract for the labor of persons held in involuntary servitude; and any person, company, or corporation so violating the provisions of this Act shall forfeit all charters, grants, or franchises for doing business in said islands, in an action or proceeding brought for that purpose in any court of competent jurisdiction by any officer of the Philippine government, or on the complaint of any citizen of the Philippines, under such regulations and rules as the Philippine Legislature shall prescribe, and in addition shall be deemed guilty of an offense, and shall be punished by a fine of not more than $10,000.

SEC. 29. That, except as in this Act otherwise provided, the salaries of all the officials of the Philippines not appointed by the President, including deputies, assistants, and other employees, shall be such and be so paid out of the revenues of the Philippines as shall from time to time be determined by the Philippine Legislature; and if the legislature shall fail to make an appropriation for such salaries, the salaries so fixed shall be paid without the necessity of further appropriations therefor. The salaries of all officers and all expenses of the offices of the various officials of the Philippines appointed as herein provided by the President shall also be paid out of the revenues of the Philippines. The annual salaries of the following-named officials appointed by the President and so to be paid shall be: The Governor General, $18,000; in addition thereto he shall be entitled to the occupancy of the buildings heretofore used by the chief executive of the Philippines, with the furniture and effects therein, free of rental; vice governor, $10,000; chief justice of the supreme court, $8,000; associate justices of the supreme court, $7,500 each;[5] auditor, $6,000; deputy auditor, $3,000.

Sec. 30. That the provisions of the foregoing section shall not apply to provincial and municipal officials; their salaries and the compensation of their deputies, assistants, and other help, as well as all other expenses incurred by the Provinces and municipalities, shall be paid out of the provincial and municipal revenues in such manner as the Philippine Legislature shall provide.

Sec. 31. That all laws or parts of laws applicable to the Philippines not in conflict with any of the provisions of this Act are hereby continued in force and effect.

Approved, August 29, 1916.

## Extracts from Act of Congress Approved February 13, 1925
### [public—no. 415—68th congress]

Sec. 7. That in any case in the Supreme Court of the Philippine Islands wherein the Constitution, or any statute or treaty of the United States is involved, or wherein the value in controversy exceeds $25,000, or wherein the title or possession of real estate exceeding in value the sum of $25,000 is involved or brought in question, it shall be competent for the Supreme Court of the United States, upon the petition of a party aggrieved by the final judgment or decree, to require, by certiorari, that the cause be certified to it for review and determination with the same

---

[5]Act of Congress of May 29, 1928, provides that following salaries shall be paid: To the chief justice of the Supreme Court of the Philippine Islands $10,500 per year, and to each of the associate justices thereof $10,000 per year.

power and authority, and with like effect, as if the cause had been brought before it on writ of error or appeal; and, except as provided in this section, the judgments and decrees of the Supreme Court of the Philippine Islands shall not be subject to appellate review.

Sec. 8. (a) That no writ of error, appeal, or writ of certiorari intended to bring any judgment or decree before the Supreme Court for review shall be allowed or entertained unless application therefor be duly made within three months after the entry of such judgment or decree, excepting that writs of certiorari to the Supreme Court of the Philippine Islands may be granted where application therefor is made within six months: *Provided,* That for good cause shown either of such periods for applying for a writ of certiorari may be extended not exceeding sixty days by a justice of the Supreme Court.

\* \* \* \* \* \* \*

(d) In any case in which the final judgment or decree of any court is subject to review by the Supreme Court on writ of certiorari, the execution and enforcement of such judgment or decree may be stayed for a reasonable time to enable the party aggrieved to apply for and to obtain a writ of certiorari from the Supreme Court. The stay may be granted by a judge of the court rendering the judgment or decree or by a justice of the Supreme Court, and may be conditioned on the giving of good and sufficient security, to be approved by such judge or justice, that if the aggrieved party fails to make application for such writ within the period allotted therefor, or fails to obtain an order granting his application, or fails to make his plea good in the Supreme Court, he shall answer for all damages and costs which the other party may sustain by reason of the stay.

Sec. 9. That in any case where the power to review, whether in the circuit courts of appeals or in the Supreme Court, depends upon the amount or value in controversy, such amount or value, if not otherwise satisfactorily disclosed upon the record, may be shown and ascertained by the oath of a party to the cause or by other competent evidence.

\* \* \* \* \* \* \*

Sec. 13. That the following statutes and parts of statutes be, and they are, repealed: \* \* \*

Section 27 of "An Act to declare the purpose of the people of the United States as to the future political status of the people of the Philippine Islands, and to provide a more autonomous government for those islands," approved August 29, 1916. \* \* \*

# III. THE TYDINGS-McDUFFIE INDEPENDENCE ACT

[PUBLIC—No. 127—73D CONGRESS]

[H. R. 8573]

## AN ACT

*To provide for the complete independence of the Philippine Islands, to provide for the adoption of a constitution and a form of government for the Philippine Islands, and for other purposes.*

*Be it enacted by the Senate and House of Representatives of the United States of America in Congress assembled,*

### CONVENTION TO FRAME CONSTITUTION FOR PHILIPPINE ISLANDS

---

SECTION 1. The Philippine Legislature is hereby authorized to provide for the election of delegates to a constitutional convention, which shall meet in the hall of the house of representatives in the capital of the Philippine Islands, at such time as the Philippine Legislature may fix, but not later than October 1, 1934, to formulate and draft a constitution for the government of the Commonwealth of the Philippine Islands, subject to the conditions and qualifications prescribed in this Act, which shall exercise jurisdiction over all the territory ceded to the United States by the treaty of peace concluded between the United States and Spain on the 10th day of December 1898, the boundaries of which are set forth in article III of said treaty, together with those islands embraced in the treaty between Spain and the United States concluded at Washington on the 7th day of November 1900. The Philippine Legislature shall provide for the necessary expenses of such convention.

### CHARACTER OF CONSTITUTION—MANDATORY PROVISIONS

SEC. 2 (a) The constitution formulated and drafted shall be republican in form, shall contain a bill of rights, and shall, either as a part thereof or in an ordinance appended thereto, contain provisions to the effect

181

that, pending the final and complete withdrawal of the sovereignty of the United States over the Philippine Islands—

(1) All citizens of the Philippine Islands shall owe allegiance to the United States.

(2) Every officer of the government of the Commonwealth of the Philippine Islands shall, before entering upon the discharge of his duties, take and subscribe an oath of office, declaring, among other things, that he recognizes and accepts the supreme authority of and will maintain true faith and allegiance to the United States.

(3) Absolute toleration of religious sentiment shall be secured and no inhabitant or religious organization shall be molested in person or property on account of religious belief or mode of worship.

(4) Property owned by the United States, cemeteries, churches, and parsonages or convents appurtenant thereto, and all lands, buildings, and improvements used exclusively for religious, charitable, or educational purposes shall be exempt from taxation.

(5) Trade relations between the Philippine Islands and the United States shall be upon the basis prescribed in section 6.

(6) The public debt of the Philippine Islands and its subordinate branches shall not exceed limits now or hereafter fixed by the Congress of the United States; and no loans shall be contracted in foreign countries without the approval of the President of the United States.

(7) The debts, liabilities, and obligations of the present Philippine government, its Provinces, municipalities, and instrumentalities, valid and subsisting at the time of the adoption of the constitution, shall be assumed and paid by the new government.

(8) Provision shall be made for the establishment and maintenance of an adequate system of public schools, primarily conducted in the English language.

(9) Acts affecting currency, coinage, imports, exports, and immigration shall not become law until approved by the President of the United States.

(10) Foreign affairs shall be under the direct supervision and control of the United States.

(11) All acts passed by the Legislature of the Commonwealth of the Philippine Islands shall be reported to the Congress of the United States.

(12) The Philippine Islands recognizes the right of the United States to expropriate property for public uses, to maintain military and other reservations and armed forces in the Philippines, and, upon order of the President, to call into the service of such armed forces all military forces organized by the Philippine government.

(13) The decisions of the courts of the Commonwealth of the Philippine Islands shall be subject to review by the Supreme Court of the United States as provided in paragraph (6) of section 7.

(14) The United States may, by Presidential proclamation, exercise the right to intervene for the preservation of the government of the Commonwealth of the Philippine Islands and for the maintenance of the government as provided in the constitution thereof, and for the protection of life, property, and individual liberty and for the discharge of government obligations under and in accordance with the provisions of the constitution.

(15) The authority of the United States High Commissioner to the government of the Commonwealth of the Philippine Islands, as provided in this Act, shall be recognized.

(16) Citizens and corporations of the United States shall enjoy in the Commonwealth of the Philippine Islands all the civil rights of the citizens and corporations, respectively, thereof.

(b) The constitution shall also contain the following provisions, effective as of the date of the proclamation of the President recognizing the independence of the Philippine Islands, as hereinafter provided:

(1) That the property rights of the United States and the Philippine Islands shall be promptly adjusted and settled, and that all existing property rights of citizens or corporations of the United States shall be acknowledged, respected, and safeguarded to the same extent as property rights of citizens of the Philippine Islands.

(2) That the officials elected and serving under the constitution adopted pursuant to the provisions of this Act shall be constitutional officers of the free and independent government of the Philippine Islands and qualified to function in all respects as if elected directly under such government, and shall serve their full terms of office as prescribed in the constitution.

(3) That the debts and liabilities of the Philippine Islands, its Provinces, cities, municipalities, and instrumentalities, which shall be valid and subsisting at the time of the final and complete withdrawal of the sovereignty of the United States, shall be assumed by the free and independent government of the Philippine Islands; and that where bonds have been issued under authority of an Act of Congress of the United States by the Philippine Islands, or any Province, city, or municipality therein, the Philippine government will make adequate provision for the necessary funds for the payment of interest and principal, and such obligations shall be a first lien on the taxes collected in the Philippine Islands.

(4) That the government of the Philippine Islands, on becoming independent of the United States, will assume all continuing obligations assumed by the United States under the treaty of peace with Spain ceding said Philippine Islands to the United States.

(5) That by way of further assurance the government of the Philippine Islands will embody the foregoing provisions (except paragraph (2)) in a treaty with the United States.

### SUBMISSION OF CONSTITUTION TO THE PRESIDENT OF THE UNITED STATES

Sec. 3. Upon the drafting and approval of the constitution by the constitutional convention in the Philippine Islands, the constitution shall be submitted within two years after the enactment of this Act to the President of the United States, who shall determine whether or not it conforms with the provisions of this Act. If the President finds that the proposed constitution conforms substantially with the provisions of this Act he shall so certify to the Governor General of the Philippine Islands, who shall so advise the constitutional convention. If the President finds that the constitution does not conform with the provisions of this Act he shall so advise the Governor General of the Philippine Islands, stating wherein in his judgment the constitution does not so conform and submitting provisions which will in his judgment make the constitution so conform. The Governor General shall in turn submit such message to the constitutional convention for further action by them pursuant to the same procedure hereinbefore defined, until the President and the constitutional convention are in agreement.

### SUBMISSION OF CONSTITUTION TO FILIPINO PEOPLE

Sec. 4. After the President of the United States has certified that the constitution conforms with the provisions of this Act, it shall be submitted to the people of the Philippine Islands for their ratification or rejection at an election to be held within four months after the date of such certification, on a date to be fixed by the Philippine Legislature, at which election the qualified voters of the Philippine Islands shall have an opportunity to vote directly for or against the proposed constitution and ordinances appended thereto. Such election shall be held in such manner as may be prescribed by the Philippine Legislature, to which the return of the election shall be made. The Philippine Legislature shall by law provide for the canvassing of the return and shall certify the result to the Governor General of the Philippine Islands, together with a statement of the votes cast, and a copy of said constitution and ordinances. If a majority of the votes cast shall be for the constitution, such vote shall be deemed an expression of the will of the people of the Philippine Islands in favor of Philippine independence, and the Governor General shall, within thirty days after receipt of the certification from the Philippine Legislature, issue a proclamation for the election of officers of the government of the Commonwealth of the Philippine Islands provided for in the constitution. The election shall take place not earlier than three months nor later than six months after the proclamation by the Governor General ordering such election. When the election of the officers provided for under the constitution has been held and the results determined, the Governor General of the Philippine Islands shall certify the results of the election to the President of the United States, who shall thereupon issue a proclamation announcing the results of the election, and upon the issuance of such proclamation by the President the existing Philippine government shall terminate and the new government shall enter upon its rights, privileges, powers, and duties, as provided under the constitution. The present government of the Philippine Islands shall provide for the orderly transfer of the functions of government.

If a majority of the votes cast are against the constitution, the existing government of the Philippine Islands shall continue without regard to the provisions of this Act.

#### TRANSFER OF PROPERTY AND RIGHTS TO PHILIPPINE COMMONWEALTH

SEC. 5. All the property and rights which may have been acquired in the Philippine Islands by the United States under the treaties mentioned in the first section of this Act, except such land or other property as has heretofore been designated by the President of the United States for Military and other reservations of the Government of the United States, and except such land or other property or rights or interests therein as may have been sold or otherwise disposed of in accordance with law, are hereby granted to the government of the Commonwealth of the Philippine Islands when constituted.

#### RELATIONS WITH THE UNITED STATES PENDING COMPLETE INDEPENDENCE

SEC. 6. After the date of the inauguration of the government of the Commonwealth of the Philippine Islands trade relations between the United States and the Philippine Islands shall be as now provided by law, subject to the following exceptions:

(a) There shall be levied, collected, and paid on all refined sugars in excess of fifty thousand long tons, and on unrefined sugars in excess of eight hundred thousand long tons, coming into the United States from the Philippine Islands in any calendar year, the same rates of duty which are required by the laws of the United States to be levied, collected, and paid upon like articles imported from foreign countries.

(b)  There shall be levied, collected, and paid on all coconut oil coming into the United States from the Philippine Islands in any calendar year in excess of two hundred thousand long tons, the same rates of duty which are required by the laws of the United States to be levied, collected, and paid upon like articles imported from foreign countries.

(c)  There shall be levied, collected, and paid on all yarn, twine, cord, cordage, rope and cable, tarred or untarred, wholly or in chief value of manila (abaca) or other hard fibers, coming into the United States from the Philippine Islands in any calendar year in excess of a collective total of three million pounds of all such articles hereinbefore enumerated, the same rates of duty which are required by the laws of the United States to be levied, collected, and paid upon like articles imported from foreign countries.

(d)  In the event that in any year the limit in the case of any article which may be exported to the United States free of duty shall be reached by the Philippine Islands, the amount or quantity of such articles produced or manufactured in the Philippine Islands thereafter that may be so exported to the United States free of duty shall be allocated, under export permits issued by the government of the Commonwealth of the Philippine Islands, to the producers or manufacturers of such articles proportionately on the basis of their exportation to the United States in the preceding year; except that in the case of unrefined sugar the amount thereof to be exported annually to the United States free of duty shall be allocated to the sugar-producing mills of the islands proportionately on the basis of their average annual production for the calendar years 1931, 1932, and 1933, and the amount of sugar from each mill which may be so exported shall be allocated in each year between the mill and the planters on the basis of the proportion of sugar to which the mill and the planters are respectively entitled. The government of the Philippine Islands is authorized to adopt the necessary laws and regulations for putting into effect the allocation hereinbefore provided.

(e)  The government of the Commonwealth of the Philippine Islands shall impose and collect an export tax on all articles that may be exported to the United States from the Philippine Islands free of duty under the provisions of existing law as modified by the foregoing provisions of this section, including the articles enumerated in subdivisions (a), (b), and (c), within the limitations therein specified, as follows:

(1) During the sixth year after the inauguration of the new government the export tax shall be 5 per centum of the rates of duty which are required by the laws of the United States to be levied, collected, and paid on like articles imported from foreign countries;

(2) During the seventh year after the inauguration of the new government the export tax shall be 10 per centum of the rates of duty which are required by the laws of the United States to be levied, collected, and paid on like articles imported from foreign countries;

(3) During the eighth year after the inauguration of the new government the export tax shall be 15 per centum of the rates of duty which are required by the laws of the United States to be levied, collected, and paid on like articles imported from foreign countries;

(4) During the ninth year after the inauguration of the new government the export tax shall be 20 per centum of the rates of duty which are required by the laws of the United States to be levied, collected, and paid on like articles imported from foreign countries;

(5) After the expiration of the ninth year after the inauguration of the new government the export tax shall be 25 per centum of the rates of duty which are required by the laws of the United States to be levied, collected, and paid on like articles imported from foreign countries.

The government of the Commonwealth of the Philippine Islands shall place all funds received from such export taxes in a sinking fund, and such funds shall, in addition to other moneys available for that purpose, be applied solely to the payment of the principal and interest on the bonded indebtedness of the Philippine Islands, its Provinces, municipalities, and instrumentalities, until such indebtedness has been fully discharged.

When used in this section in a geographical sense, the term "United States" includes all Territories and possessions of the United States, except the Philippine Islands, the Virgin Islands, American Samoa, and the island of Guam.

SEC. 7. Until the final and complete withdrawal of American sovereignty over the Philippine Islands—

(1) Every duly adopted amendment to the constitution of the government of the Commonwealth of the Philippine Islands shall be submitted to the President of the United States for approval. If the President approves the amendment or if the President fails to disapprove such amendment within six months from the time of its sub-

mission, the amendment shall take effect as a part of such constitution.

(2) The President of the United States shall have authority to suspend the taking effect of or the operation of any law, contract, or executive order of the government of the Commonwealth of the Philippine Islands, which in his judgment will result in a failure of the government of the Commonwealth of the Philippine Islands to fulfill its contracts, or to meet its bonded indebtedness and interest thereon or to provide for its sinking funds, or which seems likely to impair the reserves for the protection of the currency of the Philippine Islands, or which in his judgment will violate international obligations of the United States.

(3) The Chief Executive of the Commonwealth of the Philippine Islands shall make an annual report to the President and Congress of the United States of the proceedings and operations of the government of the Commonwealth of the Philippine Islands and shall make such other reports as the President or Congress may request.

(4) The President shall appoint, by and with the advice and consent of the Senate, a United States High Commissioner to the government of the Commonwealth of the Philippine Islands who shall hold office at the pleasure of the President and until his successor is appointed and qualified. He shall be known as the United States High Commissioner to the Philippine Islands. He shall be the representative of the President of the United States in the Philippine Islands and shall be recognized as such by the government of the Commonwealth of the Philippine Islands, by the commanding officers of the military forces of the United States, and by all civil officials of the United States in the Philippine Islands. He shall have access to all records of the government or any subdivision thereof, and shall be furnished by the Chief Executive of the Commonwealth of the Philippine Islands with such information as he shall request.

If the government of the Commonwealth of the Philippine Islands fails to pay any of its bonded or other indebtedness or the interest thereon when due or to fulfill any of its contracts, the United States High Commissioner shall immediately report the facts to the President, who may thereupon direct the High Commissioner to take over the customs offices and administration of the same, administer the same, and apply such part of the revenue received therefrom as may be necessary for the payment of such overdue indebtedness or for the fulfillment of such contracts. The United States High Commissioner shall annually, and at such other times as the President may require, render an official report to the President and Congress of the United States. He shall perform such additional duties and functions as may be delegated to him from time to time by the President under the provisions of this Act.

The United States High Commissioner shall receive the same compensation as is now received by the Governor General of the Philippine Islands, and shall have such staff and assistants as the President may deem advisable and as may be appropriated for by Congress, including a financial expert, who shall receive for submission to the High Commissioner a duplicate copy of the reports of the insular auditor. Appeals from decisions of the insular auditor may be taken to the President of the United States. The salaries and expenses of the High Commissioner and his staff and assistants shall be paid by the United States.

The first United States High Commissioner appointed under this Act shall take office upon the inauguration of the new government of the Commonwealth of the Philippine Islands.

(5) The government of the Commonwealth of the Philippine Islands shall provide for the selection of a Resident Commissioner to the United States, and shall fix his term of office. He shall be the representative of the government of the Commonwealth of the Philippine Islands and shall be entitled to official recognition as such by all departments upon presentation to the President of credentials signed by the Chief Executive of said government. He shall have a seat in the House of Representatives of the United States, with the right of debate, but without the right of voting. His salary and expenses shall be fixed and paid by the government of the Philippine Islands. Until a Resident Commissioner is selected and qualified under this section, existing law governing the appointment of Resident Commissioners from the Philippine Islands shall continue in effect.

(6) Review by the Supreme Court of the United States of cases from the Philippine Islands shall be as now provided by law; and such review shall also extend to all cases involving the constitution of the Commonwealth of the Philippine Islands.

SEC. 8. (a) Effective upon the acceptance of this Act by concurrent resolution of the Philippine Legislature or by a convention called for that purpose, as provided in section 17—

(1) For the purposes of the Immigration Act of 1917, the Immigration Act of 1924 (except section 13(c)), this section, and all other laws of the United States relating to the immigration, exclusion, or expulsion of aliens, citizens of the Philippine Islands who are not citizens of the United States shall be considered as if they were aliens. For such purposes the Philippine Islands shall be considered as a separate country and shall have for each fiscal year a quota of fifty. This para-

graph shall not apply to a person coming or seeking to come to the Territory of Hawaii who does not apply for and secure an immigration or passport visa, but such immigration shall be determined by the Department of the Interior on the basis of the needs of industries in the Territory of Hawaii.

(2) Citizens of the Philippine Islands who are not citizens of the United States shall not be admitted to the continental United States from the Territory of Hawaii (whether entering such Territory before or after the effective date of this section) unless they belong to a class declared to be nonimmigrants by section 3 of the Immigration Act of 1924 or to a class declared to be nonquota immigrants under the provisions of section 4 of such Act other than subdivision (c) thereof, or unless they were admitted to such Territory under an immigration visa. The Secretary of Labor shall by regulations provide a method for such exclusion and for the admission of such excepted classes.

(3) Any Foreign Service officer may be assigned to duty in the Philippine Islands, under a commission as a consular officer, for such period as may be necessary and under such regulations as the Secretary of State may prescribe, during which assignment such officers shall be considered as stationed in a foreign country; but his powers and duties shall be confined to the performance of such of the official acts and notarial and other services, which such officer might properly perform in respect of the administration of the immigration laws if assigned to a foreign country as a consular officer, as may be authorized by the Secretary of State.

(4) For the purposes of sections 18 and 20 of the Immigration Act of 1917, as amended, the Philippine Islands shall be considered to be a foreign country.

(b) The provisions of this section are in addition to the provisions of the immigration laws now in force, and shall be enforced as a part of such laws, and all the penal or other provisions of such laws not inapplicable, shall apply to and be enforced in connection with the provisions of this section. An alien, although admissible under the provisions of this section, shall not be admitted to the United States if he is excluded by any provision of the immigration laws other than this section, and an alien, although admissible under the provisions of the immigration laws other than this section, shall not be admitted to the United States if he is excluded by any provision of this section.

(c) Terms defined in the Immigration Act of 1924 shall, when used in this section, have the meaning assigned to such terms in that Act.

SEC. 9. There shall be no obligation on the part of the United States to meet the interest or principal of bonds and other obligations of the government of the Philippine Islands or of the Provincial and municipal governments thereof, hereafter issued during the continuance of United States sovereignty in the Philippine Islands: *Provided,* That such bonds and obligations hereafter issued shall not be exempt from taxation in the United States or by authority of the United States.

### RECOGNITION OF PHILIPPINE INDEPENDENCE AND WITHDRAWAL OF AMERICAN SOVEREIGNTY

SEC. 10.(a) On the 4th day of July immediately following the expiration of a period of ten years from the date of the inauguration of the new government under the constitution provided for in this Act the President of the United States shall by proclamation withdraw and surrender all right of possession, supervision, jurisdiction, control, or sovereignty then existing and exercised by the United States in and over the territory and people of the Philippine Islands, including all military and other reservations of the Government of the United States in the Philippines (except such naval reservations and fueling stations as are reserved under section 5), and, on behalf of the United States, shall recognize the independence of the Philippine Islands as a separate and self-governing nation and acknowledge the authority and control over the same of the government instituted by the people thereof, under the constitution then in force.

(b) The President of the United States is hereby authorized and empowered to enter into negotiations with the government of the Philippine Islands, not later than two years after his proclamation recognizing the independence of the Philippine Islands, for the adjustment and settlement of all questions relating to naval reservations and fueling stations of the United States in the Philippine Islands, and pending such adjustment and settlement the matter of naval reservations and fueling stations shall remain in its present status.

### NEUTRALIZATION OF PHILIPPINE ISLANDS

SEC. 11. The President is requested, at the earliest practicable date, to enter into negotiations with foreign powers with a view to the conclusion of a treaty for the perpetual neutralization of the Philippine Islands, if and when Philippine independence shall have been achieved.

### NOTIFICATION TO FOREIGN GOVERNMENTS

SEC. 12. Upon the proclamation and recognition of the independence of the Philippine Islands, the President shall notify the governments with which the United States is in diplomatic correspondence thereof and invite said governments to recognize the independence of the Philippine Islands.

### TARIFF DUTIES AFTER INDEPENDENCE

SEC. 13. After the Philippine Islands have become a free and independent nation there shall be levied, collected, and paid upon all articles coming into the United States from the Philippine Islands the rates of duty which are required to be levied, collected, and paid upon like articles imported from other foreign countries: *Provided,* That at least one year prior to the date fixed in this Act for the independence of the Philippine Islands, there shall be held a conference of representatives of the Government of the United States and the government of the Commonwealth of the Philippine Islands, such representatives to be appointed by the President of the United States and the Chief Executive of the Commonwealth of the Philippine Islands, respectively, for the purpose of formulating recommendations as to future trade relations between the Government of the United States and the independent government of the Philippine Islands, the time, place, and manner of holding such conference to be determined by the President of the United States; but nothing in this proviso shall be construed to modify or affect in any way any provision of this Act relating to the procedure leading up to Philippine independence or the date upon which the Philippine Islands shall become independent.

### IMMIGRATION AFTER INDEPENDENCE

SEC. 14. Upon the final and complete withdrawal of American sovereignty over the Philippine Islands the immigration laws of the United States (including all the provisions thereof relating to persons ineligible to citizenship) shall apply to persons who were born in the Philippine Islands to the same extent as in the case of other foreign countries.

### CERTAIN STATUTES CONTINUED IN FORCE

SEC. 15. Except as in this Act otherwise provided, the laws now or hereafter in force in the Philippine Islands shall continue in force in the Commonwealth of the Philippine Islands until altered, amended, or repealed by the Legislature of the Commonwealth of the Philippine Islands or by the Congress of the United States, and all references in such laws to the government or officials of the Philippines or Philippine Islands shall be construed, insofar as applicable, to refer to the government and corresponding officials respectively of the Commonwealth of the Philippine Islands. The government of the Commonwealth of the Philippine Islands shall be deemed successor to the present government of the Philippine Islands and of all the rights and obligations thereof. Except as otherwise provided in this Act, all laws or parts of laws relating to the present government of the Philippine Islands and its administration are hereby repealed as of the date of the inauguration of the government of the Commonwealth of the Philippine Islands.

SEC. 16. If any provision of this Act is declared unconstitutional or the applicability thereof to any person or circumstance is held invalid, the validity of the remainder of the Act and the applicability of such provisions to other persons and circumstances shall not be affected thereby.

### EFFECTIVE DATE

SEC. 17. The foregoing provisions of this Act shall not take effect until accepted by concurrent resolution of the Philippine Legislature or by a convention called for the purpose of passing upon that question as may be provided by the Philippine Legislature.

Approved, March 24, 1934.

# AMENDMENT TO THE TYDINGS-McDUFFIE ACT

[PUBLIC—NO. 300—76TH CONGRESS]
[CHAPTER 502—Ist SESSION]
[H. R. 7096]

## AN ACT

*To amend an Act entitled "An Act to provide for the complete independence of the Philippine Islands, to provide for the adoption of a constitution and a form of government for the Philippine Islands, and for other purposes."*

*Be it enacted by the Senate and House of Representatives of the United States of America in Congress assembled,* That section 6 of the Act of March 24, 1934, entitled "An Act to provide for the complete independence of the Philippine Islands, to provide for the adoption of a constitution and a form of government for the Philippine Islands, and for other purposes" (48 Stat. 456), is hereby amended to read as follows:

"SEC. 6. During the period beginning January 1, 1940, and ending July 3, 1946, trade relations between the United States and the Philippines shall be as now provided by law, subject to the following exceptions:

"(a) On and after January 1, 1941, the Philippine Government shall impose and collect an export tax on every Philippine article shipped from the Philippines to the United States, except as otherwise specifically provided in this section. Said tax shall be computed in the manner hereinafter set forth in this subsection and in subsection (c) of this section. During the period January 1, 1941, through December 31, 1941, the export tax on every such article shall be 5 per centum of the United States duty; on each succeeding January 1 thereafter the export tax shall be increased progressively by an additional 5 per centum of the United States duty, except that during the period January 1, 1946, through July 3, 1946, the export tax shall remain at 25 per centum of the United States duty.

"(b) (1) No export tax described in subsection (a) of this section shall be imposed or collected upon any Philippine article of a class or kind in respect of which a quota is established by subdivision (3) of this

194

subsection, nor upon copra or manila (abaca) fiber not dressed or manufactured in any manner.

"(2) The United States duty shall be levied, collected, and paid in the United States upon every article which is of a class or kind in respect of which a quota is established by subdivision (3) of this subsection and which is entered, or withdrawn from warehouse, for consumption after December 31, 1939, in excess of its respective quota: *Provided, however,* That nothing in this section or any subsection thereof shall be construed to exempt the quota of coconut oil therein provided for from the excise taxes provided for in section 2470 of the Internal Revenue Code (I. R. C., ch. 21, sec. 2470).

"(3) For the purposes indicated in subdivisions (1) and (2) of this subsection, there are hereby established the following quotas of the designated Philippine articles: For the calendar year 1940, the quotas, hereafter called original quotas, shall be as follows:

"a. cigars (exclusive of cigarettes, cheroots of all kinds, and paper cigars and cigarettes including wrappers), two hundred million cigars;

"b. scrap tobacco, and stemmed and unstemmed filler tobacco described in paragraph 602 of the Tariff Act of 1930, four million five hundred thousand pounds;

"c. coconut oil, two hundred thousand long tons;

"d. buttons of pearl or shell, eight hundred and fifty thousand gross.

For each calendar year thereafter through the calendar year 1945, each of the said quotas shall be the same as the corresponding quota for the immediately preceding calendar year, less 5 per centum of the corresponding original quota.

"For the period January 1, 1946, through July 3, 1946, each of said quotas shall be one-half of the corresponding quota specified for the calendar year 1945.

"(c) The Philippine Government, in imposing and collecting export taxes on Philippine embroideries, shall compute the tax in accordance with the formulas specified in subsection (a) of this section, except that in determining the taxable value of any such article, an allowance shall be made equal to the cost—cost, insurance, and freight the Philippines— of any cloth of United States origin used in the production thereof.

"(d) The United States duty shall be levied, collected, and paid, in the United States, upon all Philippine sugars, which are entered, or withdrawn from warehouse, for consumption in any calendar year after 1939, in excess of eight hundred and fifty thousand long tons, of which not more than fifty thousand long tons may be refined sugars: *Provided, however,* That for the period January 1, 1946, through July 3, 1946, the quota of Philippine sugars, not subject to the United States duty, shall be four hundred and twenty-five thousand long tons, of which not more than twenty-five thousand long tons may be refined sugars. Any export tax imposed and collected on Philippine sugars entered or withdrawn from warehouse for consumption in excess of the quotas established by this subsection shall be refunded by the Philippine Government.

"(e) Upon the expiration of the Act of June 14, 1935 (49 Stat. 340), as extended to May 1, 1941, by proclamation of the President, dated January 26, 1938, the total amount of all Philippine cordage coming into the United States which may be entered or withdrawn from warehouse, for consumption during the remainder of the calendar year 1941, shall not exceed four million pounds and in any calendar year after 1941 shall not exceed six million pounds: *Provided, however,* That for the period January 1, 1946, through July 3, 1946, the total amount of Philippine cordage which may be entered, or withdrawn from warehouse, for consumption shall not exceed three million pounds.

"(f) (1) The quotas for sugars established by subsection (d) of this section shall be allocated annually as prescribed in section 6 (d) of the Act of March 24, 1934 (48 Stat. 456), which section in this respect is not repealed by this amendatory Act.

"(2) The quotas for cordage, established by subsection (e) of this section, and by the Act of June 14, 1935, shall be allocated by authorities of the Philippine Government among the manufacturers of such commodities proportionately upon the basis of the shipment of each such manufacturer to the United States during the twelve months immediately preceding the inauguration of the Commonwealth of the Philippines.

"(3) The quotas for all articles for which quotas are established by this section, except sugars and cordage, shall in each instance be allocated by authorities of the Philippine Government among the manufacturers whose products were shipped to the United States during the calendar year 1937, on the basis of the proportion which each manufacturer's maximum production shipped to the United States, directly or through other persons, in any calendar year during the five-year period, 1933 through 1937, bears to the total of such maximum shipments of all such manufacturers.

"(4) If, after the first nine months of any quota year, the holder of any allotment under any of the quotas established by this Act or by the

Act of June 14, 1935, is or will be unable for any reason to ship to the United States by the end of the quota year the total amount of his allocation for that year, the Philippine Government shall apportion that amount of such allocation which it is established by sufficient evidence cannot be shipped to the United States during the remainder of the quota year in such manner and in accordance with such rules and regulations as it may prescribe.

"(g) (1) The Philippine Government shall pay to the Secretary of the Treasury of the United States, at the end of each calendar quarter, all of the moneys received during such quarter from export taxes (less refunds), imposed and collected in accordance with the provisions of this section, and said moneys shall be deposited in an account with the Treasurer of the United States and shall constitute a supplementary sinking fund for the payment of bonds of the Philippines, its Provinces, cities, and municipalities, issued prior to May 1, 1934, under authority of Acts of Congress: *Provided, however,* That moneys received from any export tax imposed on any article which is shipped from the Philippines to the United States prior to July 4, 1946, and which is entered, or withdrawn from warehouse for consumption, on or after July 4, 1946, shall be refunded by the independent Government of the Philippines.

"(2) The said Secretary of the Treasury is authorized to accept the deposits of the proceeds of the export taxes referred to in subdivision (1) of this subsection in accordance with the Act of June 11, 1934 (48 Stat. 929).

"(3) The Secretary of the Treasury of the United States, with the approval of the Philippine Government, is authorized to purchase with such supplementary sinking-fund bonds of the Philippines, its Provinces, cities, and municipalities, issued prior to May 1, 1934, under authority of Acts of Congress and to invest such fund in interest-bearing obligations of the United States or in obligations guaranteed as to both principal and interest by the United States. Whenever the Secretary of the Treasury finds that such fund is in excess of an amount adequate to meet future interest and principal payments on all such bonds, he may, with the approval of the Philippine Government, purchase with such excess any other bonds of the Philippines, its Provinces, cities, municipalities, and instrumentalities. For the purpose of this subsection obligations may be acquired on original issue at par, or by purchase of outstanding obligations at the market price. Any obligations acquired by the fund may, with the approval of the Philippine Government, be sold by the Secretary of the Treasury at the market price and the proceeds of such sale and the proceeds of the payment upon maturity or redemption of any obligations held in the supplementary sinking fund, as well as all moneys in any manner earned by such fund or on any obligations acquired by said fund, shall be paid into the said fund.

"(4) During the three months preceding July 4, 1946, the Philippine Government and the Secretary of the Treasury of the United States shall confer to ascertain that portion of the bonds of the Philippines, its Provinces, cities, and municipalities, issued prior to May 1, 1934, under authority of Acts of Congress, which will remain outstanding on July 4, 1946; and the Philippine Government shall turn over to the Secretary of the Treasury of the United States for destruction all such bonds that are then held, canceled, or uncanceled, in any of the sinking funds maintained for the payment of such bonds. After such outstanding portion of this indebtedness is thus determined, and before July 4, 1946, (i) there shall be set up with the Treasurer of the United States a special trust account in the name of the Secretary of the Treasury of the United States to pay future interest and principal payments on such bonds; (ii) the Philippine government shall pay to the Secretary of the Treasury of the United States for deposit in this special trust account all of the sinking funds maintained for the payment of such bonds; and (iii) the Secretary of the Treasury of the United States shall transfer into this special trust account all of the proceeds of the supplementary sinking fund referred to in subdivision (1) of this subsection. Any portion of such special trust account found by the Secretary of the Treasury of the United States on July 4, 1946, to be in excess of an amount adequate to meet future interest and principal payments on all such outstanding bonds shall be turned over to the Treasury of the independent Government of the Philippines to be set up as an additional sinking fund to be used for the purpose of liquidating and paying all other obligations of the Philippines, its Provinces, cities, municipalities, and instrumentalities. To the extent that such special trust account is determined by the Secretary of the Treasury of the United States to be insufficient to pay interest and principal on the outstanding bonds of the Philippines, its Provinces, cities, and municipalities, issued prior to May 1, 1934, under authority of Acts of Congress, the Philippine Government shall, on or before July 3, 1946, pay to the Secretary of the Treasury of the United States for deposit in such special trust account an amount which said Secretary of the Treasury determines is required to assure payment of principal and interest on such bonds: *Provided, however,* That if the Secretary of the Treasury of the United States finds that this requirement would impose an undue hardship upon the Philippines, then the Philippine Government shall continue to provide annually the necessary funds for the payment of interest and principal on such bonds until such time as the Secretary of the Treasury of the United States determines that the amount in the special trust account is adequate to meet interest and principal payments on such bonds.

"(5) On and after July 4, 1946, the Secretary of the Treasury of the United States is authorized, with the approval of the independent Government of the Philippines, to purchase at the market price for the special trust account bonds of the Philippines, its Provinces, cities, and municipalities, issued prior to May 1, 1934, under authority of Acts of Congress. The Secretary of the Treasury of the United States is also authorized, with the approval of the independent Government of the Philippines, to invest all or any part of such special trust account in any interest-bearing obligations of the United States or in any obligations guaranteed as to both principal and interest by the United States. Such obligations may be acquired on original issue at par or by purchase of outstanding obligations at the market price, and any obligations acquired by the special trust account may, with the approval of the independent Government of the Philippines, be sold by the Secretary of the Treasury at the market price, and the proceeds of the payment upon maturity or redemption of such obligations shall be held as a part of such special trust account. Whenever the special trust account is determined by the Secretary of the Treasury of the United States to be adequate to meet interest and principal payments on all outstanding bonds of the Philippines, its Provinces, cities, and municipalities, issued prior to May 1, 1934, under authority of Acts of Congress, the Secretary of the Treasury is authorized to pay from such trust account the principal of such outstanding bonds and to pay all interest due and owing on such bonds. All such bonds and interest coupons paid or purchased by the special trust account shall be canceled and destroyed by the Secretary of the Treasury of the United States. From time to time after July 4, 1946, any moneys in such special trust account found by the Secretary of the Treasury of the United States to be in excess of an amount adequate to meet interest and principal payments on all such bonds shall be turned over to the treasurer of the independent Government of the Philippines.

"(h) No article shipped from the Philippines to the United States on or after January 1, 1941, subject to an export tax provided for in this section, shall be admitted to entry in the United States until the importer of such article shall present to the United States collector of customs a certificate, signed by a competent authority of the Philippine Government, setting forth the value and quantity of the article and the rate and amount of the export tax paid, or shall give a bond for the production of such certificate within six months from the date of entry."

SEC. 2. Section 8 of the said Act of March 24, 1934, is hereby amended by adding thereto a new subsection as follows:

"(d) Pending the final and complete withdrawal of the sovereignty of the United States over the Philippine Islands, except as otherwise provided by this Act, citizens and corporations of the Philippine Islands shall enjoy in the United States and all places subject to its jurisdiction all of the rights and privileges which they respectively shall have enjoyed therein under the laws of the United States in force at the time of the inauguration of the Government of the Commonwealth of the Philippine Islands."

SEC. 3. Section 10 of the said Act of March 24, 1934, is hereby amended by adding the following subsection thereto:

"(c) (1) Whenever the President of the United States shall find that any properties in the Philippines, owned by the Philippine Government or by private persons, would be suitable for diplomatic or consular establishments of the United States after the inauguration of the independent Government, he may, with the approval of the Philippine Government, and in exchange for the conveyance of title to the United States, transfer to the said Government or private persons any properties of the United States in the Philippines. Title to any properties so transferred to private persons, and title to any properties so acquired by the United States, shall be vested in fee simple in such persons and the United States, respectively, notwithstanding the provisions contained in subsection (a) of this section.

"(2) Whenever, prior to July 4, 1946, the President of the United States shall find that any properties of the United States in the Philippines would be suitable for diplomatic and consular establishments of the United States after the inauguration of the independent Government, he shall designate the same by the issuance of a proclamation or proclamations, and title to any properties so designated shall continue to be vested in fee simple in the United States notwithstanding the provisions contained in subsection (a) of this section.

"(3) Title to the lands and buildings pertaining to the official residences of the United States High Commissioner to the Philippine Islands in the cities of Manila and Baguio, together with all fixtures and movable objects, shall continue to be vested in the United States after July 4, 1946, notwithstanding the provisions contained in subsection (a) of this section.

"(4) Administrative supervision and control over any properties acquired or designated by the President of the United States pursuant to this subsection, and over the official residences in the Philippines of the High Commissioner, shall, on and after July 4, 1946, be exercised by the Secretary of State, in accordance with Acts of Congress relating to property held by the United States in foreign countries for official establishments."

SEC. 4. Section 13 of the said Act of March 24, 1934, is hereby amended by striking out the proviso and inserting in lieu thereof the following: "*Provided*, That at least two years prior to the date fixed in this Act for the independence of the Philippine Islands, there shall be held a conference of representatives of the Government of the United States and the Government of the Commonwealth of the Philippine Islands, such representatives, on the part of the United States, to consist of three United States Senators appointed by the President of the Senate, three Members of the House of Representatives appointed by the Speaker of the House, and three persons appointed by the President of the United States, and, on the part of the Philippines, to consist of nine representatives to be appointed by the President of the Commonwealth of the Philippines, with the consent of the Commission on Appointments of the National Assembly, for the purpose of formulating recommendations as to future trade relations between the United States and the independent Philippine Republic, the time, place, and manner of holding such conference to be determined by the President of the United States; but nothing in this proviso shall be construed to modify or affect in any way any provision of this Act relating to the procedure leading up to Philippine independence or the date upon which the Philippine Islands shall become independent.

"In the event any vacancy occurs in the Commission by reason of the death, resignation, or retirement of any member thereof, such vacancy may be filled by the authority appointing the member whose death, resignation, or retirement caused the vacancy."

SEC. 5. The said Act of March 24, 1934, is further amended by the addition of the following new section:

"SEC. 18. (a) As used in sections 6 and 10 of this Act—

"(1) The term 'United States', when used in a geographical sense, but not the term 'continental United States', includes all Territories and possessions of the United States, other than the Philippines.

"(2) The term 'cordage' includes yarns, twines (including binding twine described in paragraph 1622 of the Tariff Act of 1930 (46 Stat. 675)), cords, cordage, rope and cable, tarred or untarred, wholly or in chief value of manila (abaca) or other hard fiber.

"(3) The term 'Philippine Government' means the Government of the Commonwealth of the Philippines.

"(4) The term 'United States duty', when used in connection with the computation of export taxes, means the lowest rate of ordinary customs duty in effect at the time of the shipment of the article concerned from the Philippines and applicable to like articles imported into the continental United States from any foreign country, except Cuba, or when more than one rate of ordinary customs duty is applicable to such like articles, the aggregate of such rates.

"(5) The term 'refined sugars' possesses the same meaning as the term 'direct-consumption sugar' as defined in section 101 of the Sugar Act of 1937.

"(6) The term 'Philippine article' means an article the growth, produce, or manufacture of the Philippines, in the production of which no materials of other than Philippine or United States origin valued in excess of 20 per centum of the total value of such article was used and which is brought into the United States from the Philippines.

"(7) The term 'American article' means an article the growth, produce, or manufacture of the United States, in the production of which no materials of other than Philippine or United States origin valued in excess of 20 per centum of the total value of such article was used and which is brought into the Philippines from the United States.

"(8) The term 'Philippine import duty' means the lowest rate of ordinary customs duty applicable at the port of arrival, at the time of entry, or withdrawal from warehouse, for consumption of the article concerned, to like articles imported into the Philippines from any other foreign country, or when more than one rate of ordinary customs duty is applicable to such like articles, the aggregate of such rates.

"(b) As used in subsection (a) of this section:

"(1) The terms 'includes' and 'including' shall not be deemed to exclude other things otherwise within the meaning of the term defined.

"(2) The term 'ordinary customs duty' shall not include any import duty or charge which is imposed to compensate for an internal tax imposed in respect of a like domestic product or in respect of a commodity from which the imported product has been manufactured or produced in whole or in part."

SEC. 6. The said Act of March 24, 1934, is further amended by the addition of the following new section:

"SEC. 19. (a) The proceeds of the excise taxes imposed by section 2470 of the Internal Revenue Code (I. R. C., ch. 21, sec. 2470), and of the import taxes imposed by sections 2490 and 2491 of the Internal

Revenue Code (I. R. C., ch. 22, secs. 2490, 2491), collected on or after January 1, 1939, and accrued prior to July 4, 1946, and required to be held in separate or special funds and paid into the Treasury of the Philippines, together with any moneys hereafter appropriated in accordance with the authorization contained in section 503 of the Sugar Act of 1937 (50 Stat. 915) by virtue of accruals of excise and import taxes prior to July 4, 1946, shall be held as separate funds and paid into the treasury of the Philippines to be used for the purpose of meeting new or additional expenditures which will be necessary in adjusting Philippine economy to a position independent of trade preferences in the United States and in preparing the Philippines for the assumption of the responsibilities of an independent state: *Provided, however,* That the portion of such funds expended by the Government of the Commonwealth of the Philippines shall be budgeted, appropriated, and accounted for separately from other moneys of that Government.

"(b) If the President of the United States finds that the Government of the Commonwealth of the Philippines has failed or is about to fail to comply with any requirement of subsections (a) and (c) of this section, he shall direct the Secretary of the Treasury of the United States to withhold or discontinue, during any period or periods of time specified by the President of the United States further payments in whole or in part.

"(c) The provisions contained in section 2476 of the Internal Revenue Code (I. R. C., ch. 21, sec. 2476), prohibiting further payments in the event that the Government of the Commonwealth of the Philippines should provide by law for the subsidization of producers of copra, coconut oil, or allied products, and the provisions contained in the Sugar Act of 1937, specifying the purpose for which such appropriations could be used by the said government and the manner and condition of transfer, shall not apply to any moneys collected or appropriated pursuant to said Acts on or after January 1, 1939, and to this extent are hereby repealed: *Provided, however,* That the restriction contained in the proviso to section 503 of the Sugar Act of 1937 shall continue in full force and effect: *And provided further,* That no part of the proceeds of the excise taxes herein referred to shall be paid directly or indirectly as a subsidy to the producers or processors of copra, coconut oil or allied products, except that this provision shall not be construed as prohibiting the use of a portion of said funds for facilities for better curing of copra, or for bona fide production loans to Philippine copra producers.

"(d) Nothing contained herein shall be construed as obligating the

United States to continue for any period of time any or all of the excise and import taxes imposed by sections 2470, 2490, 2491 of the Internal Revenue Code or by sections 3490, 3500, 3501 of the Internal Revenue Code (I. R. C., ch. 32, secs. 3490, 3500, 3501).

"(e) Notwithstanding the provisions of section 4 of the Act of March 8, 1902 (32 Stat. 54), or of any other provision of law, on or after the first day of the second month following the passage of this amendatory Act, except as otherwise provided in this section, all customs duties collected in accordance with sections 6 and 13 of this Act, on any article the growth, produce, or manufacture of the Philippines, in the production of which no materials of other than Philippine or United States origin valued in excess of 20 per centum of the total value of such article, was used and which is brought into the United States from the Philippines, and all customs duties collected on any other article brought into the United States from the Philippines, shall be covered into the general fund of the Treasury of the United States and shall not be paid into the Treasury of the Philippines."

SEC. 7. (a) Sections 1 to 5, inclusive, of this amendatory Act shall become effective on January 1, 1940, if before that date—

(1) Subsection 5 of section 1 of the Ordinance Appended to the Constitution of the Philippines shall have been amended in the manner now provided by law, by changing the final period of said subsection to a comma, and by adding thereto the words: "as amended by the Act of Congress of the United States approved (followed by the date of the approval of this amendatory Act)", and section 3 of the said ordinance shall have been amended by inserting immediately after the words "approved March 24, 1934" the same amendatory language mentioned above.

(2) The President of the United States shall have found and proclaimed that the Philippine Government has enacted, subsequent to the adoption of the amendments to the Constitution of the Philippines (as provided in subdivision (1) of this subsection), a law relating to export taxes (as provided in section 1), and has retained those Philippine laws relating to sinking-fund and currency matters which were in effect on May 20, 1938.

(b) Section 1 of this amendatory Act shall remain in full force and effect from the effective date thereof until July 4, 1946, unless the President of the United States shall, prior to July 4, 1946, have found and proclaimed that the Philippine Government has, in any substantial respect, repealed or amended, or failed or refused to enforce or administer any Philippine law referred to in subdivision (2) of subsection (a) of this section. In the event of such a finding and proclamation, section 1 shall immediately become ineffective and trade relations between the United States and the Philippines shall be as provided by section 6 of the Act of March 24, 1934, prior to the enactment of this amendatory Act and by section 13 of the said Act.

(c) Sections 6 and 7 of this amendatory Act shall become effective upon its enactment.

SEC. 8. Notwithstanding the provisions contained in section 8 (a) (3) of the Act of March 24, 1934 (48 Stat. 456), entitled "An Act to provide for the complete independence of the Philippine Islands, to provide for the adoption of a constitution and a form of government for the Philippine Islands, and for other purposes", Foreign Service officers may, under commissions as diplomatic and consular officers, be assigned to the Philippine Islands, during which assignments such officers shall be considered as stationed in a foreign country, for such periods of time and under such regulations as the Secretary of State may prescribe for the performance of any of the duties customarily performed by Foreign Service officers stationed in foreign countries and of additional duties in connection with advising and assisting the United States High Commissioner to the Philippine Islands in the supervision and control of the foreign affairs of the Commonwealth of the Philippines in accordance with section 2 (a) (10) of the Act approved March 24, 1934, and section 1 (10) of the ordinance appended to the constitution of the Philippines adopted February 8, 1935.

This section shall become effective upon its enactment.

Approved, August 7, 1939.

# IV. CONSTITUTION OF THE PHILIPPINES

---

*Adopted by the Philippine Constitutional Convention at the City of Manila, Philippine Islands, on the eighth day of February, nineteen hundred and thirty-five, and approved by the President of the United States on the twenty-third day of March, nineteen hundred and thirty five.*

The Filipino people, imploring the aid of Divine Providence, in order to establish a government that shall embody their ideals, conserve and develop the patrimony of the nation, promote the general welfare, and secure to themselves and their posterity the blessings of independence under a régime of justice, liberty, and democracy, do ordain and promulgate this Constitution.

### ARTICLE I.—THE NATIONAL TERRITORY

SECTION 1. The Philippines comprises all the territory ceded to the United States by the treaty of Paris concluded between the United States and Spain on the tenth day of December, eighteen hundred and ninety-eight, the limits of which are set forth in Article III of said treaty, together with all the islands embraced in the treaty concluded at Washington, between the United States and Spain on the seventh day of November, nineteen hundred, and in the treaty concluded between the United States and Great Britain on the second day of January, nineteen hundred and thirty, and all territory over which the present Government of the Philippine Islands exercises jurisdiction.

### ARTICLE II.—DECLARATION OF PRINCIPLES

SECTION 1. The Philippines is a republican state. Sovereignty resides in the people and all government authority emanates from them.

SEC. 2. The defense of the State is a prime duty of government, and in the fulfillment of this duty all citizens may be required by law to render personal military or civil service.

SEC. 3. The Philippines renounces war as an instrument of national policy, and adopts the generally accepted principles of international law as a part of the law of the Nation.

SEC. 4. The natural right and duty of parents in the rearing of the youth for civic efficiency should receive the aid and support of the Government.

SEC. 5. The promotion of social justice to insure the well-being and economic security of all the people should be the concern of the State.

### ARTICLE III.—BILL OF RIGHTS

SECTION 1. (1) No person shall be deprived of life, liberty, or property without due process of law, nor shall any person be denied the equal protection of the laws.

(2) Private property shall not be taken for public use without just compensation.

(3) The right of the people to be secure in their persons, houses, papers, and effects against unreasonable searches and seizures shall not be violated, and no warrants shall issue but upon probable cause, to be determined by the judge after examination under oath or affirmation of the complainant and the witnesses he may produce, and particularly describing the place to be searched, and the persons or thing to be seized.

(4) The liberty of abode and of changing the same within the limits prescribed by law shall not be impaired.

(5) The privacy of communication and correspondence shall be inviolable except upon lawful order of the court or when public safety and order require otherwise.

(6) The right to form associations or societies for purposes not contrary to law shall not be abridged.

(7) No law shall be made respecting an establishment of religion, or prohibiting the free exercise thereof, and the free exercise and enjoyment of religious profession and worship, without discrimination or preference, shall forever be allowed. No religious test shall be required for the exercise of civil or political rights.

(8) No law shall be passed abridging the freedom of speech, or of the press, or the right of the people peaceably to assemble and petition the Government for redress of grievances.

(9) No law granting a title of nobility shall be enacted, and no per-

son holding any office of profit or trust shall, without the consent of the National Assembly, accept any present, emolument, office, or title of any kind whatever from any foreign state.

(10) No law impairing the obligation of contracts shall be passed.

(11) No *ex post facto* law or bill of attainder shall be enacted.

(12) No person shall be imprisoned for debt or nonpayment of a poll tax.

(13) No involuntary servitude in any form shall exist except as a punishment for crime whereof the party shall have been duly convicted.

(14) The privilege of the writ of *habeas corpus* shall not be suspended except in cases of invasion, insurrection, or rebellion, when the public safety requires it, in any of which events the same may be suspended wherever during such period the necessity for such suspension shall exist.

(15) No person shall be held to answer for a criminal offense without due process of law.

(16) All persons shall before conviction be bailable by sufficient sureties, except those charged with capital offenses when evidence of guilt is strong. Excessive bail shall not be required.

(17) In all criminal prosecutions the accused shall be presumed to be innocent until the contrary is proved, and shall enjoy the right to be heard by himself and counsel, to be informed of the nature and cause of the accusation against him, to have a speedy and public trial, to meet the witnesses face to face, and to have compulsory process to secure the attendance of witnesses in his behalf.

(18) No person shall be compelled to be a witness against himself.

(19) Excessive fines shall not be imposed, nor cruel and unusual punishment inflicted.

(20) No person shall be twice put in jeopardy of punishment for the same offense. If an act is punished by a law and an ordinance, conviction or acquittal under either shall constitute a bar to another prosecution for the same act.

(21) Free access to the courts shall not be denied to any person by reason of poverty.

### ARTICLE IV.—CITIZENSHIP

SECTION 1. The following are citizens of the Philippines.

(1) Those who are citizens of the Philippine Islands at the time of the adoption of this Constitution.

(2) Those born in the Philippine Islands of foreign parents who, be-

fore the adoption of this Constitution, had been elected to public office in the Philippine Islands.

(3) Those whose fathers are citizens of the Philippines.

(4) Those whose mothers are citizens of the Philippines and, upon reaching the age of majority, elect Philippine citizenship.

(5) Those who are naturalized in accordance with law.

SEC. 2. Philippine citizenship may be lost or reacquired in the manner provided by law.

ARTICLE V.—SUFFRAGE

SECTION 1. Suffrage may be exercised by male citizens of the Philippines not otherwise disqualified by law, who are twenty-one years of age or over and are able to read and write, and who shall have resided in the Philippines for one year and in the municipality wherein they propose to vote for at least six months preceding the election. The National Assembly shall extend the right of suffrage to women, if in a plebiscite which shall be held for that purpose within two years after the adoption of this Constitution, not less than three hundred thousand women possessing the necessary qualifications shall vote affirmatively on the question.

ARTICLE VI.—LEGISLATIVE DEPARTMENT

SECTION 1. The Legislative power shall be vested in a National Assembly. The Members of the National Assembly shall not exceed one hundred and twenty, shall be chosen every three years, and shall be apportioned among the several provinces as nearly as may be according to the number of their respective inhabitants, but each province shall have at least one Member. The National Assembly shall by law make an apportionment within three years after the return of every enumeration, and not otherwise. Until such apportionment shall have been made, the National Assembly shall consist of ninety-eight Members, of whom eighty-seven shall be elected by the representative districts as now provided by law; and three by the Mountain Province, and one by each of the other eight existing special provinces. The Members of the National Assembly in the provinces of Sulu, Lanao, and Cotabato shall be chosen as may be determined by law; in all other provinces they shall be elected by the qualified voters therein.

SEC. 2. No person shall be a Member of the National Assembly unless he has been five years a citizen of the Philippines, is at least thirty years of age, and, at the time of his election, a qualified elector, and a resident of the province in which he is chosen for not less than one year immediately prior to his election.

SEC. 3. (1) In case of vacancy in the National Assembly a special election may be called in the corresponding district, in the manner prescribed by law, but the Member thus elected shall serve only for the unexpired term.

(2) Elections for the National Assembly shall be held on the dates fixed by law.

(3) The National Assembly shall convene in regular session once every year, on the second Monday of the month immediately following that on which the election of its Members was held, unless a different date is fixed by law. The National Assembly may be called in special session at any time by the President to consider general legislation or only such subjects as he may designate. No special session shall continue longer than thirty days and no regular session longer than one hundred days, exclusive of Sundays.

(4) The National Assembly shall choose its Speaker, a secretary, a sergeant-at-arms, and such other officers as may be required. A majority of all the Members shall constitute a quorum to do business, but a smaller number may adjourn from day to day, and may compel the attendance of absent Members, in such manner and under such penalties as the National Assembly may provide.

(5) The National Assembly may determine the rules of its proceedings, punish its Members for disorderly behavior, and, with the concurrence of two-thirds, expel a Member. It shall keep a journal of its proceedings, and from time to time publish the same, excepting such parts as may in its judgment require secrecy; and the *yeas* and *nays* on any question shall, at the request of one-fifth of its Members present, be entered in the Journal.

SEC. 4. There shall be an Electoral Commission composed of three Justices of the Supreme Court designated by the Chief Justice, and of six Members chosen by the National Assembly, three of whom shall be nominated by the party having the largest number of votes, and three by the party having the second largest number of votes therein. The senior Justice in the Commission shall be its Chairman. The Electoral Commission shall be the sole judge of all contests relating to the election, returns, and qualifications of the Members of the National Assembly.

SEC. 5. The Members of the National Assembly shall, unless otherwise provided by law, receive an annual compensation of five thousand pesos each including per diems and other emoluments or allowances and exclusive only of traveling expenses to and from their respective districts when attending sessions of the National Assembly. No increase in said compensation shall take effect until after the expiration of the full term of the Members of the National Assembly elected subsequent to the approval of such increase. The Speaker of the National Assembly shall receive an annual compensation of sixteen thousand pesos until otherwise provided by law.

Sec. 6. The Members of the National Assembly shall in all cases except treason, felony, and breach of the peace, be privileged from arrest during their attendance at the sessions of the National Assembly, and in going to and returning from the same; and for any speech or debate therein, they shall not be questioned in any other place.

Sec. 7. The National Assembly shall elect from among its Members, on the basis of proportional representation of the political parties therein, a Commission on Appointments and a Commission on Impeachment, each to consist of twenty-one members. These Commissions shall be constituted within thirty days after the National Assembly shall have been organized with the election of its Speaker, and shall meet only while the National Assembly is in session, at the call of their respective Chairmen or a majority of their members, to discharge such powers and functions as are herein conferred upon them.

Sec. 8. (1) No Member of the National Assembly may hold any other office or employment in the Government without forfeiting his seat, nor shall any such Member during the time for which he was elected, be appointed to any civil office which may have been created or the emoluments whereof shall have been increased while he was a Member of the National Assembly.

(2) No Member of the National Assembly shall directly or indirectly be financially interested in any contract with the Government or any subdivision or instrumentality thereof, or in any franchise or special privilege granted by the National Assembly during his term of office; nor shall any such Member appear as counsel before the Electoral Commission or any court in any civil case wherein the Government or any subdivision or instrumentality thereof is the adverse party, or collect any fee for his appearance in any administrative proceedings or in any criminal case wherein an officer or employee of the Government is accused of an offense committed in relation to his office. No Member of the Commission on Appointments of the National Assembly shall appear as counsel before any court inferior to the Supreme Court.

Sec. 9. (1) The President shall submit within fifteen days of the opening of each regular session of the National Assembly a budget of receipts and expenditures, which shall be the basis of the general appropriation bill. The National Assembly may not increase the appropriations recommended by the President for the operation of the Government as specified in the Budget, except the appropriations for the National Assembly and the Judicial Department. The form of the Budget and the information that it should contain shall be prescribed by law.

(2) No provision or enactment shall be embraced in the general appropriation, unless it relates specifically to some particular appropriation in the bill; and any such provision or enactment shall be limited in its operation to such appropriation.

SEC. 10. The heads of departments upon their own initiative or upon the request of the National Assembly may appear before and be heard by the National Assembly or any matter pertaining to their departments, unless the public interest shall require otherwise and the President shall so state in writing.

SEC. 11. (1) Every bill which shall have passed the National Assembly shall, before it becomes a law, be presented to the President. If he approve the same, he shall sign it; but if not, he shall return it with his objections to the National Assembly, which shall enter the objections at large on its Journal and proceed to reconsider it. If, after such reconsideration, two-thirds of all the Members of the National Assembly shall agree to pass the bill, it shall become a law. In all such cases the votes of the National Assembly shall be determined by *yeas* and *nays*, and the names of the Members voting for and against shall be entered on the Journal. If any bill shall not be returned by the President as herein provided within twenty days (Sundays excepted) after it shall have been presented to him, the same shall become a law in like manner as if he had signed it, unless the National Assembly by adjournment prevent its return, in which case it shall become a law unless vetoed by the President within thirty days after adjournment.

(2) The President shall have the power to veto any particular item or items of an appropriation bill, but the veto shall not affect the item or items to which he does not object. When a provision of an appropriation bill affects one or more items of the same, the President cannot veto the provision without at the same time vetoing the particular item or items to which it relates. The item or items objected to shall not take effect except in the manner heretofore provided as to bills returned to the National Assembly without the approval of the President. If the veto refers to a bill or any item of an appropriation bill which appropriates a sum in excess of ten *per centum* of the total amount voted in the appropriation bill for the general expenses of the Government for the preceding year, or if it should refer to a bill authorizing an increase of

the public debt, the same shall not become a law unless approved by three-fourths of all the Members of the National Assembly.

(3) The President shall have the power to veto any separate item or items in a revenue or tariff bill, and the item or items vetoed shall not take effect except in the manner provided as to bill vetoed by the President.

SEC. 12. (1) No bill which may be enacted into law shall embrace more than one subject which shall be expressed in the title of the bill.

(2) No bill shall be passed or become a law unless it shall have been printed and copies thereof in its final form furnished the Members at least three calendar days prior to its passage by the National Assembly, except when the President shall have certified to the necessity of its immediate enactment. Upon the last reading of a bill no amendment thereof shall be allowed, and the question upon its final passage shall be taken immediately thereafter, and the *yeas* and *nays* entered on the Journal.

SEC. 13. (1) All money collected on any tax levied for a special purpose shall be treated as a special fund and paid out for such purpose only. If the purpose for which a special fund was created has been fulfilled or abandoned, the balance, if any, shall be transferred to the general funds of the Government.

(2) No money shall be paid out of the Treasury except in pursuance of an appropriation made by law.

(3) No public money or property shall ever be appropriated, applied, or used, directly or indirectly, for the use, benefit, or support of any sect, church, denomination, sectarian institution, or system of religion, or for the use, benefit, or support of any priest, preacher, minister, or other religious teacher or dignitary as such, except when such priest, preacher, minister, or dignitary is assigned to the armed forces or to any penal institution, orphanage, or leprosarium.

SEC. 14. (1) The rule of taxation shall be uniform.

(2) The National Assembly may by law authorize the President, subject to such limitations and restrictions as it may impose, to fix within specified limits, tariff rates, import or export quotas, and tonnage and wharfage dues.

(3) Cemeteries, churches, and parsonages or convents appurtenant thereto, and all lands, buildings, and improvements used exclusively for religious, charitable, or educational purposes shall be exempt from taxation.

SEC. 15. The National Assembly shall, with the concurrence of two-thirds of all its Members, have the sole power to declare war.

Sec. 16. In times of war or other national emergency, the National Assembly may by law authorize the President, for a limited period and subject to such restrictions as it may prescribe, to promulgate rules and regulations to carry out a declared national policy.

ARTICLE VII.—EXECUTIVE DEPARTMENT

Section 1. The Executive power shall be vested in a President of the Philippines.

Sec. 2. The President shall hold his office during a term of six years, and together with the Vice-President chosen for the same term, shall be elected by direct vote of the people. The election returns for President and Vice-President, duly certified by the board of canvassers of each province, shall be transmitted to the National Assembly. Upon receipt of such returns the National Assembly shall forthwith, in public session, count the votes, and proclaim the persons elected President and Vice-President. The persons respectively having the highest number of votes for President and Vice-President shall be declared elected, but in case two or more shall have an equal and the highest number of votes for either office, the National Assembly shall, by a majority vote of all its Members, elect one of said persons as President or Vice-President.

Sec. 3. No person may be elected to the office of President or Vice-President unless he be a natural-born citizen of the Philippines, a qualified voter, forty years of age or over, and has been a resident of the Philippines for at least ten years immediately preceding the election.

Sec. 4. No person elected President may be reëlected for the following term, nor shall the Vice-President or any other person who may have succeeded to the office of President as herein provided at least one year before the election, be eligible to the office of President at such election.

Sec. 5. Elections for President and Vice-President shall be held once every six years on a date to be fixed by the National Assembly.

Sec. 6. The terms of the President and Vice-President shall end at noon on the thirtieth day of December following the expiration of six years after the election, and the terms of their successors shall begin from such time.

Sec. 7. If, at the time fixed for the beginning of the term of the President, the President-elect shall have died, the Vice-President-elect shall become President. If a President shall not have been chosen before the time fixed for the beginning of his term, or if the President-elect shall have failed to qualify, then the Vice-President shall act as President until a President shall have qualified, and the National Assembly may by law provide for the case wherein neither a President-elect nor a Vice-President-elect shall have qualified, declaring who shall then act as President, or the manner in which one who is to act shall be selected, and such person shall act accordingly until a President or Vice-President shall have qualified.

SEC. 8. Before he enter on the execution of his office, the President shall take the following oath or affirmation:

"I do solemnly swear (or affirm) that I will faithfully and conscientiously fulfill my duties as President of the Philippines, preserve and defend its Constitution, execute its laws, do justice to every man, and consecrate myself to the service of the Nation. So help me God." (In case of affirmation, last sentence will be omitted.)

SEC. 9. In the event of the removal of the President from office or of his death, resignation, or inability to discharge the powers and duties of the said office, the same shall devolve on the Vice-President, and the National Assembly shall by law provide for the case of removal, death, resignation, or inability, both of the President and Vice-President, declaring what officer shall then act as President, and such officer shall act accordingly, until the disability be removed, or a President shall be elected.

SEC. 10. The President shall have an official residence and receive a compensation to be ascertained by law which shall be neither increased nor diminished during the period for which he shall have been elected, and he shall not receive within that period any other emolument from the Government or any of its subdivisions or instrumentalities. Until the National Assembly shall provide otherwise, the President shall receive an annual salary of thirty thousand pesos. The Vice-President, when not acting as President, shall receive an annual compensation of fifteen thousand pesos until otherwise provided by law.

SEC. 11. (1) The President shall have control of all the executive departments, bureaus, or offices, exercise general supervision over all local governments as may be provided by law, and take care that the laws be faithfully executed.

(2) The President shall be commander-in-chief of all armed forces of the Philippines and, whenever it becomes necessary, he may call out such armed forces to prevent or suppress lawless violence, invasion, insurrection, or rebellion. In case of invasion, insurrection, or rebellion, or imminent danger thereof, when the public safety requires it, he may

suspend the privileges of the writ of *habeas corpus*, or place the Philippines or any part thereof under martial law.

(3) The President shall nominate and with the consent of the Commission on Appointments of the National Assembly, shall appoint the heads of the executive departments and bureaus, officers of the Army from the rank of colonel, of the Navy and air forces from the rank of captain or commander, and all other officers of the Government whose appointments are not herein otherwise provided for, and those whom he may be authorized by law to appoint; but the National Assembly may by law vest the appointment of inferior officers, in the President alone, in the courts, or in the heads of departments.

(4) The President shall have the power to make appointments during the recess of the National Assembly, but such appointments shall be effective only until disapproval by the Commission on Appointments or until the next adjournment of the National Assembly.

(5) The President shall from time to time give to the National Assembly information of the state of the Nation, and recommend to its consideration such measures as he shall judge necessary and expedient.

(6) The President shall have the power to grant reprieves, commutations, and pardons, and remit fines and forfeitures, after conviction, for all offenses, except in cases of impeachment, upon such conditions and with such restrictions and limitations as he may deem proper to impose. He shall have the power to grant amnesty with the concurrence of the National Assembly.

(7) The President shall have the power, with the concurrence of a majority of all Members of the National Assembly, to make treaties, and with the consent of the Commission on Appointments, he shall appoint ambassadors, other public ministers, and consuls. He shall receive ambassadors and other ministers duly accredited to the Government of the Philippines.

Sec. 12. (1) The executive departments of the present Government of the Philippine Islands shall continue as now authorized by law until the National Assembly shall provide otherwise.

(2) The heads of the departments and chiefs of bureaus or offices and their assistants shall not, during their continuance in office, engage in the practice of any profession, or intervene, directly or indirectly, in the management or control of any private enterprise which in any way may be affected by the functions of their office; nor shall they, directly or indirectly, be financially interested in any contract with the Government, or any subdivision or instrumentality thereof.

(3) The President may appoint the Vice-President as a member of his cabinet and also as head of an executive department.

ARTICLE VIII.—JUDICIAL DEPARTMENT

SECTION 1. The Judicial power shall be vested in one Supreme Court and in such inferior courts as may be established by law.

SEC. 2. The National Assembly shall have the power to define, prescribe, and apportion the jurisdiction of the various courts, but may not deprive the Supreme Court of its original jurisdiction over cases affecting ambassadors, other public ministers, and consuls, nor of its jurisdiction to review, revise, reverse, modify, or affirm on appeal, certiorari, or writ of error, as the law or the rules of court may provide, final judgments and decrees of inferior courts in—

(1) All cases in which the constitutionality or validity of any treaty, law, ordinance, or executive order or regulation is in question.

(2) All cases involving the legality of any tax, impost, assessment, or toll, or any penalty imposed in relation thereto.

(3) All cases in which the jurisdiction of any trial court is in issue.

(4) All criminal cases in which the penalty imposed is death or life imprisonment.

(5) All cases in which an error or question of law is involved.

SEC. 3. Until the National Assembly shall provide otherwise, the Supreme Court shall have such original and appellate jurisdiction as may be possessed and exercised by the Supreme Court of the Philippine Islands at the time of the adoption of this Constitution. The original jurisdiction of the Supreme Court shall include all cases affecting ambassadors, other public ministers, and consuls.

SEC. 4. The Supreme Court shall be composed of a Chief Justice and ten Associate Justices and may sit either *in banc* or in two divisions unless otherwise provided by law.

SEC. 5. The members of the Supreme Court and all judges of inferior courts shall be appointed by the President with the consent of the Commission on Appointments of the National Assembly.

SEC. 6. No person may be appointed member of the Supreme Court unless he has been five years a citizen of the Philippines, is at least forty years of age, and has for ten years or more been a judge of a court of record or engaged in the practice of law in the Philippines.

SEC. 7. No judge appointed for a particular district shall be designated or transferred to another district without the approval of the

Supreme Court. The National Assembly shall by law determine the residence of judges of inferior courts.

SEC. 8. The National Assembly shall prescribe the qualifications of judges of inferior courts, but no person may be appointed judge of any such courts unless he is a citizen of the Philippines and has been admitted to the practice of law in the Philippines.

SEC. 9. The members of the Supreme Court and all judges of inferior courts shall hold office during good behavior, until they reach the age of seventy years, or become incapacitated to discharge the duties of their office. They shall receive such compensation as may be fixed by law, which shall not be diminished during their continuance in office. Until the National Assembly shall provide otherwise, the Chief Justice of the Supreme Court shall receive an annual compensation of sixteen thousand pesos, and each Associate Justice, fifteen thousand pesos.

SEC. 10. All cases involving the constitutionality of a treaty or law shall be heard and decided by the Supreme Court *in banc*, and no treaty or law may be declared unconstitutional without the concurrence of two-thirds of all the members of the Court.

SEC. 11. The conclusions of the Supreme Court in any case submitted to it for decision shall be reached in consultation before the case is assigned to a Justice for the writing of the opinion of the Court. Any Justice dissenting from a decision shall state the reasons for his dissent.

SEC. 12. No decision shall be rendered by any court of record without expressing therein clearly and distinctly the facts and the law on which it is based.

SEC. 13. The Supreme Court shall have the power to promulgate rules concerning pleading, practice, and procedure in all courts, and the admission to the practice of law. Said rules shall be uniform for all courts of the same grade and shall not diminish, increase, or modify substantive rights. The existing laws on pleading, practice, and procedure are hereby repealed as statutes, and are declared Rules of Courts, subject to the power of the Supreme Court to alter and modify the same. The National Assembly shall have the power to repeal, alter, or supplement the rules concerning pleading, practice, and procedure, and the admission to the practice of law in the Philippines.

### ARTICLE IX.—IMPEACHMENT

SECTION 1. The President, the Vice-President, the Justices of the Supreme Court, and the Auditor General, shall be removed from office on impeachment for, and conviction of, culpable violation of the Constitution, treason, bribery, or other high crimes.

SEC. 2. The Commission on Impeachment of the National Assembly, by a vote of two-thirds of its Members, shall have the sole power of impeachment.

SEC. 3. The National Assembly shall have the sole power to try all impeachments. When sitting for that purpose the Members shall be on oath or affirmation. When the President of the Philippines is on trial, the Chief Justice of the Supreme Court shall preside. No person shall be convicted without the concurrence of three-fourths of all the Members who do not belong to the Commission on Impeachment.

SEC. 4. Judgment in cases of impeachment shall not extend further than to removal from office and disqualification to hold and enjoy any office of honor, trust, or profit under the Government of the Philippines, but the party convicted shall nevertheless be liable and subject to prosecution, trial, and punishment according to law.

ARTICLE X.—GENERAL AUDITING OFFICE

SECTION 1. There shall be a General Auditing Office under the direction and control of an Auditor General, who shall hold office for a term of ten years and may not be reappointed. The Auditor General shall be appointed by the President with the consent of the Commission on Appointments, and shall receive an annual compensation to be fixed by law which shall not be diminished during his continuance in office. Until the National Assembly shall provide otherwise, the Auditor General shall receive an annual compensation of twelve thousand pesos.

SEC. 2. The Auditor General shall examine, audit, and settle all accounts pertaining to the revenues and receipts from whatever source, including trust funds derived from bond issues; and audit, in accordance with law and administrative regulations, all expenditures of funds or property pertaining to or held in trust by the Government or the provinces or municipalities thereof. He shall keep the general accounts of the Government and preserve the vouchers pertaining thereto. It shall be the duty of the Auditor General to bring to the attention of the proper administrative officer expenditures of funds or property which, in his opinion, are irregular, unnecessary, excessive, or extravagant. He shall also perform such other functions as may be prescribed by law.

SEC. 3. The decisions of the Auditor General shall be rendered within the time fixed by law, and the same may be appealed to the President whose action shall be final. When the aggrieved party is a private person or entity, an appeal from the decision of the Auditor General may be taken directly to a court of record in the manner provided by law.

Sec. 4. The Auditor General shall submit to the President and the National Assembly an annual report covering the financial condition and operations of the Government, and such other reports as may be required.

### ARTICLE XI.—CIVIL SERVICE

Section 1. A Civil Service embracing all branches and subdivisions of the Government shall be provided by law. Appointments in the Civil Service, except as to those which are policy-determining, primarily confidential or highly technical in nature, shall be made only according to merit and fitness, to be determined as far as practicable by competitive examination.

Sec. 2. Officers and employees in the Civil Service, including members of the armed forces, shall not engage directly or indirectly in partisan political activities or take part in any election except to vote.

Sec. 3. No officer or employee of the Government shall receive additional or double compensation unless specifically authorized by law.

Sec. 4. No officer or employee in the Civil Service shall be removed or suspended except for cause as provided by law.

### ARTICLE XII.—CONSERVATION AND UTILIZATION OF NATURAL RESOURCES

Section 1. All agricultural, timber, and mineral lands of the public domain, waters, minerals, coal, petroleum, and other mineral oils, all forces of potential energy, and other natural resources of the Philippines belong to the State, and their disposition, exploitation, development, or utilization shall be limited to citizens of the Philippines, or to corporations or associations at least sixty *per centum* of the capital of which is owned by such citizens, subject to any existing right, grant, lease, or concession at the time of the inauguration of the Government established under this Constitution. Natural resources, with the exception of public agricultural land, shall not be alienated, and no license, concession, or lease for the exploitation, development, or utilization of any of the natural resources shall be granted for a period exceeding twenty-five years, renewable for another twenty-five years, except as to water rights for irrigation, water supply, fisheries, or industrial uses other than the development of water power, in which cases beneficial use may be the measure and the limit of the grant.

SEC. 2. No private corporation or association may acquire, lease, or hold public agricultural lands in excess of one thousand and twenty-four hectares, nor may any individual acquire such lands by purchase in excess of one hundred and forty-four hectares, or by lease in excess of one thousand and twenty-four hectares, or by homestead in excess of twenty-four hectares. Lands adapted to grazing, not exceeding two thousand hectares, may be leased to an individual, private corporation, or association.

SEC. 3. The National Assembly may determine by law the size of private agricultural land which individuals, corporations, or associations may acquire and hold, subject to rights existing prior to the enactment of such law.

SEC. 4. The National Assembly may authorize, upon payment of just compensation, the expropriation of lands to be subdivided into small lots and conveyed at cost to individuals.

SEC. 5. Save in cases of hereditary succession, no private agricultural land shall be transferred or assigned except to individuals, corporations, or associations qualified to acquire or hold lands of the public domain in the Philippines.

SEC. 6. The State may, in the interest of national welfare and defense, establish and operate industries and means of transportation and communication, and, upon payment of just compensation, transfer to public ownership utilities and other private enterprises to be operated by the Government.


### ARTICLE XIII.—GENERAL PROVISIONS

SECTION 1. The flag of the Philippines shall be red, white, and blue, with a sun and three stars, as consecrated and honored by the people and recognized by law.

SEC. 2. All public officers and members of the armed forces shall take an oath to support and defend the Constitution.

SEC. 3. The National Assembly shall take steps toward the development and adoption of a common national language based on one of the existing native languages. Until otherwise provided by law, English and Spanish shall continue as official languages.

SEC. 4. The State shall promote scientific research and invention. Arts and letters shall be under its patronage. The exclusive right to writings and inventions shall be secured to authors and inventors for a limited period.

SEC. 5. All educational institutions shall be under the supervision of and subject to regulation by the State. The Government shall establish and maintain a complete and adequate system of public education, and shall provide at least free public primary instruction, and citizenship training to adult citizens. All schools shall aim to develop moral character, personal discipline, civic conscience, and vocational efficiency, and to teach the duties of citizenship. Optional religious instruction shall be maintained in the public schools as now authorized by law. Universities established by the State shall enjoy academic freedom. The State shall create scholarships in arts, science, and letters for specially gifted citizens.

SEC. 6. The State shall afford protection to labor, especially to working women and minors, and shall regulate the relations between landowner and tenant, and between labor and capital in industry and in agriculture. The State may provide for compulsory arbitration.

SEC. 7. The National Assembly shall not, except by general law, provide for the formation, organization, or regulation of private corporations, unless such corporations are owned or controlled by the Government or any subdivision or instrumentality thereof.

SEC. 8. No franchise, certificate, or any other form of authorization for the operation of a public utility shall be granted except to citizens of the Philippines or to corporations or other entities organized under the laws of the Philippines, sixty *per centum* of the capital of which is owned by citizens of the Philippines, nor shall such franchise, certificate, or authorization be exclusive in character or for a longer period than fifty years. No franchise or right shall be granted to any individual, firm, or corporation, except under the condition that it shall be subject to amendment, alteration, or repeal by the National Assembly when the public interest so requires.

SEC. 9. The Government shall organize and maintain a national police force to preserve public order and enforce the law.

SEC. 10. This Constitution shall be officially promulgated in English and Spanish, but in case of conflict the English text shall prevail.

### ARTICLE XIV.—AMENDMENTS

SECTION 1. The National Assembly, by a vote of three-fourths of all its Members, may propose amendments to this Constitution or call a convention for that purpose. Such amendments shall be valid as part of this Constitution when approved by a majority of the votes cast at an election at which the amendments are submitted to the people for their ratification.

ARTICLE XV.—TRANSITORY PROVISIONS

SECTION 1. The first election of the officers provided in this Constitution and the inauguration of the Government of the Commonwealth of the Philippines shall take place as provided in Public Act Numbered One hundred and twenty-seven of the Congress of the United States, approved March twenty-four, nineteen hundred and thirty-four.

SEC. 2. All laws of the Philippine Islands shall continue in force until the inauguration of the Commonwealth of the Philippines; thereafter, such laws shall remain operative, unless inconsistent with this Constitution, until amended, altered, modified, or repealed by the National Assembly, and all references in such laws to the Government or officials of the Philippine Islands shall be construed, in so far as applicable, to refer to the Government and corresponding officials under this Constitution.

SEC. 3. All courts existing at the time of the adoption of this Constitution shall continue and exercise their jurisdiction, until otherwise provided by law in accordance with this Constitution, and all cases, civil and criminal, pending in said courts, shall be heard, tried, and determined under the laws then in force.

SEC. 4. All officers and employees in the existing Government of the Philippine Islands shall continue in office until the National Assembly shall provide otherwise, but all officers whose appointments are by this Constitution vested in the President shall vacate their respective offices upon the appointment and qualification of their successors, if such appointment is made within a period of one year from the date of the inauguration of the Commonwealth of the Philippines.

SEC. 5. The Members of the National Assembly for the Mountain Province shall be elected as may be provided by law. The voters of municipalities and municipal districts formerly belonging to a special province and now forming part of regular provinces shall vote in the election for Members of the National Assembly in such districts as may be provided by law.

SEC. 6. The provisions of this Constitution, except those contained in this article and in Article V, and those which refer to the election and qualifications of officers to be elected under this Constitution, shall not take effect until the inauguration of the Commonwealth of the Philippines.

### ARTICLE XVI.—SPECIAL PROVISIONS EFFECTIVE UPON THE PROCLAMATION OF THE INDEPENDENCE OF THE PHILIPPINES

SECTION 1. Upon the proclamation of the President of the United States recognizing the independence of the Philippines—

(1) The property rights of the United States and the Philippines shall be promptly adjusted and settled, and all existing property rights of citizens or corporations of the United States shall be acknowledged, respected, and safeguarded to the same extent as property rights of citizens of the Philippines.

(2) The officials elected and serving under this Constitution shall be constitutional officers of the free and independent government of the Philippines and qualified to function in all respects as if elected directly under such Government, and shall serve their full terms of office as prescribed in this Constitution.

(3) The debts and liabilities of the Philippines, its provinces, cities, municipalities, and instrumentalities, which shall be valid and subsisting at the time of the final and complete withdrawal of the sovereignty of the United States, shall be assumed by the free and independent government of the Philippines; and where bonds have been issued under authority of an Act of Congress of the United States by the Philippine Islands, or any province, city, or municipality therein, the Government of the Philippines will make adequate provision for the necessary funds for the payment of interest and principal, and such obligations shall be a first lien on all taxes collected.

(4) The Government of the Philippines will assume all continuing obligations of the United States under the Treaty of Peace with Spain ceding the Philippine Islands to the United States.

(5) The Government of the Philippines will embody the foregoing provisions of this article (except subsection (2)) in a treaty with the United States.

### ARTICLE XVII.—THE COMMONWEALTH AND THE REPUBLIC

SECTION 1. The government established by this Constitution shall be known as the Commonwealth of the Philippines. Upon the final and complete withdrawal of the sovereignty of the United States and the proclamation of Philippine independence, the Commonwealth of the

Philippines shall thenceforth be known as the Republic of the Philippines.

## ORDINANCE APPENDED TO THE CONSTITUTION

SECTION 1. Notwithstanding the provisions of the foregoing Constitution, pending the final and complete withdrawal of the sovereignty of the United States over the Philippines—

(1) All citizens of the Philippines shall owe allegiance to the United States.

(2) Every officer of the Government of the Commonwealth of the Philippines shall, before entering upon the discharge of his duties, take and subscribe an oath of office, declaring, among other things, that he recognizes and accepts the supreme authority of and will maintain true faith and allegiance to the United States.

(3) Absolute toleration of religious sentiment shall be secured and no inhabitant or religious organization shall be molested in person or property on account of religious belief or mode of worship.

(4) Property owned by the United States, cemeteries, churches, and parsonages or convents appurtenant thereto, and all lands, buildings, and improvements used exclusively for religious, charitable, or educational purposes shall be exempt from taxation.

(5) Trade relations between the Philippines and the United States shall be upon the basis prescribed in section six of Public Act Numbered One hundred and twenty-seven of the Congress of the United States approved March twenty-four, nineteen hundred and thirty-four.

(6) The public debt of the Philippines and its subordinate branches shall not exceed limits now or hereafter fixed by the Congress of the United States, and no loans shall be contracted in foreign countries without the approval of the President of the United States.

(7) The debts, liabilities, and obligations of the present Government of the Philippine Islands, its provinces, municipalities, and instrumentalities, valid and subsisting at the time of the adoption of the Constitution, shall be assumed and paid by the Government of the Commonwealth of the Philippines.

(8) The Government of the Commonwealth of the Philippines shall establish and maintain an adequate system of public schools, primarily conducted in the English language.

(9) Acts affecting currency, coinage, imports, exports, and immigration shall not become law until approved by the President of the United States.

(10) Foreign affairs shall be under the direct supervision and control of the United States.

(11) All acts passed by the National Assembly of the Commonwealth of the Philippines shall be reported to the Congress of the United States.

(12) The Philippines recognizes the right of the United States to expropriate property for public uses, to maintain military and other reservations and armed forces in the Philippines, and, upon order of the President of the United States, to call into the service of such armed forces all military forces organized by the Government of the Commonwealth of the Philippines.

(13) The decisions of the courts of the Philippines shall be subject to review by the Supreme Court of the United States as now provided by law, and such review shall also extend to all cases involving the Constitution of the Philippines.

(14) Appeals from decisions of the Auditor General may be taken to the President of the United States.

(15) The United States may, by Presidential proclamation, exercise the right to intervene for the preservation of the Government of the Commonwealth of the Philippines and for the maintenance of the Government as provided in the Constitution thereof, and for the protection of life, property, and individual liberty and for the discharge of Government obligations under and in accordance with the provisions of the Constitution.

(16) The authority of the United States High Commissioner to the Government of the Commonwealth of the Philippines as provided in Public Act Numbered One hundred and twenty-seven of the Congress of the United States approved March twenty-four, nineteen hundred and thirty-four, is hereby recognized.

(17) Citizens and corporations of the United States shall enjoy in the Commonwealth of the Philippines all the civil rights of the citizens and corporations, respectively, thereof.

(18) Every duly adopted amendment to the Constitution of the Philippines shall be submitted to the President of the United States for approval. If the President approve the amendment or if the President fail to disapprove such amendment within six months from the time of its submission, the amendment shall take effect as a part of such Constitution.

(19) The President of the United States shall have authority to suspend the taking effect of or the operation of any law, contract, or executive order of the Government of the Commonwealth of the

Philippines, which in his judgment will result in a failure of the Government of the Commonwealth of the Philippines to fulfill its contracts, or to meet its bonded indebtedness and interest thereon or to provide for its sinking funds, or which seems likely to impair the reserves for the protection of the currency of the Philippines, or which in his judgment will violate international obligations of the United States.

(20) The President of the Commonwealth of the Philippines shall make an annual report to the President and Congress of the United States of the proceedings and operations of the Government of the Commonwealth of the Philippines and shall make such other reports as the President or Congress may request.

SEC. 2. Pending the final and complete withdrawal of the sovereignty of the United States over the Philippines, there shall be a Resident Commissioner of the Philippines to the United States who shall be appointed by the President of the Commonwealth of the Philippines with the consent of the Commission on Appointments. The powers and duties of the Resident Commissioner shall be as provided in section seven, paragraph five of Public Act Numbered One hundred and twenty-seven of the Congress of the United States, approved March twenty-four nineteen hundred and thirty-four, together with such other duties as the National Assembly may determine. The qualifications, compensation, and expenses of the Resident Commissioner shall be fixed by law.

SEC. 3. All other provisions of Public Act Numbered One hundred and twenty-seven of the Congress of the United States, approved March twenty-four, nineteen hundred and thirty-four, applicable to the Government of the Commonwealth of the Philippines are hereby made a part of this Ordinance as if such provisions were expressly inserted therein.

# V. THE MIND OF A NEW COMMONWEALTH

*Address delivered in the University of Notre Dame, December 9, 1935.*

---

## By Carlos Peña Romulo

One would be dull of wit, indeed, and slow of heart who could be unresponsive to the fortunate coincidence of historic influences brought to this occasion at Notre Dame. I refer to the apt confluence of the faith and freedom that have streamed through the history of the Philippines, nurturing our people to the maturity of independence. Today, both are given representative testimony in a joint gesture of remembrance and the concerned congratulation of amicable hope.

His Excellency, the President of the United States, bespeaks the freedom of a nation dedicated to the proposition that all men, and all groups of men, are created equal *before the law;* a nation which controls itself through democratic institutions so designed as to serve evenly the rights of all—their liberties and opportunities; that each may live without servitude and without envy; protected in domestic security and confirmed in the inalienable, proprietary powers of citizens.

The sovereignty of this Republic is shared by all, possessed by none, that the authority of government may never be presumptive or arbitrary but only representative and revocable. A democracy may vote away its powers—as it has in Germany and, recently, in Greece; but a republic cannot do likewise without ceasing to exist. In the United States, freedom is not limited to the franchise of suffrage but extended to all elements of political and social function. The State, then, can never become co-equal with the community; as could be if processes of government were accepted as embracing the structure and form of society. The community is greater, as well as antecedent to the State. It creates the State to control and order its multiple interests; interests which citizens never relinquish whether to kings, princes, or parliaments. To mistake this relation, to misread the genealogy of government, is to induce the subservience of the popular to the governmental will.

"Of the people, by the people, for the people," is, therefore, a prepositional summary of the concept of that freedom which the United States enjoys and which, with singular magnanimity, it has conveyed and bequeathed to the Filipino people.

Among a people so naturally disposed as the Filipinos to independence, this doctrine of freedom, taught with the conviction of discovery, found widespread and lively acceptance. Small wonder that we should have desired for ourselves what the Americans taught was the pre-eminent blessing of national existence!

There are some now, however, who would caution us (and not imprudently) that autonomy may prove precipitate; that we are unskilled in statecraft; lacking the consciousness of organic unity; infantile in the arbitrament of arms; that we are economically overweighted by the past preferment of export; in short, that freedom may mean famine, if it will not mean worse.

To such counsel of caution we reply that freedom is an essential condition of national, as of individual, expression. The Revolutionary Americans so believed and, risking all, died in the hallowed name of Liberty. Bunker Hill, Valley Forge, Saratoga, are the immortal watchwords of an ideal and a lasting record of its price. The Filipinos, too, have their battlefields of freedom and they shall bear, I trust, with equanimity the trials that independence imposes. Indeed, misfortune and dangers are but the transient if inescapable circumstances of living; to strive to overcome them is to live valiantly. We desire no more!

And in our freedom we shall be fortified by that faith which outlasts because it transcends time. This greater heritage of the vast majority of our people is given witness today by Notre Dame and the prelates of the Catholic Church. Like freedom, faith reached us through conquest. Centuries ago, with the crown of Spain came the cross of Christ; both borne on the vehement and masterful exuberance of those dauntless adventurers who foreshortened the earth. They sought silver for their king and subjects for their God. Among us they found both. But the crown was really buried with them; we have almost forgotten how or when. The cross remains throughout our islands, a symbol and an evidence of the *radical* culture of our minds.

For no one can believe human life foreshadows, through mysteries, a more ample and intimate existence with God; no one can believe that Jesus Christ is the Son of God Who saved us by His death and sanctifies us by His Sacraments; no one can believe himself a conscious soul under the commandment of Divine love; no one, I repeat, can believe these things without having altered profoundly the quality of his thought and the direction of his outlook. Such belief is a tradition among the Filipinos. It distinguishes us among the peoples of the Far East; and it will be a vital, creative agent in the formation of our new nation. By this I do not wish to imply that Catholicism is the religion of the State. It is *much more;* it is the religion of the people. And the people, not the State, are sovereign. To constrain religion as an instrumentality of Government and to adopt the anomalous thing called "State Religion" is to consider religion falsely and abandon it, as contemporary events elsewhere prove, to the mercy of a government which may not be representative of the people whom it rules. To permit the State to adopt a religion is to concede to the State its potential extension to all functions of society; it is to conceive the State as the ultimate framework of the social organism. The contrary is, of course, true in the very nature of things. Government, unless it be tyranny, is but an instrument variously chosen by the community for its own social purposes.

So the Philippine constitution instructs its future government that there shall be freedom of worship, indicating thereby that its power shall be limited to control manifestations affecting public discipline; and indicating, too, that the practice of religion shall in no way be considered as dependent on legislative concession. The phrase "freedom of worship" places religion outside the basic law rather than within it; and properly so, since a constitution is projected to restrict government, not society.

The Catholic faith will be, accordingly, free to inspire, develop, and modify our institutions conformably to its supreme law of charity. Through charity we should achieve obedience without servility; authority without autocracy; justice without favoritism; equality of respect without the anarchy of no distinctions. A legalistic mechanism never has been nor will be devised to attain *per se* the ends of social justice. Nor are these ends furthered substantially, as some maintain, by racial temperament, geographical position, or contingent relationships. Only the assurance of Christian charity enables us to forecast the direction that the exercise of sovereignty will take. Faith, then, gives sustenance to our freedom.

Graced with this double gift of constructive forces, the Philippine Commonwealth initiates a new national effort for the realization of an ordered and equivalent society. It would be presumptuous to say we shall achieve it; it would be supine not to try. We shall begin our task with an enthusiasm sobered by historical perspective. If we are a newborn nation, we are not, thereby, newborn to the perception of realities. We can be careful not to be misled by ardent apostles of fatuous panaceas, infallible in appearance because tested only against the unanswering vacuity of their authors' minds. We can be docile before facts and mindful that systems, however finely sculptured, can be broken by inordinate hearts and tempestuous wills. We can put forth a modest, well-principled effort to approximate a solution of the harassing problem of economic balance and distribution.

Until lately the Philippines had a plantation economy such as once obtained in the southeastern states of the Union. Now we have moved, though in a limited degree, toward the complexities of agrarian and industrial capitalism. There is in capitalism much that is still immature and, therefore, maladjusted to the existing social order.

But there is nothing inherently vicious in capitalism. This pooling of wealth for production needs to be counterbalanced by pooling of resources of consumption; only so can capitalism be wholesome and beneficial. We do not share the views of those who would prevent the acquirement of wealth by distributing it gratuitously. We believe such a process would either destroy wealth for all or concentrate it in the hands of some group who would call themselves, euphemistically, the State.

We do not accept the Marxian dialectic that classes are *economically* formed and that the road to security is through the liquidation of those classes in favor of the proletariat. Every Oriental knows that there *is* scarcely any proletariat in the Far East; and knows, too, that classes are formed there by educational discrimination as in China, by social heredity as in Malaya, by religious modalities as in India where no amount of acquired wealth would warrant infringement of class privileges. True, the Far East is mildly sensitive to communism, but not because the Far East is class conscious; rather because it is land conscious. Communism in the East is not a philosophy; it is an illegitimate hope for unearned increment. Economic class warfare is a myth of the Communists. But economic conflict, as a disorder of the whole social body, is no myth and we shall strive to eliminate it from our commonwealth by what I have referred to as a modest, well-principled effort.

The approach to this must be realistic; not patronizing and crusading. It is grandiose and anarchial nonsense to pretend that all elements of society must enjoy equality of identity. "Every man a king" is the motto of a fool's paradise and the catch phrase of political trumpery. There is in society a natural diversity of gifts and function, and where there is distinction of ability, there will be distinction of reward. The coalescing of sundry groups composes the pattern of communal living; and communal living is not an artificial result produced by one class for its own advantage but the inevitable expression of man's social character.

Accordingly, we believe economic factors possess social as well as individual significance. Men are not free to ignore these; nor have we the power by legislative fiat to abolish them. We shall maintain, then, that ownership is a right derived from nature, not from law, and its use or misuse cannot destroy, or cause to be forfeited, the right itself. Wealth invested in capital should have a return, but the return should be related to the economy of the nation current at the period of the deposition. Income should be as thermal as the discount rate. A fixed interest or a fixed wage for profit, determined over any but a short period, is obviously unsocial since economic conditions will have altered before the loan or the contract has expired. Contracts for interest or labor once outmoded destroy the equilibrium of the economic field in which the incidence of their fulfillment occurs. The fixed element in economics should be the equation of justice; the variable element is price.

Like ownership and its rewards, labor, too, has its social obligations. Labor must attain its individual rights without infringement of the common good. It is false that the worth of labor is the worth of its net result; false that labor exercised on the property of another begets ownership; false even that all profits not needed for repair and replacement belong to the workingman. To assert the contrary is to lose sight of the social aspect of labor and the right of ownership. But labor does create a right to profit sharing—a right that is again individual and social. It is the right of labor to share in profits on the basis of a living wage. If capital does not pay this, social justice demands that employment be prohibited. But if employers cannot pay this because of unfair competition or unethical imposition of taxes, then the controlling laws of the State should be abrogated. Such considerations will form the basis of our principled effort to obtain the peace of economic security within our own country.

But for the assurance of that larger peace which depends not on us but on the nations of the world, we must await a more enlightened internationalism. In international affairs, the Darwinian theory seems still to persist though long since dispossessed from its native habitat in biology. The survival of the fittest appears to be the law of national existence; and actions which, in the domestic ambient, would be corrected by police power, are glorified and given the support of armies in the international arena. When will we learn to apply to nations the same principles of morality we apply to individuals? When will we learn that nations, as well as men, are created equal before the law? Until we do, all nations, the great as well as the small, are in jeopardy; the great may repel invasion; they have yet to succeed in repelling war. The present competition for mathematical equality is a trepidating evidence of mutual distrust and a proof of reliance in strength for the enforcement of claims. We must inveigh against and deplore the conditions which warrant this cynicism of preparedness. And I venture to propose that, of these conditions, the most pernicious is the prevailing concept of the State as a political and economic, rather than a moral, entity. When Louis Quatorze said, "I am the State," he at least made the State a responsible person. Today, State absolutism is impersonal and neuter. Unless this is corrected, the Congress of nations will continue to be regulated by a diplomatic, rather than a moral, code; governments will be recognized as great or small; the voice of power, instead of truth, will continue to be the decisive voice; and the freedom of little nations will depend on their ability to remain unnoticed or undesirable.

Against the aggression of arms, the Philippines will have no fortress on land or sea. Competitive armament would be a tragic error. The only defense of the Philippines will be its spirit—its articulated cultural unity which will give it protection in the indestructible integration of character. If war comes, or fresh conquest from whatever source, we shall oppose it to the death; but we shall oppose it alone. We shall not ask the shedding of another's blood to spare our own. We shall not make the Philippines the Sarajevo of another world Armageddon. Let no one fear it. To the Philippines, the United States has been a generous benefactor; a loyal and true friend; and if, Mr. President, we can honor that debt in no other way, we can pay with our lives, if need be, lest any act of ours should be a prelude to the weeping of American mothers for their dead. We are a poor nation but not, I hope, without valor and gratitude.

We have requested independence; the American people have granted it. So let it be; and may it prove a blessing for both and a pledge of friendship through the years that are to come. We shall go forward bulwarked with abiding faith in God; confident of the particular good will of the United States and the amity of our Far Eastern neighbors; and we shall take our place glorying in our freedom, with restrained courage, ambitious of peace, with malice toward none and with charity toward all.

We thank you, Mr. President, Prelates, the Faculty of Notre Dame, for the honor you have this day conferred upon us; and we bring to each and all the expression of high regard and cordial esteem from the Honorable Manuel Quezon, President of the Philippine Commonwealth.